return on or before th^ '^ ' stamped below

Am… …n in London in 196… educa… …School in Wiltshire and Unive… College, … from where she graduated with … First Class Honours …gree in English in 1982. After working in advertising for three years she accompanied her husband on a posting to Buenos Aires where she worked as a freelance journalist and wrote her first novel. She now lives in London with her husband where she divides her time between writing fiction and looking after their two sons. Her earlier novels, *Alice Alone, A Cast of Smiles, Walls of Glass, A Summer Affair*, and *The Godmother*, are all available from Hodder & Stoughton paperbacks.

RVC
LEARNING CENTRE

Also by Amanda Brookfield

Alice Alone
A Cast of Smiles
Walls of Glass
A Summer Affair
The Godmother

Marriage Games

Amanda Brookfield

FLAME
Hodder & Stoughton

Copyright © 1998 Amanda Brookfield

First published in 1998 by Hodder and Stoughton
First published in paperback in 1998 by
Hodder and Stoughton
This edition published in 2001 by Hodder and Stoughton
A division of Hodder Headline
A Flame Paperback

The right of Amanda Brookfield to be identified as the Author of the Work has been asserted by her in accordance with the Copyright, Designs and Patents Act 1988.

10 9 8 7 6

All rights reserved. No part of this publication may be reproduced, stored in a retrieval system or transmitted in any form or by any means without the prior written permission of the publisher, nor be otherwise circulated in any form of binding or cover other than that in which it is published and without a similar condition being imposed on the subsequent purchaser.

All characters in this publication are fictitious and any resemblance to real persons, living or dead, is purely coincidental.

A CIP catalogue record for this book is available from the British Library.

ISBN 0 340 67152 1

Typeset by Palimpsest Book Production Limited
Polmont, Stirlingshire
Printed and bound in Great Britain by
Mackays of Chatham plc, Chatham, Kent

Hodder and Stoughton
A division of Hodder Headline
338 Euston Road
London NW1 3BH

JUNE 10
0041464
General Fiction BRO

In loving memory of my dear father

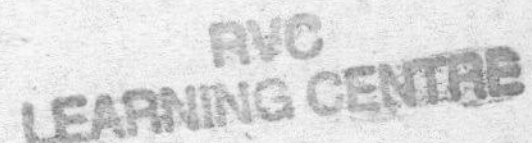
RVC
LEARNING CENTRE

Special thanks must go to my sister, Fiona Ballantine Dykes, and to Sara Westcott and Christine Goodall for all the time and trouble they took in advising me over subjects on which their knowledge vastly exceeded mine.

1

A fresh fall of snow, faintly blue under the velvet glower of the night sky, masked the ancient uneven cobbles of Torbridge's market square. In its centre, the weathered frame of the poultry cross seemed to sag under the weight of the whiteness layered on top. Only the dim strains of the string quartet performing in the domed apse of St Cuthbert's church penetrated the muffled stillness of the scene. As the last chords were stroked and held, the town hall clock struck an imperious chime, as if to assert itself against the silent mountain of Torbridge cathedral towering behind, its giant illuminated triangle quite dwarfing the chattering clusters as they spilled out of St Cuthbert's cosy Norman doorway into the square below.

'Christ, I hate concerts in churches,' declared Juliet Howard cheerfully, linking arms with her husband, and blowing on the knuckles of her other hand. 'Frozen bum, frozen fingers and a streaming nose. Even my hair feels cold,' she added with a sniff, tugging the black velvet rim of her beret to a more rakish angle over her left ear and putting up the collar of her coat so that her frizz of bleached curls bunched round her neck like a scarf.

'No you don't,' soothed James Howard good-humouredly, patting her hand. 'Besides, a little discomfort is good for the soul – not to mention some fine music. I thought it was fabulous. Great acoustics.'

'Hmm,' murmured Juliet, who nurtured a fond scepticism for her husband's judgment when it came to the echoing qualities of draughty old buildings, and musical excellence of any kind. His throaty performances in the shower each morning could make even their children – undiscerning musicians of nine and seven years old – go bolting for cover under the bedclothes. Their intermittent support of the Torbridge winter concert programme stemmed, as Juliet well knew, more from a keen sense of the social role expected of a local GP rather than from any real desire to feed a musical habit that had latched on to Pink Floyd a couple of decades before and never quite let go. Such wifely wisdom in no way diminished Juliet's respect or affection for the man to whom she had been married for ten of the twelve years they had been acquainted. As if to underline this fact for herself, she curled her left hand up into a fist and pressed it into his large warm palm. James responded at once by closing his fingers round the fist and giving a tender squeeze. The gesture was an old friend, an echo of a mutual attraction which time had mellowed, but never yet called into serious question.

'Oh look, there's Ben and Isobel – do let's catch up and persuade them to have a drink.' Juliet wriggled her hand free and started to elbow her way through the throng loitering round the railings guarding the haggard stone front of the church.

Isobel Tarrant was walking half a stride behind her husband, absently placing her feet in the imprint left by his heavy-soled shoes while she thought about the music and the snow and the mystifying fact that profoundly beautiful things were somehow sad. Her head was still ringing with sound and her throat ached from the lump that had blocked it from the start of the final slow movement, when the man on the viola closed his eyes and kept them shut till the last reverberation of the final note had died away.

To Isobel, snow was a treat at any stage of the winter, let alone in mid-January when there was nothing to look forward to but weeks of damp drizzle and false starts to the spring. The recent weather had thrilled the girls too, making them late for school that morning because of snowballing and having to stop at every wall and gatepost to shovel white clods off the top. Both sets of mittens had been so sodden by the time they reached the playground that Isobel had taken them home for a spin through the tumble-drier, providing company for a consignment of towels and a beloved bed-toy of Sophie's that had been salvaged from an altercation with a leaky felt pen and which went coarse and bobbly if left to dry on its own.

Ben Tarrant was the first to stop and turn to acknowledge the Howards, merely grinning and shrugging his broad shoulders so as not to have to remove his hands from the ragged but warm interiors of his anorak pockets.

'Hey, you two. Good, wasn't it? That violinist . . .' He rolled his eyes in admiration. 'So much talent. And only nineteen. I think these winter concerts get better every year.' Famous himself for a lively ability at the piano – reserved for increasingly infrequent displays during late evenings in the company of friends – Ben Tarrant pronounced such views with a confidence that was both well received and quite uncalculated.

'I liked the viola best,' murmured Isobel, recalling again the enchanting concentration of the player, how each twitch of his face had altered with the mood swings of the music, how the tips of his slim fingers had seemed to tease out the notes by touch alone. The violinist had been too much of an extrovert for her tastes, swaying all over the place, like a kite straining to get off the ground; all elbows and showing off.

'Can we continue this discussion somewhere warm?' suggested Juliet, tucking her hands under armpits. 'Like the Stag, for instance? If we hurry we might even persuade them to serve up a plate of chips.'

'Did you walk?'

The women had fallen into step behind the men, their conversation creating wispy swirls of vapour that rose on the cold air.

'I did, yes. But Ben came on his bike straight from school, as usual. I wonder where he left it?' As Isobel paused to look back in the direction from which they had come, she was struck again by the stark beauty of the square under its vast duvet of snow. 'I say, isn't this lovely?' she sighed. 'The children are behaving as if they've never seen the stuff before. For the first time in months they wanted to be outside instead of watching the telly. We spent all afternoon building a lopsided snowman with mean eyes and a leering grin.'

'Lovely,' echoed Juliet, with a dismissive sniff, 'for anyone considering retirement to the North Pole. I tell you, it's like Ice Station bloody Zebra where we are, but with none of the heroics. The school bus got wedged between snow banks at the bottom of our lane and James's car made one measly whir before subsiding into an icy silence that made him very late and horribly cross.'

Isobel smiled. 'Serves you right for moving out of town and becoming dependent on such things.'

'And the AA wouldn't come because we'd broken down outside our own home instead of half a mile down the road.' She beat her hands together, scowling good-naturedly at Isobel, who was laughing. 'What on earth kept Ben in the staffroom on a Friday night anyway?'

'Play rehearsals. What else?'

'Already? But it's months till his play, isn't it?'

Isobel sighed. 'It'll be at the last weekend of term, as usual. But Ben says it's got all the makings of a complete disaster . . .'

'Well, bollocks to that,' interrupted Juliet brightly, 'it's what he always says. It's what directors are supposed to say, it goes with the territory,' she added, by way of an oblique reference to her own considerable – if somewhat distant – experience of thespian life. 'Do you remember last year and the Miranda whose voice broke?'

Isobel giggled. 'From treble to bass in one week . . . oh, poor Ben, he agonised for nights about what to do. But no, this time it really does sound bad,' she persisted earnestly and with a loyalty which Juliet, in her more critical moments, could find quite infuriatingly dogged. 'Julius Caesar is being played by that boy who got suspended last term – Giles Turner – the one found having glue hallucinations on a bench in the close. Do you remember? Terribly talented but difficult as hell, Ben says. He's sort of taken him on,' she added, her heart twisting with a familiar confusion of pride and resentment at the relentless alacrity with which her husband was drawn to such causes.

The Stag was a low-beamed den of a pub with horse brasses and prints of milk carts and old shopfronts decorating its walls. Since it was Friday night at an hour when Torbridge's one theatre and two cinemas had ejected full audiences into the streets, the single-roomed bar was more packed than usual. After having jostled for drinks, Ben led their small party, with some triumph, to a single empty stool and sufficient space to stand right beside the fiery mouth of a huge hearth. Juliet, at first eager to toast herself before the flames, was soon stripping off layers and fanning her cheeks with her concert programme. They piled their coats and sweaters in a precarious tower on the stool and took it in turns to stand in the hottest spot.

As Juliet set off to retrieve her order of chips, James embarked on a funny story about a bashful patient with haemorrhoids. At the punch line Ben laughed more heartily than his wife, who caught herself savouring an old gratitude that she had had the sense to register herself at the practice in Farley Road once it became clear that the Howards were to become close acquaintances. Stethoscopes and friends didn't go together, she felt, although James was undeniably marvellous with the girls, and Ben had no qualms whatsoever about consulting his keenest squash rival on the rare occasion when he admitted the need of medical intervention beyond that offered by the bathroom cabinet.

'Oh dear, now I've offended Isobel,' remarked James, running his hand through his handsome grey-blond hair in a show of despair. At fifty, he was considerably older than his wife and most of their friends, but never in danger of showing it. Thanks to a genuine fondness for ball games and a lifetime of caution about desserts, his waistline was still so trim that he had recently taken to tucking his sweaters into the waistband of his trousers in order to advertise the fact.

'Don't be silly,' she replied quickly, feeling caught out. 'I'm quite used to you and your stories, James.'

'I certainly hope so.' He looked almost serious for a second. 'I should hate to lose the respect of your wife, Ben—'

'What makes you so sure you had it in the first place?' The two men were still laughing when Juliet returned. 'Did I miss something funny?'

'I was just telling them about—'

'Oh no, not again,' groaned Isobel, helping herself to a chip from the heap on Juliet's plate. 'Stop him, Juliet, please. It's all about a poor man with piles . . .'

'Don't be tedious, James,' Juliet scolded, passing the plate round. 'Anyway, I want to hear more about this play, Ben. Isobel says it's bound for disaster.'

'Well, thanks for the wifely support, darling.'

'I only meant that you had said it was . . .' she began, but he had already turned away to answer Juliet.

'. . . a Brutus who can't act, a Caesar who won't act and a Mark Antony who thinks he can act but can't at all. Only a couple of months till curtain-up and I've got a field trip to Wales to contend with as well.'

'Have you?'

'The lower sixth spring term treat in Pembrokeshire. Remember?' Ben shook his head in wonder at his wife's forgetfulness.

'Oh, of course,' Isobel murmured absently, suddenly feeling awash with tiredness.

'Don't worry, Isobel, I have to phone Vera at the practice to find out what's going on in James's life, don't I, darling?'

'She certainly doesn't,' retorted her husband with mock indignation. 'Keep your wife informed of your movements at all times, Tarrant, it's the secret of a happy marriage, I assure you.'

'Oh, we already know the secret, thanks, James,' quipped Ben, slipping his arm round Isobel and pulling him to her. Caught off balance, she half stepped, half fell against him and clung to his shirt for a moment to steady herself. He took her hand and lightly kissed the fingers. 'You look tired, my love. Do you want to go home?'

'No, I'm fine, as long as you are, Ben,' Isobel lied, defeated as always by his tenderness, and wishing that such shows of affection could be both more frequent and more dependable. Having accepted the offer of a second glass of wine, she concentrated on maintaining an expression of interest while Juliet embarked on an entertaining but lengthy account of the healing power of aromatic oils, the latest in a long string of flirtations with life-enhancing hobbies. As her thoughts drifted, Isobel found herself trying to imagine what it would feel like to be as confiding as Juliet, who released anxieties about husbands, children and life in general with an ease that was almost gleeful. Whereas in her own case, to talk so freely about Ben would, she knew, feel like disloyalty, or, worse still, an admission of defeat.

Aware of Ben laughing, as the two men sparred happily on familiar topics, Isobel experienced a sudden spurt of envy towards James, for the casual friendship that he could enjoy with a man whom every instinct in her being still loved, but whose friendship seemed to be slipping from her grasp. From there, her thoughts plummeted towards the even more unsettling notion that friends like the Howards, so casual, but seen so often, might in some way have contributed to such problems, by minimising the need to confront them.

In a bid to divert herself from such gloominess, Isobel proceeded to offer a volley of penetrating questions on the subject of aromatherapy, now so excelling in the art of appearing interested that she quite forgot to listen to any of Juliet's answers.

Meanwhile, the mask of snow outside was beginning to melt, sliding with slow elegance from roofs and crevices throughout southern England. By morning all that remained of Torbridge's postcard prettiness was a gravelly sludge, pushed into ugly drifts along pavements and walls by car wheels and hurrying feet.

2

Ben Tarrant threw a piece of blue chalk at the boy reading a magazine under his desk and emitted a rumbling growl. The child jumped visibly as the chalk landed squarely on the tarbrush crown of his head before bouncing once on his desk and then rolling on to the floor. Titters of amusement rippled round the classroom.

'Perhaps Marcel Proust back there could spare some time to share with us his views on the infinitely fascinating subject of glacier formations. How the thing moves, for instance. You may use the blackboard – and that writing aid now situated near your trailing shoelaces. If I draw a boulder – here' – Ben drew a ragged circle in the centre of the board – 'perhaps you would be so good as to describe for us how the ice gets past it?'

The boy slouched to the front of the class and stood for several moments staring disconsolately at the ring of chalk.

'Take your time, Martin,' said Ben, pretending to shake himself awake. The rest of the class laughed again, more loudly this time.

'Does it sort of melt, sir?'

Ben folded his arms and cocked his head. 'Yes,' he said slowly, 'it sort of does.'

'And then it freezes again round the other side of the rock, sir, I think. But I haven't the foggiest how to draw it.'

There were more muffled giggles which Ben silenced with a stern look. 'You seem to have grasped the basic principles quite well, Martin, by miraculous osmosis, I'd say, given that you have been so ungraciously distracted by other literature since the start of the lesson.'

'Yes, sir. Sorry, sir.'

'OK, go back to your seat. And Martin . . .'

The boy stopped and turned, fresh worry creasing his freckled blushing face. 'Yes, sir?'

'My chalk. Do you think I could have it back?' Ben smiled, aiming to convey that the sin had been forgiven, but still hoping that the memory of the discomfort suffered for it would be sufficient to prevent similar occurrences in the future.

At the sound of the bell for lunch, desk lids slammed and the room emptied in seconds. Ben sighed and began slowly rubbing his dubious representation of a boulder off the blackboard. He worked with unnecessary diligence, erasing every trace of chalk, distracted now by the concern that he might have been too harsh. The boy's parents had separated the year before and a slow deterioration in concentration had been in evidence ever since. Fifteen was a tough age, he reflected grimly, a watershed time when even the most promising pupils could drop beyond reach of reason or help, overwhelmed by adolescent confusions or peer pressure to be defiant and lazy.

Perhaps getting Martin involved in a spot of set-painting would help, he mused, putting down the board rubber and absently dusting white streaks of chalk on to his trousers. God knew, they needed all the help they could get. He wrote the boy's name on a scrap of paper to remind himself and opened the first of a tall pile of blue exercise books which he needed to return to their owners that afternoon. A sausage of an ox-bow lake greeted him, floating between two smudged blue felt-pen streaks.

Use coloured pencils, please, he wrote, before scowling at the miniature spider writing that accompanied the drawing. Tempted to put a red line through the lot, he resisted, knowing both that his impatience rose from his own fatigue more than anything justifiable and that, if deciphered, the spider scrawl could comprise comments that were lucid and sometimes illuminating. *Well tried,* he wrote after a few minutes, before putting down the pen and rubbing his eyes with his fingertips. With the bustle of the morning behind him, a terrible tiredness began to take hold. He felt as if he could sleep for ever. Pushing the books back to one side, Ben crossed his arms on the desk and laid his head upon them with a heavy sigh. Specks of colour danced before his eyes, jigging to a half-remembered tune from the concert the week before. For a few minutes he grappled with the sensation of being pulled in several conflicting directions at once; as the music merged with the sound of school bells, images of Isobel joined the fray in his head, her lips pursed with disappointment, her lovely eyes twitching with unspoken challenges that he recognised but for which there seemed to be no appropriate response. Then, at last, a glorious blackness took hold, pulling him down into a pleasurably vacant womb of a world where nobody required anything of him at all.

Having made a mug of coffee, Isobel took the brochures upstairs with her to the small attic which they had converted into a cubby-hole of a study bedroom the year before. It took several minutes to clear a space for herself on the desk, minutes which she did not resent at all, since they delayed still further the moment when she would have to try and pretend to herself that she was being serious. A moment which she had been avoiding all morning, first by returning a couple of children's books to the library and then by an impromptu and not altogether necessary cleaning of the lavatory. She had frowned as she scrubbed, holding her long auburn hair back from her face with one hand and rigorously jabbing the brush up round and under the rim with the other. Then a splodge of something suspiciously sticky had caught her eye round the back under the pipes and before she knew it she was on her knees with a J-cloth and a bottle of Jif. Though such frenzied activity might have fooled any onlookers, Isobel herself knew very well that she was merely taking a cowardly detour round the large white envelope which had been forced through their narrow letterbox that morning. Housework had never been a major priority in her life, not even before she had acquired the assistance of dear Mrs Beety, who behaved as if the very foundations of human happiness were threatened by fluff balls or undetected grime of any kind.

With the desk cleared, there was only the view of neighbouring rooftops and terraced gardens to distract her, together with the couple of framed photographs that lived on either side of the letter-stand. Ben and the girls building sandcastles on a

Suffolk beach; the wind blowing their hair in flat strands across their faces, their eyes screwed up against the glare of the sun; brandishing spades and buckets in cheerful salute at the camera. The image provoked a lump of nostalgia which Isobel impatiently swallowed away. That particular day had been as fraught with petty domestic dramas as any other, she recalled wryly. Ben in a bad mood as he invariably was when they stayed with her parents, smiling through gritted teeth while they waited for her mother to find her reading glasses and her father rootled about in the back of the garage for a fishing rod that would never get used. By the time they set off it was almost lunch-time; the girls, still at an age when food dictated states of euphoria or despair, had bickered and moaned so relentlessly that they had undertaken a lengthy diversion round a sleepy village in search of ice creams. Though eventual success in this quest had produced silence for the remainder of the journey, the price paid was a punishingly tight-lipped grandmotherly anxiety about children being given sweets just before a meal and the notion of ice-cream dribbles staining the upholstery of the car. The sandcastle episode had taken place just a few minutes after they had all finally staggered through some grass-tufted dunes on to the beach, when all adult parties had thrown themselves into the taxing business of having fun. It seemed to Isobel now that even as she had taken the picture she had felt the duplicity of it, the play-acting rigmarole of snapshots and smiles.

The other photograph, which was much older, showed her, sitting on a five-bar gate in muddied wellingtons and a crumpled T-shirt and shorts. Ben had taken it one glorious September afternoon on their honeymoon, when they had just tumbled out of a draughty Cotswold bed and breakfast, groaning at the heaviness of the fried food in their stomachs and teasingly chiding each other for their shameful failure to commune with anything but themselves. Her hair was tied back in a loose ponytail that had broken free round the sides. She was grinning broadly, her head cocked towards one shoulder, her eyes locked with quite audacious intensity on the centre of the lens, or rather the person behind it. Looking now from one photo to the other, Isobel was struck, more forcefully than ever before, by the great chasm of experiences that divided them. She would not look like that now if Ben were to take her picture, she reflected sadly. She would look questioning and unsure. But Ben never did take her picture. These days their albums were full of photos of the girls. These days she felt increasingly as if she were waiting for affection from her husband, like a dog begging for scraps from a table. Still so eager for a show of love, but powerless to inspire it.

And they had begun so well. Isobel closed her eyes, letting the nostalgia flood through her, knowing from experience that it would run its course if allowed to. Ben's affection had seemed infinite, enough for lifetimes and more. A shiver of recollected ecstasy tiptoed from the nape of her neck and down her spine. Ben Tarrant. She would have died for him. Robbed grannies. Gone to hell.

Isobel seized the honeymoon photograph and scowled at it, hating the image for reminding her of what she missed, of what she had hoped their marriage would be. Of what it had been. She rubbed her temples, trying and failing to pinpoint the origin of her husband's declining interest, knowing only that it had worsened considerably in recent months. Impatient with herself, she turned both photographs to face the window before tearing open the flap of the white envelope and tipping its contents out on to the desk. *Open University: Courses, Diplomas and BA/BSc Degrees*, she read, before her eyes skipped to a scrutiny of the collage of pictures below, in which earnest-looking men and women of politically correct skin colours and sexes assumed false poses round charts and test tubes and books.

Absently twisting one tress of hair round her index finger, Isobel creased her brow in concentration, wishing she could muster something approximating to enthusiasm for the subjects and vocations described inside. Instead, the sense of pointlessness that had inspired her to reach for the loo brush rather than race to study prospects for self-improvement mushroomed obstinately inside.

She had known pointlessness before, as a student; a more angry, energetic kind, generated by three years of trying to develop a liking for the law and a lack of funds with which to enjoy the distractions offered by London in her spare time. With her finals behind her and a resolution never to open a legal book again, the future had shimmered alarmingly out of focus. A cousin of her mother's invited her to New Zealand, a godfather talked about introducing her to colleagues in Hong Kong. While Isobel feigned interest in such possibilities, in her heart she knew she was waiting for something else, something altogether more momentous, to vault her into the gaping next stage of her life.

She met Ben Tarrant thanks to a flatmate's undeclared passion for a wiry, blond German who spent his spare time shifting scenery and painting backdrops for a motley group of part-time thespians in East London. Much against her better judgment, Isobel allowed herself to be coerced into offering moral support for the development of this unpromising relationship by attending a lesser-known Lorca play in a dingy basement theatre next to a warehouse on the Old Kent Road. Isobel's own love life had been disappointingly uneventful since a brief and ugly fling with a tutor who turned out to be in possession not only of a wife, four children and a dog, but also of a notoriety of which everyone had apparently been aware but herself. The episode had done little to endear her to the course. Nor had it heightened the dubious attractions of her male fellow students, most of whose lives seemed to revolve around an unrestrainable passion for beer and ball games.

Ben Tarrant stormed into her consciousness in the few instants it took him to stride into the spotlight on the stage. He was tall, with glossy dark hair and startled blue eyes that looked almost comical under the heavy line of his eyebrows. Isobel, sliding forward on to the edge of her seat, was at once transfixed, not only by his physical presence, but also by the unintelligible Spanish poetry tumbling with evident sing-song fluency from his wide, agile mouth. All the pretension of performing such an incomprehensible play in a hot shoe box of a theatre on a sticky August night was forgiven in an instant. And when her companion suggested they gatecrash the cast party scheduled to take place afterwards, Isobel's initial reluctance to do so arose only from a regret that she should be wearing her most unflattering knee-bagged jeans, instead of the newish purple dress hanging, with most of her clothes, round the dado rail skirting the high-ceilinged wall of her Camberwell bedsit.

As she later discovered, Ben Tarrant liked the faded jeans

almost as much as the shimmering conker colour of her long hair and what some regarded as the unhealthy pallor of her skin. He said that with the light behind her she looked as if her head were on fire. She was wearing a T-shirt saying 'Save The Whales' and a thin gold bangle that fell down her forearm every time she tried to tuck some flyaway wisps of hair behind her ears. The trainers on her feet were flecked with dried mud and there were ink stains on her two middle fingers. Then involved in a highly unsatisfactory liaison with a woman addicted to the transforming powers of curling tongs and self-tanning lotion, Ben was instantly charmed by such scruffiness. While Isobel, never having met a man so clearly aware of his abilities and yet so reluctant to admit to them, was equally awestruck. The discovery that he had a Chilean mother and had spent his boyhood in South America added a wonderfully exotic edge both to his appeal and Isobel's determination to become better acquainted. Incoherent with ardour and too much wine, the pair of them had flirted outrageously, much to the disgust of the lovelorn flatmate, whose own romantic expectations had been dashed by a rival with studs in her nostrils and electric-blue hair.

From such unglamorous beginnings, however, had sprung a connection of more lasting quality, based not simply on mutual physical attraction, but on instinctive feelings quite unlike anything Isobel had experienced before or since. Wonderful when it worked, but hopeless when it didn't, she reflected sadly, abandoning the desk and shaking her head at the realisation that not understanding something rendered one powerless to mend it.

When Ben left for a teaching exchange at a school in Madrid, just a few weeks after their first meeting, she had accompanied him. After an intense and idyllic twelve months spent mostly in each other's company, they returned to England and got married. By the time Ben had successfully nailed the job of geography master at Torbridge Cathedral School, Isobel was several months into her first pregnancy, struggling to readjust both to a cold climate and the realisation that her husband had many things in his life to attend to other than her.

The sound of yapping drew her to the window. Down below she could see a wiry terrier sniping at one of Druscilla Carew's treasured cats through the hole in the bottom of her front fence. After a few moments Druscilla herself scurried out through her front door, clapping her hands and making small screeching noises designed to attract her pet back into the safety of the house. She was dressed in one of her pastel-coloured track suits, with pom-pommed slippers on her feet and a large velvet bow tied on the crown of her head. Like an Easter egg, mused Isobel, trying and failing to skip out of view.

'Halloo, up there!' Druscilla shrieked, waving hard. 'I've been neglecting you, I know . . .'

Isobel stepped back into the frame of the window with an acknowledging smile and wave.

'. . . simply *must* have one of our chats soon . . . been far too long.' She scooped up the cat and retreated back inside her house amidst a flurry of coughing, designed to remind anyone within earshot that pets were the cause of both her greatest allergy and her greatest love.

'But not long enough,' muttered Isobel to herself, turning her back on the window and returning to the desk with a sense of stoical determination that had seen her through many a crisis in the past.

Juliet Howard stood for a few moments at her bedroom window, watching the young man pushing a wheelbarrow of stones down her garden path. In spite of the foul weather, he wore only a T-shirt and a pair of paint-encrusted jeans. His long, bushy blond hair was tied back in a ponytail, revealing earlobes pierced with gold and silver loops. He walked nicely, she decided, with that faint roll of the hips which she associated with masculine confidence of the most enticing kind. His fellow workers, with whom he was responsible for repointing the outer walls of the house and constructing a large semicircular patio in the back garden, were far less gratifying to have around; all bottom cleavages and ugly pot-bellies that hung below the hem-lines of their T-shirts.

Turning her attention to the blobs of hand cream in her hands, Juliet started to massage them into her palms. She hummed quietly under her breath as she did so, savouring the prospect of the day ahead: a morning at her aromatherapy course, a sandwich with one of her fellow students – granary with bacon and avocado inside, or maybe egg mayonnaise. She licked her lips. Then some shopping – just the top-up kind round Torbridge's central square mile – before picking the children up from school and ferrying them home for *Blue Peter* and her non-beef version of spaghetti bolognaise. Tilly would groan and Eddie would have seconds, she thought with one of those pangs of fond maternal indulgence that came so easily at a distance, and could be so elusive when the little darlings were actually around.

Having combed the zigzags of her perm into a more satisfactory shape, Juliet set about applying her make-up for the day. One of the more obvious pleasures arising from their recent move out of Torbridge had been the discovery of the school bus. Though occasionally envious of Isobel Tarrant's ability to look fresh-faced and windswept without trying at all, Juliet herself was as likely to leave the house without lipstick and mascara as she would have been to parade naked up the aisle of the cathedral. But then Isobel, at the measly age of thirty two, was almost ten years younger, she reminded herself with a sigh that was accepting rather than envious. Juliet was far too fond of Isobel to let jealousy get in the way. Besides which, there were other aspects to the woman which she would not have wanted for the world; like her shyness amongst crowds, and the flickers of unhappiness that sometimes glazed her eyes when she imagined she was alone. Juliet, on the other hand, not only adored people, but had also developed a singular capacity for being cheerful in the face of almost anything. Not even growing old was going to get her down, she decided, working creams and powders into her face with a practised efficiency that bore testimony to her days on the stage; days on which she frequently looked back with affection, but no longing at all. Apart from a Pam Ayers-style voice-over for a commercial for clotted cream, she had never really earned any serious money. By her mid-thirties it had been nothing short of a relief to give up the struggle with agents and diets and surrender at last to the tug of marriage and motherhood with James. Dearest James, waiting patiently in the wings for two long years, putting up with all those premarital tantrums and panics, and then agreeing so readily with her plea to abandon his lucrative Holland Park practice and make a fresh start. As things turned out, Torbridge life had suited them both beautifully right from the beginning. Bumping into Isobel Tarrant so early on had helped enormously, Juliet reflected, smiling at the recollection of the antenatal class in which they had met and the repugnantly zealous representative of the NCT, who breast-fed a precocious two-year-old during sessions and handed out price lists for birthing pools together with sachets of raspberry leaf tea. United by near-hysterical aversion to such things – confessed to over coffee and wedges of cheesecake in Royles Coffee House afterwards – the two women had struck up a friendship that had lasted ever since.

Juliet sighed contentedly as she applied a final stroke of pink dust across the cheekbones which, she knew, would hold her face in place for many a year to come. The sight of her full-length image in the mirror on the landing, however, brought a less rapturous sense of wellbeing. She did a little shimmy to recover some of her sense of self-worth, before reminding herself that the loss of figure had been traded for regular indulgences of her favourite foods and two enchanting children. And my husband still loves me, she thought suddenly, her heart surging with fondness and her legs tripping down the stairs in a rush of schoolgirl eagerness to be on her way. As she stepped outside into a blaze of unexpected sunshine, it occurred to Juliet that she was probably as happy as she had ever been in her life; that, apart from the patio, things were pretty well complete. The thought made her feel both pleased and faintly worried. To want for nothing but a patio was, she suspected, not terribly admirable; not something she was sure she would own up to, not even to Isobel, to whom she told most things.

At the sight of the bushy-haired workman tipping something sludgy into the skip parked outside their front door, all such potentially self-critical thoughts flitted out of Juliet's head. She tooted twice as she drove off, enjoying the look of pleased surprise that preceded the impish smile he offered in return.

James Howard studied his list of patients booked in for the morning and groaned quietly. He was in no mood for Arthur Hackett's rickety hips, Mrs Reeves's gluey sinuses, or the obese

Grigson boy's fantastical abdominal pains, invariably brought on by the prospect of the classroom and the enticing alternative of keeping his mother company behind the sweet counter in the mini-market next to the chemist.

It was harder to feel inspired these days, he thought wearily, recalling with a small twist of envy the evident passion of the young quartet to whom they had listened the week before. Such intensity and commitment. Such fiendish energy. James stooped to check his appearance in the small mirror that hung behind the door in reception, running a small black comb through his handsome sweep of hair and baring his teeth to check for specks. The sight of his reflection did lift the doctor's spirits a little; many a fifty-year-old would, he knew, have been glad of the solidity of his hairline and the way the tiredness round his grey eyes manifested itself in small lines that could look quite becoming when he smiled. That he felt heavier and moved more slowly these days was due not so much to additional kilograms as a fundamental sense of prudence. He could still beat Ben Tarrant on the squash court, but only once in a while and only because the dear man had a habit of throwing himself at everything without reference to logic or intelligence. The thought made James smile. He liked Ben enormously, without believing – even after almost nine years' acquaintance – that he knew him very well. Several shared family holidays in a variety of cottages and caravan parks had brought them to a state of mutual affection that never seemed duty-bound to develop into anything else. Which was precisely what he liked about it, decided James, slotting his comb back into the pocket of his white coat and returning to his desk.

In contrast, the superior intimacy evident between their wives had at times made him uneasy. Not just because it was clear that Juliet did most of the talking, but also because Isobel Tarrant seemed to be one of those quiet, unknowable women, content to sit well within the shadow of her very able husband and to let everyone else commit to the risky business of expressing opinions. That she had opinions, James was in no doubt; though he had yet fully to decide whether such reticence made her interesting or merely devious.

As he scrolled through files on his computer screen, James

found his mind drifting from the welfare of his patients back to a vivid snapshot of his wife's best friend, tipping water over herself early one sticky morning in Brittany the year before, when the rest of the campsite was still asleep. James, peering out from a small smeary caravan window for an early weather check, had, somewhat to his surprise, found himself spying with all the guile and curiosity of the true voyeur. She was too slight and freckled for his tastes, hollow-cheeked and pale, with an almost childlike slimness to her arms and legs. James had always preferred his women to come in larger portions, to have bodies that could quiver and crush, with flesh that could cushion his. Yet there was something about the sight of Isobel that morning, ladling water over herself from a bucket, that was mesmerising. Her hair, usually so red, blackened under the water, until it dripped down her back in long dark tails that soaked through her shirt. He could see the pink of her skin, protected so studiously during the day with creams and covers and shades, pressing through the damp white cloth. So delicate compared to the deep honey tan of Juliet, he had thought, tearing his eyes from the window for a moment to check that the splayed body of his wife still heaved with the deep sighs of genuine sleep. When Isobel had finished with the water, she bound her hair in a tight towering turban with a towel, so tight that it slanted the corners of her green eyes and showed a line of chalky whiteness along the top of her forehead, where the sun hadn't reached the skin.

Such was James's immersion in this reverie that he jerked visibly when the phone rang. More disconcerting still was the fact than the voice on the other end proved to belong to Isobel Tarrant herself. Blushing profusely, James had leapt to his feet to take the call, knocking over his mug of coffee in the process.

'Isobel – bugger – sorry. Hello. I've just spilt a drop of coffee. Not at all, no . . . just a drop . . .' He mopped with his handkerchief as he talked, failing to notice the brown stream trickling down the desk leg and forming a dark puddle on the green-carpeted floor. 'To what do I owe the pleasure?'

'James – sorry. This is a real cheek. The receptionist said you were fully booked, so I thought I'd make a direct appeal. Could you squeeze Megan in later on this morning? It's probably just the start of a bad cold – we got caught in all that dreadful rain at the weekend – but she's so floppy and hot that I can't help being worried. And she says she's got a horrible headache, which of course makes me think of meningitis, though she can still look up and down which is supposed to be the main thing, isn't it?'

James could not help smiling at such a wonderfully simplistic mode of diagnosis for a disease which even the most competent doctor could struggle to detect. 'I doubt it's meningitis, Isobel.'

'I was wondering if I could bring her in when you've finished all your appointments. If you call me I can be there in five minutes if I come in the car. But of course I'll understand if you're too busy. Now that she's older we don't get same-day appointments any more, which I quite understand. Like I said, it's probably only a bad cold . . .'

'I'll come myself,' he said kindly. 'As soon as I'm done here. Will you be at home?'

'Oh no, I didn't mean to put you out in any way—'

'It won't be putting me out at all, Isobel, honestly,' he lied, spurred on by a sudden impulse to atone for the thoroughly uncharacteristic bout of daydreaming that had preceded the phone call. He looked at his watch and frowned. 'But I've got to get on now, I'm afraid. I'll see you around lunch-time. Junior Disprin and lots of liquid in the meantime.'

Having wrung out his handkerchief over the bin, James then returned to his desk and pressed the buzzer that would indicate he was ready, for by no means the first time in their long acquaintance, to discuss hip replacement surgery with Arthur Hackett in the certain knowledge that the old man would limp away refusing to commit himself to anything of the kind.

3

'You're delivering a speech, Leon, not reading out a shopping list,' wailed Ben, rolling his eyes in despair. The group of boys gathered on the stage at one end of Crofton College's impressive oak-panelled hall giggled and exchanged glances while the would-be Mark Antony frowned in genuine surprise.

'But I thought you said I was to sound gentle, sir . . .'

'Gentle, yes, but firm. You want this lot to trust you. You're trying to win them over. You want them – improbable though it may seem – to think you are noble, so that they realise quite how dishonourable Brutus has been.'

'But he says Brutus is honourable, sir,' replied the boy, pointing at the page in front of him with a wide-eyed desire to be helpful.

'Yes, Leon, I am well aware of that.' Ben spoke in a tone of weary patience. 'But he means the opposite. He's saying Brutus is honourable, but by describing Caesar's virtues he is communicating precisely the opposite sentiment. OK?'

'Right you are, sir.' The boy shrugged, clearly mystified by such a perversely complex interpretation of something potentially so very simple.

Ben concentrated on pushing back the cuticles of his fingernails in order to prevent himself from interrupting the speech again. He studied the white flecks on his nails and told himself to pour more milk on his cornflakes while Mark Antony delivered a new version of instructions to his countrymen, this time employing a loud, clipped tone suggestive of little more than a desire to make his voice echo round the hall. They were already fast approaching the point, as Ben well knew, when any wise director resorted to encouragement rather than overt criticism of any kind. Egos mattered terribly, especially amongst teenaged boys. Experience had taught him that a little self-confidence could uplift even the most abysmal performance.

Leon was barking 'my heart is in the coffin' and pointing for no discernible reason at a portrait of the lugubrious face of the school's founder when Ben, with equal illogicality, remembered Aunt Violet. Or rather, he remembered that he had forgotten her.

'Isobel, darling, can you do me a huge favour.' Overwhelmed again by the grogginess that had prompted his unscheduled nap during break that morning, Ben leant back against the wall beside the pay-phone and ran his hand across his eyes.

'I expect so,' Isobel replied cautiously, wanting to please but made wary by the breathy impatience in his voice.

'It's Aunt Violet. Would you have time to drive over and see her?'

'Aunt Violet? Today? Oh, Ben, don't be ridiculous.' Ben's spinster aunt, who had recently suffered a stroke, was a relatively new addition to the Tarrant family duties and one about which Isobel retained well-aired and highly negative views. To ship the poor dear, after years of voluntary and mutually satisfactory exile in the wilds of Scotland, to a nursing home on the far side of Ilcombe seemed to her to constitute nephewly philanthropy of the most misguided kind. Not only had she quailed at the responsibility on her own account, but she also felt that Aunt Violet's very small contribution and involvement in Ben's childhood did not warrant such a massive return of effort. That the old dear had clearly lost touch with most of her mental faculties only reinforced such views.

'I've just remembered that I forgot her birthday—'

'Ben, you said you were going to deal with all this sort of thing—'

'I know, I will, I just forgot this time. Please, Isobel. Couldn't you pop over with a card and some flowers or something? . . . please.'

'You could phone her. Extend your greetings in person.'

'It's not the same . . . she hates the phone . . . and probably wouldn't recognise my voice.'

'Well, she probably won't recognise it's her birthday either,' snapped Isobel with a cruelty she did not quite feel.

'Oh, darling, please.'

'But Megan's not well and Mrs Beety has only just got here—'

'Then surely you could leave Meg for a couple of hours with Mrs Beety?'

'Well, I suppose I could, but James has kindly agreed to come round . . .'

'When?'

'Lunch-time,' she mumbled, wishing she had the courage to lie.

'So there is time, then?'

'Yes, I suppose there is,' she conceded, wondering if she were being kind or merely weak for caving in and thinking that once upon a time he had at least pretended that the demands of her life were of parallel as opposed to subordinate importance to his.

'Ben, we need to talk,' she stammered, interrupting the warm expostulations of gratitude that followed.

'What about . . . ? Hang on, the money's going to run out. I've got to go. I left a rehearsal in full swing. Thank you again, Isobel, I really appreciate it—'

Isobel stared for a few seconds at the receiver in her hand, before returning it to its slot on the wall beside the kitchen window. Appreciation isn't love, she thought glumly, rummaging in drawers for a box of chocolates she knew she had but couldn't find. Had her husband's affections slumped to the point where he could only feel positive emotions towards her if she actually did things for him, she wondered, but not during the times in between? Isobel paused, chocolates now in hand, thinking again that gratitude wasn't love, that it was unsustaining and one-dimensional and led nowhere.

As the car lurched reluctantly out of its parking space, Isobel found herself drawing somewhat hysterical and uncharitable parallels between her husband's aunt and her eldest daughter's guinea pig. There had been promises to assume responsibility there too, she recalled with a sigh, waving at Megan's pasty face framed in the sitting-room window and doing a mental calculation as to exactly when anyone but herself had last cleaned out the smelly interior of the hutch, or filled the small plastic feeding bowl with nutrients of any kind. Though Aunt Violet did not require quite such personal or frequent attention, she reflected wryly, her very presence, just thirty minutes' drive away, was somehow just as insidiously demanding.

I don't have a life, Isobel decided with a certain sense of self-drama, as she sat waiting for a space in the traffic streaming round Torbridge's busy ring-road roundabout; I have everybody else's. 'Good for guinea pigs and decrepit great-aunts,' she muttered, hooting at a motorcyclist who swerved in front of her, and blushing at the gesture she received in return.

Any idealistic hopes that the burden of visiting an ancient aunt might be redeemed by a sense of having done some good, of having brought a little happiness into an otherwise clouded and diminishing life, had been dashed almost at once. On their very first trip to the home, made jointly with Ben on the day following Aunt Violet's arrival from the North, it became clear that the old lady was either too mentally damaged, or too riddled with the self-centredness peculiar to old age, to disclose any emotions beyond a liking for boiled sweets and large-print true romances. She liked watching boxing on the telly too, Isobel had since discovered, but was seldom allowed to by her more queasy fellow residents.

'You look peaky,' announced Aunt Violet in a querulous voice, waving a lacy handkerchief at the sight of Isobel and then looking round as if in search of a more pleasing view.

'Happy birthday.' She kissed the sagging powdered cheek and held out the present. 'Ben is sorry he couldn't come himself. He'll be over soon.'

'I don't know a Ben,' she retorted, ignoring the box of chocolates and turning her attention to the large window beside her chair.

'Pretty, isn't it?' murmured Isobel, following the old lady's gaze to the tall silver maple that swayed in the gusty breeze outside. 'It'll be flowering before too long, I expect, with spring just around the corner.' Since the chocolates had been ignored, she delved into her bag for a packet of wine gums.

'How lovely,' exclaimed Aunt Violet, her face breaking instantly into an enchanted smile at the sight of the tube of sweets. Though the white fortress of her false teeth was flawless, the structure moved slightly under the pressure of her lips when she talked. She had been quite beautiful once, Isobel could see, though the face now, beneath its mask of glistening powder, was furrowed with wrinkles and splodgy liver spots. Most disconcerting of all were her eyes, of faded turquoise with pupils as sharp as stones, and the heart-shaped curve of her upper lip, which that morning had been clumsily accentuated with a daub of pearly lipstick.

There were several smudges of pink on the teeth, Isobel noticed, watching the smile broaden as the packet of pastilles was handed over for unwrapping. Experience had already taught her to resist the temptation to offer help. Whatever insanity afflicted the old bird, her pride, cruelly, had survived it intact. Isobel concerned herself instead with the dancing maple in the garden outside, studying the grace of its gnarled branches while, in the lap beside her, the knotted fingers struggled for command over the tiny twists and folds of the sweet wrappers.

Another resident came into the room, moving slowly with the help of two sticks, her head bent towards the floor in concentration. Her legs, Isobel noticed, were not much thicker than the sticks themselves. At the sight of Isobel and Violet her face lit up.

'Ah, a visitor!' she exclaimed delightedly, pausing to rest on her props.

Violet shrugged and turned her back on the door, hoicking her cardigan over her shoulders with a loud, contemptuous grunt. 'They're all women here, you know. No men at all,' she confided in a whisper of foghorn proportions.

Isobel smiled apologetically at the woman in the doorway, who nodded and went to sit down in an armchair next to a table of newspapers and magazines.

'Do you know any men?' asked Violet suddenly, feverishly gripping Isobel's arm, her eyes ablaze.

'I know my husband,' replied Isobel gently, wondering as she spoke whether this was in fact true. 'Ben Tarrant, your nephew. The one you used to visit sometimes at boarding school. His father Albert was your brother. He went to live in Chile.' Isobel spoke very slowly and clearly, as she might address a foreigner with a limited understanding of English.

Aunt Violet was nodding her head. 'Albert left the Diplomatic

Service, to marry that woman. Silly boy. He's dead now, of course. *Everyone is, you know,*' she added archly, popping a second sweet in her mouth and giving it a noisy suck. 'That's why I'm here, of course; to die.'

Isobel looked at her hands and smoothed at imaginary creases in her brown corduroy skirt.

'I was born in Dorset, you know,' Aunt Violet proceeded airily. 'As a little girl I grew up in Poole, near the sea and all those heavenly white rocks.'

'Poole's not far from here at all,' exclaimed Isobel, with an eagerness that betrayed her discomfort.

'Silly Albert, staying away like that. And she died too, you know.'

'His wife?'

'That's what I said. The wife, Louisa. Died in a car crash.'

'I know,' said Isobel gently, remembering how moved she had been the first time Ben had referred to this childhood tragedy, using the steely tone of voice that he reserved for any references to his family. With his subsequent exile to boarding school in England at the age of seven, had come an estrangement from his father from which neither of them had ever quite recovered. Albert Tarrant's death, several years before they met, had been a relief, Ben said, the final cutting of a tie that had never meant anything anyway.

'I visited them once, you know . . . such heat . . . and the insects . . .' Aunt Violet sighed and pressed her handkerchief to her cheek, her eyes suddenly dreamy, lost in the kaleidoscope of her past.

Isobel sighed too, feeling helpless and a little bored.

'Isn't it time you were going?' Aunt Violet declared a few moments later, just as Isobel was wondering if she might venture the same opinion herself.

'Yes, probably.' The prospect of escape caused a rush of guilty tenderness. 'Don't forget the chocolates, will you? They're for your birthday.'

'Birthdays are hell,' came the retort, delivered through half-closed eyes that revealed tiny rivulets of blue where the morning's smudge of eyeshadow had collected. 'And if you meet any men, remember not to chase them. They don't like that, though they pretend to. And for heaven's sake do something with your hair,' she hissed, as Isobel scurried away, minding and wishing she didn't that the lady in the corner had probably heard every word of these curious farewells.

As she hurried across the gravelled driveway to her car, Isobel found herself putting her hands to her head, raking back the long tresses of her hair and pushing her fringe out of her eyelashes. But the wind only whisked it back again, tossing it round her ears and eyes so that she could barely see to put the key in the lock.

4

At a quarter to four, the Torbridge school rush-hour traffic was at its worst. Another good reason never to move out of town, thought Isobel with a scowl at the car clock as she realised that by the time they had had tea with the Howards and driven home again, it would be at least six thirty. She had done nothing about supper and the girls were bound to need cajoling through their homework. Sophie, who was six, was studying the body. Why did poor children look so fat? she had enquired at breakfast that morning, her mouth bulging with Coco-pops as she squinted at a pot-bellied famine victim pictured on the front of the newspaper. Isobel stumbled through several answers about air and emptiness before conceding that she could not offer a precise explanation as to why the human stomach should behave in such a contradictory fashion. 'And couldn't Father Christmas have left them some food?' had been the more challenging follow-up, much to the silent but manifest disgust of her elder, more worldy-wise sister. In the interests of protecting such endearing naïvety for another twelve months at least, Isobel took rather longer to complete her answer, right up to the end of the walk to school, in fact; by which time Megan, squirming at her sibling's relentless inquisitions, had wrapped her scarf around her ears by way of a protest. All that could be seen were her angry blue eyes, so like Ben's under the dark arches of her brows, and the tip of her nose, still pink from quite the worst cold that Isobel could remember. At the grand age of nine, she was showing increasing signs of tolerating rather than enjoying the company of her younger sibling. A fact which Sophie, a much more precocious and volatile six-year-old than

Megan had ever been, seemed to interpret as a challenge to be as annoying as possible at every opportunity.

On the back seat boredom had prompted a potentially explosive discussion concerning ownership of a comic whose battered covers had been littering the car for weeks. Sophie, having won possession of what remained of its pages, was in the process of rolling it up in preparation for use as a weapon. Unable to face the prospect of the rumpus that would ensue, Isobel, by endangering all their lives for several seconds, managed to turn and swipe the disputed item from her daughter's hands, tearing several more of its pages in the process.

'That's enough,' she shouted, venting rage that was as much connected to the traffic as her offspring. 'You two do not deserve to be going to tea with anybody. You have been behaving like animals and I'm sick of it. If you don't start being more considerate towards each other then I shall have to think up some serious punishments . . .' She faltered for a moment at the thought of quite what such castigation might entail. 'My big sister was my best friend when we were little,' she added weakly, thinking as she spoke that this was not an outright lie since she and Angela had always managed a façade of respect for each other's differences in preference to an open declaration of war.

'But she's not your best friend now, is she?' mumbled Sophie. 'Tilly and Ed's mum is.'

'That's right, Juliet is my best friend,' conceded Isobel, thinking somewhat ruefully that intimacy with a workaholic sister, whose prime passions were money markets and Swedish exercise machines, was not something that could be expected to come naturally to anybody.

The submissive silence behind her made Isobel feel guilty for her outburst. The children were the only people she dared to shout at, she realised with a start, the only people whose love she trusted with enough conviction to know that something as futile as a raised voice could do nothing to jeopardise it. When it came to Ben, she only shouted inside her head, where it was safe to make a noise, where nothing could be said that would make things any worse than they were already.

The Howards, on the other hand, had never been shy of the

occasional display of mutual antagonism. As their handsome new red-bricked Georgian home came into view, Isobel was reminded of several public marital spats about wallpaper designs and the space required to accommodate a downstairs lavatory. The house, which had been half restored by the previous owners until their funds had dried up and they were forced to sell, was set half a mile down the back route to Ilcombe village, along a pretty road lined with silver birches. By the time Isobel reached the Howards' drive their silvery trunks were gleaming in the late afternoon sun, casting a light that seemed to come from within the trees themselves rather than from the sky.

Was it simply a question of self-confidence? Isobel wondered, as she edged cautiously between the two gateposts, whose separating width seemed to narrow mysteriously as she approached. Was Juliet able to bare her teeth at James just because she possessed enough conviction – in both herself and her marriage – to do so? But then Juliet had other helpful character traits in her favour, she reflected; like a cunning knack for owning up to any doubts or shortcomings with such cheerful and open resignation that they instantly seemed irrelevant or endearing. In fact, thought Isobel, praying through half-closed eyes on her wing mirror's behalf as she edged forward, the only thing that ever seemed to cause Juliet any genuine exasperation were the eccentricities of her offspring – a pleasant, if boisterous, pair whom their mother had cast into the rigours of full-time school with a much-advertised and unabashed relief.

Isobel jerked up the handbrake, and winked at Megan's sulky reflection in the rear-view mirror. By contrast, motherhood was the one area of her own life with which she felt entirely at ease. From the first scissor-thrust of pain that would, some eight hours later, result in the birth of Megan – so different from the quick wrenching of the miscarriage the year before – Isobel had known instinctively that childbirth was something she would manage rather well, something she could even excel at. Mothering had followed with as much ease, all the well-publicised difficulties, like shortage of sleep and adapting domestic routines, being underpinned by a fundamental sureness of touch; a self-belief that came from nowhere and which she recognised as being as much a gift as the children themselves.

Miscarriages happened all the time, Isobel reminded herself, as the ache swelled inside. Caught by surprise, a part of her regarded the strength of the emotion with something like curiosity. So many years on from the event, such stabs of grief were fortunately few and far between. Unstrapping her belt in a businesslike way, she turned and managed a grin at the girls.

'Out you get.' But for a moment all she could see was the space on the seat between them. They were nearing the anniversary. He would have been ten; a big brother, tall and dark like Ben and Sophie.

'Mummy, are you going to cry?'

'No, Sophie, I am not,' she retorted, making a silly face and then smiling more genuinely as the pain eased away.

'I'm lusting after one of the workmen,' declared Juliet cheerfully a little while later, after the children had demolished platefuls of crusty jam sandwiches and two-thirds of a large chocolate cake. 'The short one with the deliciously long curly hair,' she went on, enjoying the expression on her friend's face as she ploughed up a blob of buttery icing from the rim of the cake board.

'Oh, Juliet, really, you're impossible.' Isobel shook her head with a smile and set about clearing dirty plates and mugs from the table.

'I've told James, naturally.'

'Naturally.'

'He took it very well. I think he finds it reassuring to know that the menopause has not yet affected my libido.'

'The menopause?'

'Well, not yet, I know. But it looms, my dear, it looms.' Having seen to all the excess icing on the board, Juliet embarked on a modest assault of the cake itself.

'Anyway, James says sex in the head is quite normal after a certain age.'

'Sex in the head?'

'Fantasy for the faithful, you know.'

'Oh yes.' Isobel, scraping crumbs into Juliet's large green plastic dustbin, wondered if the way she felt about Harrison Ford at the end of *Witness* counted. She didn't experience many sexual longings these days, except towards her husband, which she suspected wasn't what Juliet meant at all. And even then they weren't fantasies so much as memories, of how things once had been, when any faltering in their sex life had been something to apologise for instead of ignore. The steady decrease of physical intimacy between them – dwindling in recent months to barely any contact at all – was something which Isobel found hard to regard in any terms other than those of personal failure. Ben's angry reticence on the rare occasions she had dared to broach the subject had only driven the wedge between them deeper still. A deadlock of silence had been reached in consequence; an unwilling surrender, on her part anyway, which brought some relief, but considerable anxiety too. Sex had once seemed so very important. To have given up fighting for its reinstatement into their married life seemed the worst defeat so far.

'By the way, do thank James for coming to see Megan the other day.' Having loaded the dishwasher, Isobel returned to the table with a cloth and began steering crumbs into manageable piles. 'I was out, unfortunately – but Mrs Beety said by the time he got there she was, needless to say, sitting up looking horribly perky – though it really was flu and quite a bad bout at that—'

'Stop clearing up, for God's sake, Isobel,' interjected Juliet through a mouthful of cake. 'You're making me dizzy.' She had now cut herself a proper slice and was eating it with a fork; chiselling off mouse-sized mouthfuls, so as to delay the sad prospect of its disappearance for as long as possible.

'James mentioned he'd paid a house call. He adores playing the good Samaritan, it's how he gets his kicks. He's an old-fashioned dear at heart, you know, loves all that Dr Finlay business – doing his rounds with a black leather case and an avuncular smile. Loves hearing about his patients' private lives and all that. It's why he left hospital medicine so early on and opted for the GP routine.' She gave her fork one last lick and sighed. 'There was no real follow-up, he used to say.'

'Well, I was extremely grateful, so please tell him. The antibiotics did the trick at once.'

'So much gratitude – it'll go to his head.' Juliet got up to put the cake out of reach. 'They've got a date on Crofton College squash courts tonight, our men, haven't they,' she said absently, before being distracted by the view from the window above the sink. 'I say, do look at the children, they're playing like lambs.'

Isobel went to stand beside her. Although it was already quite dark, their four offspring, whose many years of acquaintance was no guarantee of harmony of any kind, had unanimously insisted on going outside. They were playing tag round the piles of rubble and mud, completely ignoring the swing and the spacious stretch of lawn beyond.

'We ought to go,' murmured Isobel, trying and failing to think what might be extracted from the fridge to form the basis of an evening meal. Megan being ill had thrown the whole week off course. She had achieved nothing positive at all, apart from visiting Aunt Violet. She opened her mouth to confide as much to Juliet and then closed it again, unwilling to sound as if she were angling for sympathy.

'What about a Greek island for our hols this year?' announced Juliet suddenly, reaching for a pile of magazines stacked on top of the fridge. 'It would be wonderfully hot and you can get villas at quite reasonable prices if you share. I've got a brochure here somewhere,' she muttered, flicking with some impatience through old copies of *Good Housekeeping* and unread parish magazines. 'It's almost spring after all, and you know how these things get booked up. Make a change, don't you think?'

'Yes, maybe. I'll talk to Ben about it.' Isobel smiled to make up for the lack of conviction in her voice. Attracted though she was to the idea of allowing Juliet to organise them all for a third summer in a row, other deeper instincts told her that to accept such an invitation might be unwise. A proper family holiday alone could be just what she and Ben needed. 'Might be a bit too hot,' she ventured, by way of further justification for her reticence. 'Oh, and good luck with your dashing workman,' she teased, mainly to change the subject, as she was pulling on her coat. 'Though I thought James still kept you far too happy to think about such things.'

'Oh, don't worry, James makes me deliriously happy . . . at least twice a year.' Shrieking with amusement at her own wit, Juliet disappeared to the back of the house to summon the children.

'I'll never get used to your living out here,' Isobel complained, as they sorted through the satchels and precarious items of artwork piled round a spindly chair in the hall.

'Well, you'll just have to move closer, then, won't you,' retorted Juliet, unable to stifle a tut-tut at the wedges of mud being scattered by the Tarrant children's shoes across her newly laid parquet floor.

Knowing this to be a remote possibility, Isobel kept her response to a smile, wondering all the while if the subtle but growing distance evident between her and Juliet was purely geographical, or whether it related to more complicated matters, like specks of mud on hall floors and worrying about the bricks of a house instead of the things it contained. She would hate to leave Torbridge, even if Ben could have afforded it. Unlike Juliet, who had always regarded even the short walk to St Leonard's as painful aerobic exercise, she loved having no need of a vehicle beyond the demands of Aunt Violet and the supermarket. She loved too, for equally passionate but less easily explained reasons, the fact that her husband still cycled everywhere on a bicycle with two working gears and a rusting mudguard.

Isobel had successfully negotiated her way back out on to the road when Juliet scurried out of the front door and through the gates, rubbing her elbows against the cold. 'By the way, I forgot to tell you – that week Ben's going camping in the wilds of Wales . . .'

'They go to a youth hostel, but never mind . . .'

'I was just going to say that it looks like I might be away then too.'

'Lucky old you. Whatever for?' Isobel hoped she didn't sound envious.

'A girl called Shelley, who's in my aromatherapy class, has invited me to go on a course with her – aromatherapy and reflexology, which is all about feet.' Juliet made a face. 'Bound to be interesting, though. Apparently it's in a fab hotel just outside Peterford. Quite a drive, but a great excuse to remind James of why he needs me,' she added, flexing the pretty crescents of her eyebrows at the dark sky, oblivious of the elegant silver birches swaying beside her, their limbs shimmering in the paltry half-light of the moon. 'Anyway' – she was now hopping from one foot to the other in an attempt to ward off the cold – 'I thought you two ought to get together, seeing as Ben's away as well. Being over the weekend and so on, it might be nice to organise something for the children.'

'Juliet, go inside this minute, you're freezing to death. We can talk about this on the phone.'

'I was only going to say Torbridge Theatre's putting on *Wind in the Willows* that Saturday afternoon – might be a nice treat for the children . . .'

'Sounds great. Now go inside,' commanded Isobel, winding up the window.

'I'll get tickets, then,' Juliet called, stepping back into a pile of workmen's sludge on the roadside, which caused her to think rather less enthusiastically of the youth whose charms she had been praising so freely just half an hour before.

5

Ben took his hands off the handlebars and settled back in his saddle to enjoy the rush of freewheeling down the tarmac slope that led from the main school, past the rugby pitches, to the sports hall. *La Traviata* pumped through the headphones of his Walkman. The music heightened the thrill of the ride: the black sky, the brilliant patterns of stars, the energising bite of the air. Ben breathed deeply and closed his eyes for an instant. Of all Verdi's operas, this was by far his favourite. A light pressure from his left thigh and he was taking the bend. Across the playing field on his right he could see a single light on in the science block. Dick Caulder, no doubt, the only member of staff ever to work as late as he did. Though in Caulder's case everyone knew it was a question of killing time, until the caretaker locked up and there were no more excuses to prevent him going home. Mrs Caulder had died the year before and the poor man was still in shock. Other staff said it was just as well there were no children. But Ben wasn't so sure. Sophie and Megan lit up his world in a way that he found both awesome and quite indescribable. His family was everything, he thought with a gulp of sentiment, a concrete backdrop without which he would function with even less coherence than he did already.

A squirrel scuttled across his path, making him swerve and almost fall. In the same instant the battery in his front light flickered and died. Unwillingly, Ben replaced his hands on the bars. He wanted to live after all. He had a squash match to win, a play to produce, a field trip to organise, a family to return to. The handsome square clock set in the stone façade of the science buildings warned he was already five minutes late – enough to make James irritated but not irredeemably so, thought Ben, grinning to himself as he brought his bike to a skidding halt outside the double swing doors that led past the swimming pool to the squash courts.

Apart from the thwack of rubber on wood and squeaks from the soles of their shoes, the two men played in a silence that was fraught with an intense but quite unmentionable sense of serious competition. The tactical pattern of their games seldom varied: Ben set the pace and did all the running, while James made up for their fifteen-year age difference and his own relative slowness with brazen cunning. On this occasion, however, Ben found his usual fount of energy seriously lacking. Rather than owning up to it, he fought on, charging from wall to wall with ever-diminishing hope or sense, feeling like some insect flapping against the confines of an airless box, the victim of some cruel schoolboy game. Smiling at defeat over the handshake afterwards felt unbearably hard, as did the inevitable gloating banter that accompanied their stroll back to the changing rooms. It was a relief to step under the hot jet of the showers. Ben turned his face up to the coursing water, full of frustration at himself, not for losing – which happened from time to time – but for minding so badly, for failing to be amused by the predictability of James's pleasure.

'How's Megan?' enquired James, stepping out of the next-door cubicle and wrapping his towel around his waist.

'Megan? Fine. Why?' Ben was already pulling on his clothes, tugging them impatiently over the numerous sections of his body that he hadn't dried properly.

James rolled his eyes in despair. 'Your daughter was ill last week, Tarrant. I had to pay a house call. Ring any bells?'

'Oh, of course – Isobel mentioned something about you coming round.' He wrestled his jumper over his head and began combing his fingers through his hair in a vain attempt to smooth down the wet curls. 'Meg's fine. Bit of a cold. Bolshie as a bloody teenager. God knows what we're going to have to put up with in a few years' time. She'll be consulting you about contraception before we know it,' he added, wrenching the show of good humour from somewhere deep inside.

'And Isobel's all right, is she?'

'Isobel?' Ben dropped his hands from his head and glanced up in genuine surprise. 'Isobel's absolutely fine,' he replied carefully. 'Had a bit of a cough a week or two ago, if I recall . . .'

'Good, good.' James slipped on his watch and busied himself with stuffing his sweat-soaked clothes in his holdall. 'Just thought she wasn't looking quite herself, that's all. A bit pale.'

Ben laughed. 'Isobel's always pale. She eats red meat like a Trojan. Hey, how about a drink?' he added, in a sudden burst of determination to blow his ill-humour away.

James, though sorely tempted, managed to refuse. 'Promised I'd be back by eight – more than my life's worth to be late.' He shot Ben a wry grin. 'Bitter experience and all that.'

Though Ben knew that he too should be getting home, his thirst remained quite unassuaged by the water fountain outside the sports hall. As he wheeled his bike back up the path, he found his gaze wandering once more across the playing fields. The light was still on. If Caulder didn't leave soon he'd be kicked out by Macgraw, the school's crusty old caretaker, who was thirsting for a pint himself by eight o clock.

When the sitting-room clock struck nine, Isobel's feelings towards the tired tail-end of stew she had rushed to unearth from the ice-packed recesses of her deep-freeze turned from apology to righteous indignation. Though hungry, she decided not to eat, as if such punishment of herself might punish Ben too, through guilt if nothing else. He had said nothing about being late. After his squash games he was usually back by eight at the latest. She stared at the handsome gilt-edged face of their carriage clock for a few minutes, thinking about her parents, who had given it to them as a wedding present, and wondering whether to call them or not. It would be a useful thing to do to fill the time; possibly pleasant too if her mother was in the mood to chat. Which she usually wasn't, she reminded herself, returning to the kitchen. A second glass of wine seemed a surer form of consolation for an evening that was turning out to be unpleasantly empty. A documentary on heart transplants saw her through the next hour, together with another glass of wine, drunk guiltily now, since she usually waited for Ben before opening a bottle at all. At ten o'clock she found herself peeking out of the sitting-room curtains at the empty street outside. A pretty dusting of frost covered the pavement and cars. A streetlamp flickering on and off a few yards past Druscilla's house lent a certain eeriness to the scene. Isobel dropped the curtain with a shiver and retreated once more to the back of the house and the uninspiring challenge of clearing a swathe through the clutter on the kitchen table. Even if supper never took place there was still breakfast to consider. The mess depressed her spirits further. The whole house needed a thorough sorting out, she told herself, staring morosely at the haphazard but cosy arrangement of the room and finding it impossible to imagine having things any other way.

A few minutes of prodding disconsolately at the lumpy contents of the saucepan convinced Isobel that her hunger had genuinely evaporated anyway. Having turned off the stove, she found herself traipsing to the bookcase that lived squashed up against the umbrella stand in the hall. After a moment, she pulled out the slim pocket-book-sized photo album, which she kept tucked between some old theatre programmes and a book called *Meals in Thirty Seconds* – a slim, useless directory which she had bought for Ben as a joke shortly after their return from Spain.

There weren't many pictures and what few there were had the blurred, overexposed look of bad flash photography. Being neither equipped nor in the mood to wield cameras themselves at the time, the nurses had performed the honours, explaining softly that parents were usually grateful in the end, even the ones that said they wanted only to forget. Isobel liked the one in the blanket the best, the brown pixie face peeping over the top of the silky trimming, as if he were merely dozing. On the opposite page she had stuck the death certificate, together with a tiny handprint – again done without request or fuss by one of the nurses – and his identity tag. *Toby Tarrant.* For a while Isobel felt nothing, which was disappointing. To fuel her emotions, she plyed her memory, dredging up every last detail, right down to the glassy eyes of the pale nurse, and the earnest young doctor who had talked so unfeelingly and at such length about the needs of a uterus to expel an 'infected product'. In cases of listeria infection, survival at twenty-four weeks was highly unlikely, it was explained, time and time again, until the words sounded meaningless. The blanket picture had been taken right at the end, before the portly hospital chaplain floated in offering kindly, hushed condolences and leaflets on bereavement.

Isobel rocked slowly, still on her knees beside the bookcase, holding the album to her chest, inviting her heart to burst and feeling some frustration at its failure to co-operate. During the months following their loss, crying alone was something at which she had become rather proficient; partly because she grew embarrassed at her own aptitude for tears, and partly because of the alienating effect it gradually seemed to have on Ben. As the weeks went by, the increasingly detectable effort behind his attempts at sympathy during her bouts of weeping undermined any solace he sought to provide. Though he would sit with one arm draped dutifully round her heaving shoulders, Isobel sensed something in his silence that felt like impatience, as if one surreptitious eye never left the clock; as if he were merely sitting it out rather than riding alongside. Sometimes, during the bad early days, she had even caught herself wondering whether these stoical silences in fact contained any recognisable human emotions at all. Such crises of hostility passed, however, aided both by the speed with which she got pregnant again, and the realisation that the person least likely to be equipped to offer any help was the one closest to her own suffering. In the end, time had proved the most effective aid to convalescence, assisted greatly by Juliet Howard, whom she had met while attending breathing lessons for Megan.

After a while – and somewhat to Isobel's relief – the tears came. Self-inflicted pain, but nonetheless carthartic for that, she told herself, letting the sobs take over, and rather relishing the images of sweet baby innocence that danced across her mind. She thought of the approaching anniversary and wept harder. For years now, the date had passed unnoticed save by her and Ben. Though he probably only remembered it because she reminded him, Isobel reflected bitterly, gripping the book in her lap more tightly and vowing, with a sniff of self-pity, never to mention the subject of their lost firstborn again. Somewhere in the midst of this last indulgence, however, burst the uncomfortable realisation that she was crying not about the miscarriage at all, but about Ben himself and the fact that he seemed to have stopped loving her. The effect was sobering. Finding a wife in a gibbering heap on the hall carpet would do little to increase a husband's waning ardour, she scolded herself, slamming the album shut and roughly shoving it back into its slot.

The familiar creak of the rusty hinge of their front gate roused Isobel still further from this nosedive into self-inflicted misery. Hurriedly, she tugged at her hair and wiped her nose with the back of her hand in a bid to appear welcoming; self-disgust having by now dispelled all other, less friendly emotions. I just want him to love me, she thought weakly, splashing water on her face from the kitchen tap before returning to the hall, the picture of fresh-faced fortitude. If they had weathered losing a baby, they could certainly weather whatever storm was besetting them now, she told herself, wondering whether she had it in her to smile as he opened the door.

Ben Tarrant had always made a meek and rather endearing drunk, particularly when his handsome features were suffused with the smiling penitence of one who, even as he crawls for remission, does so in the delightful certainty that forgiveness is just around the corner. Such was the expression on his face as he approached his front door, having, with considerable difficulty, locked his bike to the railings separating their scrawny rose beds from Druscilla Carew's. The simplest movements were becoming tantalisingly hard, Ben observed, recalling with some indignation all Caulder's game attempts to assist him in the challenge of mounting his bicycle in the empty carpark behind the Red Lion pub. The recollection of the demise of his front light had eventually provided an honourable pretext for admitting to the necessity of wheeling as opposed to cycling the bike home. He had set off very carefully, taking the dainty, exaggeratedly high steps of one whose perceptions of ground level have been somewhat distorted by the effect of six pints of real ale on an empty stomach. He crossed roads only when little green men indicated that he was permitted to do so, even though this necessitated standing on one empty street corner for so long that a watchful policeman reached for his notebook.

At the sight of Isobel, who opened the door while he was still waiting for the keyhole to co-operate with the modest demands of his key, he experienced a rush of choking and largely incoherent remorse.

'Darling – so late – so sorry.' He put his arms round her and pulled her close. She could smell the beer on his breath and the pub smoke in his clothes. 'Got sidetracked – sorry.'

'Did you have a drink with James, then?' she asked, melting at such penitence, but feeling that a little frostiness was called for all the same.

'No, with Dick Caulder. Chap whose wife died, you know. Dreadfully cut up. Can't bear to go home, poor devil. Kept him company.' Ben threw his coat on to the hall chair and stifled a burp. It took revenge a few moments later in the form of noisy hiccoughs, which had an annoyingly deflating effect on the gravitas of anything he tried to say.

'Poor Mr Caulder,' she murmured, leading the way into the kitchen in search of water.

'Sorry for being late, love,' he muttered, shuffling after her and proceeding to take grateful gulps of water between hiccoughs.

Watching him, Isobel could not help smiling.

'Still love me?' He cocked his head at her sheepishly.

'Yes, silly,' she whispered, stepping into his outstretched arms.

'Christ, I love you Isobel, so very much,' he rasped, spilling water on the floor as they kissed.

'We can't go on like this Ben . . . we need to talk . . .'

He had to lean on her for the walk upstairs.

'To talk . . . absolutely . . .'

A few minutes later he was sound asleep, leaving his wife to converse with the muffled clicks issuing from the airing cupboard on the landing. The clicks, which were generated by their old but perfectly functioning boiler, had so unnerved Megan at one stage of her early childhood that she had gone to sleep for weeks with sections of her nightie stuffed into her ears.

Alone in the dark, all Isobel's doubts resurfaced, charged by the unhappy acknowledgment of the fact that it had taken alcohol to prompt the kind of passionate declaration for which she had been longing; the kind of declaration to which once, a long time ago, she had been treated almost every day. The past rose like a wall again, reminding her of what she had lost, not as a mother, but as a wife. She missed the certainty of his love. The intensity of it. I need to feel that I am loved, she thought hopelessly, all inward recriminations that such emotions might be naïve as well as self-indulgent for middle-aged housewives with busy husbands doing nothing to blow any of them away.

She started to count the noises coming from the boiler in the hope of lulling herself to sleep. But that night, the clicks, usually so steady and companionable, seemed to have a menacing ring, like the inexorable countdown to calamity.

6

Torbridge library was housed in a smudgy red-bricked Victorian building that was said to have once been an asylum for the mentally insane. While its interior had received enough coats of pastel paints over the years to obliterate any trace of this disturbing history, there was still something ominous about the high metal balustrade that ran round its perimeters and the poky windows of its upper floors, where the less popular subjects like philosophy and economics were housed. Isobel, whose patchy interest in literature had never quite recovered from the interruption of motherhood, had only really become familiar with the place on account of the children. During earlier, difficult days, before videos and board games had been sufficient child-care props for wet afternoons, she had frequently wheeled prams and pushchairs the mile or so from her front door to the library's imposing entrance, grateful for the change of scenery, if nothing else.

On visiting the library a couple of weeks after her husband's unscheduled drink with Dick Caulder, Isobel found some of these early memories coming back at her with unusual poignancy, reminding her of other ways in which times had changed. There had been workshops on puppets and mask-making, she remembered fondly, and rowdy percussion sessions with a girl with café-au-lait skin and glittery blue nails that curled over her fingertips.

Peering through the glass doors of the children's section on this occasion, however, she could see that the place was deserted apart from a lanky-haired woman breast-feeding a baby, and a ruddy-faced toddler rolling and moaning round the floor space at her feet. It was almost lunch-time – not the hour for small children to visit libraries, Isobel reminded herself, withdrawing to the adults' section and rummaging in the side pocket of her handbag for the list she had forced herself to compose during a brief session in the study that morning.

19th Cent. eg Jane Austen, George Eliot, Thomas Hardy, Charles Dickens
Literature & Gender eg Wilkie Collins, Ibsen, Louisa May Alcott, Tolstoy

Such were Isobel's modest extrapolations from the description of a course under the Arts and Languages section, entitled *Approaching literature: authors, readers, texts.* The course was coded A310 and, if Isobel understood the accompanying symbols and numbers correctly, it cost three hundred and twenty pounds, took one academic year to complete and would give her sixty points towards the three hundred and sixty required for a fully fledged degree. Since it sounded like quite a mountain to climb, and a potentially pretentious one at that, she had come to the library with the vague aim of getting a better feel for precisely what she would be letting herself in for. The other option – suggested in one of her booklets – of seeking guidance from a member of staff at her nearest Open University Regional Centre, was simply too daunting to contemplate.

Isobel had alighted upon A310 for the embarrassingly pedestrian reason that most of the names of the authors were recognisable. That this was thanks largely to a spate of recent dramatisations of the classics on television did not exactly fan the embers of her self-conviction over the project. 'You're doing it for something to do,' sneered a voice inside her head, while another countered, more reasonably, that this was better than doing nothing at all. So it was with some trepidation that Isobel approached the section headed *A – D Fiction* and began skimming her eyes along the shelves in search of the works of Jane Austen. When *Pride and Prejudice* had been on the telly she had got as far as hovering in front of the stack of reissued paperbacks on the bestseller stand in Smith's, tempted but resisting, hating the notion of being driven towards a purchase like a sheep being herded into a pen.

If only they hadn't all written so much, she thought with a

sigh, her courage faltering as her trailing fingers reached the fat spines of Eliot and Dickens, while the sneering voice reminded her that these days it was all she could do to flip through a magazine from the weekend papers before falling asleep. A book Juliet had recommended at the end of the summer still sat beside her bed, underneath a travelogue about the Himalayas given to her by her parents that Christmas; it had breathtaking photographs, but tiny compressed lines of print that made her squint. Juliet's book was one of a series written by an author whose chief protaganist was both a female detective and a gourmet cook. Every murder was intricately and skilfully tied up with food, the blurb said, which put Isobel off for a start; though Juliet had been so enthusiastic she still felt she ought to read the thing before handing it back.

Archibald Heighton-Jones, the new young curate at St Cuthbert's, who was not as engrossed as he would have liked to have been in some haphazard research for an ambitious sermon on the subject of poverty, caught sight of Isobel and wondered if he dared offer a nod of greeting. Though she was by no means a regular churchgoer, he knew her well enough by sight. He knew several other things about her too: that she had two daughters, one dark and one with copper curls, who attended St Leonards, the Church of England school on the road past the old bus station; that her husband was head of geography at Torbridge's illustrious Crofton College; and that they lived in Fox's Crescent next to the mad lady with the cats. Whether such information, acquired indirectly and even a little deviously, constituted a sufficient pretext for a direct approach, however, was a matter on which Archie felt altogether less certain. Pressing his index finger to the bridge of his long nose, as if literally to pin himself to his task, he sighed heavily and returned his gaze to the atlas open on the table in front of him. Beside his books lay a blank sponsor form for a twenty-five-mile walk in aid of breast cancer. Flora Dobbs, who organised the St Cuthbert's flower rota, a woman of intimidatingly vast proportions, had asked – or rather commanded – that he offer his support, regaling him with details of sick and dying victims with a directness that had been both harrowing and a little embarrassing. Submission had offered the only immediate release. Though in the longer term he had found himself more ensnared than ever: with the common bond of the walk to bind them, the woman now assailed him at every opportunity, summoning him to teas and Sunday lunches with a voracious enthusiasm that made Archie afraid. No young curate was safe with such widows around, he decided, with a shudder of pity for the husband whose uncooperative heart valves had apparently released him to an early grave. The thought caused Archie's eyes to stray from his papers again, whereupon he discovered – with a flush of alarm and pleasure – that the object of his earlier speculations was staring right at him.

Isobel nodded and smiled, recognising at once the new addition to the bottom ranks of the complicated religious hierarchy that governed all matters relating to St Cuthbert's. As he eagerly nodded back, she caught herself wondering fondly whether the defiant springiness of his ginger hair stemmed from defeat or a lack of vanity.

'It's Isobel, isn't it?' ventured Archie, scraping back his chair so loudly as he stood up that several studious faces glared in his direction. He considered holding out his hand, but at the last minute changed his mind and stuffed it into his jacket pocket instead. He was never sure about shaking hands, or kissing for that matter, which seemed to be of increasing vogue amongst the most lightweight acquaintances. He still found the Peace in church awkward enough, though had high hopes of it improving alongside his familiarity with St Cuthbert's parishioners. 'A lover of literature, I see,' he said, indicating the books in her basket and inwardly kicking himself for saying something so inept and pompous.

'Oh no.' Isobel smiled and shook her head. 'Though I'm considering trying to be. I'm thinking of doing a course – improving my mind,' she added with a self-deprecating grin that made Archie sure her mind needed no improving whatsoever.

'What's that, a sponsor form?' She cocked her head at the piece of paper dangling in his left hand.

'Oh, this . . .' He frowned at the form, as if its presence between his finger and thumb was a matter of pure coincidence. 'This . . .'

'Breast cancer. What a worthy cause. Would you like me to sign?' She set her basket on the table and began digging in her handbag for a pen, irritably pushing her hair out of her eyes as she did so. 'Do you promise not to do more than twenty-five miles? I mean, is it safe for me to say ten pence a mile? . . .'

It was a moment or two before he realised she was teasing him. 'Oh, I promise – don't worry at all – I'm a devilishly slow walker – probably won't even get that far.'

'Let me see, that will make my final bill – oh, heavens – two pounds fifty. That is right, isn't it? It's not twenty-five pounds? I'm so hopeless at decimal points . . . I just know I've got a pen in here somewhere,' she murmured, seizing a battered tampon by mistake and hurriedly burying it again.

'Good heavens, use mine,' exclaimed Archie, handing over the Biro with which he had been making notes and happily wringing his hands while Isobel wrote her name and pledge in neat capitals.

'I'm completely useless at sums of any kind,' he volunteered cheerfully. 'And my general knowledge is lousy too.' He nodded at his books and papers. 'Can't write a thing without help. But I do think it's so important to get the facts right.' He scowled, his thoughts straying for a moment to the exact whereabouts of Zaire, one of the many reasons for his presence in the library. Somewhere amongst his possessions was an atlas, but his digs were so small that he had had to ship a lot of things back to his parents in Cheshire. Most of the books and ornaments he had kept were still in boxes as it was.

'But I bet you know the Bible,' said Isobel kindly, responding to the look of dejection that flashed across his face. 'All that time at theological college or whatever.'

'Oh yes, I know that pretty well. Though how to use it – with people, I mean – is – can be – tricky.'

'I'm sure it can.'

'Have you read this?' Seeing she was about to go, Archie seized a book at random from the collection in her basket.

'No. Have you?'

'Well, no . . . but I've heard of it . . . of course . . . *Anna Karenina* . . . ah yes, very famous.'

'All I know is she gets married and then commits passionate adultery with a glamorous count.'

'Does she? Oh dear.'

'Lives in sin and causes a frightful scandal,' continued Isobel matter-of-factly, taking the book from him and returning it to her basket. Upon glancing up, she was astonished to find that the young priest was blushing; his ears were a particularly vibrant red. 'Well, I'd better get on . . .' she murmured, not knowing whether to be impressed or concerned by evidence of such fragile sensibilities.

'Thank you for your support,' he whispered loudly, flapping his sponsor form in appreciation as she moved away. 'And best of luck with all that reading.'

'Thanks,' she mouthed back, feeling an absurd spurt of encouragement and wishing that Ben's reaction could have been as simple and positive. Instead, he had grilled her about her long-term motives and the time and money it would involve, echoing all the reservations she had been fighting to overcome herself. Every trace of the tipsy affection demonstrated on the night of the squash game had clearly been blasted away by the headache to which he awoke the following morning. Ever hopeful, Isobel had taken care to be obviously tender herself for the next few days, showing in every word and look that a show of love would be welcome, that her affection only needed the light of his to be sparked into life. But Ben, if he noticed such invitations, gave no indication of doing so, coming home each night with ever-darkening looks and a briefcase full of marking for the following day.

He had left for Wales that morning, amidst the usual last-minute flurry of sandwich-making and locating vital, missing items. The disappearance of his cagoule from the peg in the hall caused such a stir of ill-temper that both girls were drafted to join in the hunt. Just as they were all on the point of giving up, Sophie extracted it with a triumphant squeal from the bottom of the old crate in which Isobel kept their wellingtons.

'It must have fallen in.'

'Must have,' he muttered, glowering at her before turning a beam of gratitude on his gleeful daughter.

Outside, some drifting grey clouds were beginning to drizzle with rain.

'At least they can't go without you,' Isobel reassured him, by way of reference to the white minibus parked outside their own front door.

Ben hugged the girls goodbye and swung his rucksack over one shoulder.

'I'll come out and wave you off,' she volunteered, grabbing an umbrella.

She stood, within the safe dripping circle of her brolly, while Ben stowed away his belongings, ignoring all attempts of hers to shield his head. Soon, his hair was soaked to a shining black and the shoulders of his jacket were sodden.

'Don't forget your picnic.' She held out a plastic box containing four beef sandwiches and a pear. She raised the umbrella several inches so that he could step under it to say goodbye. 'Give me a ring, won't you?'

'Of course, but you've got the number of the hostel in any case.' His voice was impatient, his mind already on the few days ahead, on the taxing but rewarding business of herding a group of seventeen-year-olds round cliff-faces and pubs.

'Yes,' she murmured dutifuly, all the while thinking that if past years were anything to go by, there was never a good time to call. And if he ever got around to phoning her it was usually quite some time after she had fallen asleep.

'See you Sunday night, then. Have fun at the theatre or whatever. Look after the girls. And if Miss Harris rings about any costume problems tell her I don't want to know.'

Isobel had nodded, wishing he would hug her instead of talking, and wondering how long a love that got nothing in return could last. Even a very deep love, which had started with all the blinding conviction of a religious conversion.

The memory of her husband's brief kiss of farewell was not inspiring, reflected Isobel gloomily, dumping a pile of books beside the computer on the librarian's desk and thinking that the rain on Ben's face had left more of an impression than the touch of his lips on her cheek.

7

Druscilla Carew was practising the tango with a cushion clasped between her arms when she caught sight of Isobel Tarrant between a gap in her net curtains. Pretty hair, but such a dismal taste in clothes, she thought, sliding one step closer to her unsuspecting neighbour, who was clutching a pair of secateurs and staring doubtfully at the brown stumps of rosebushes in their adjoining shoe box of a front garden. Such was Druscilla's pity for these poor mismanaged plants that she had on occasions been known to nurture them with some secret recipes of her own. Tea leaves and milk in particular. Without such clandestine care she was certain they would never have produced any buds at all. Withdrawing her eyes from her window for a moment, Druscilla stamped her left foot back alongside her right and brought her warbling accompaniment to a vibrato flourish of a finale, squeezing the cushion to her chest like a lover.

'Now don't look so jealous and silly,' she scolded, addressing a honey-coloured Persian cat draped across the closed lid of her piano. Wagging her index finger at the animal, she left the room in search of the pink scarf she had knitted herself that winter by way of an inspired precaution against the cold. The wool was a delicious furry fluorescent pink, spangled with myriad flecks of silver. The pattern had included a hat too, but Druscilla distrusted hats; even the prettiest ones seemed to squash all the bounce out of her hair and make her scalp itch like the devil.

'Isobel, how nice.'

Druscilla's head appearing so suddenly over the flimsy wind-blown fence dividing their properties made Isobel jump. She was wearing her awful scarf – a neck brace of candy floss, as

Ben had so wickedly dubbed it – and clashing gashes of scarlet across her lips.

'How are you, Druscilla? Enjoying all this sunshine?' Isobel squinted up at the inky blue which had appeared as if by magic that morning, its dazzle quite making up for the grey blur of all the weeks that had gone before. 'Spring is here at last,' she murmured, continuing to lop off any stems that didn't look a perfect green.

'The girls on holiday yet?'

'Oh no, not for a while . . .'

'Time for a cup of coffee?'

'I don't think so, I'm afraid, Druscilla. Thank you – sweet of you to ask – but I've heaps to do.' Isobel paused in her snipping in order to make a show of looking at her watch.

'You're cutting too low,' exclaimed her neighbour, wringing her hands in a drama of compassion.

'Oh, they'll survive,' replied Isobel with an airiness she did not quite feel and, driven by some wicked instinct, starting to cut lower still.

Druscilla turned away and picked up a black cat for comfort. 'On your own, then?' she remarked slyly. She had witnessed Ben's departure the previous morning for herself, from the slit in the curtains of her front bedroom window.

'Yes. Ben's taken his upper-sixth group to the Welsh coast to study rock formations and things. Lots of limestone layers and so on to help them through their A-levels.'

'I could bring the coffee out here,' declared Druscilla suddenly, as if the response to her earlier invitation had never been made. 'It's really quite nice, isn't it? Milk no sugar, I know,' she added briskly as she trotted back inside her house, leaving Isobel to roll her eyes heavenward, cursing whichever omniscient creature had been responsible for awarding them such a co-resident in an otherwise very amicable and undemanding street. Being an end-of-terrace house, they at least enjoyed the luxury of having no one to worry about on the other side; though Isobel sometimes thought it would take quite a lot more than that to make up for the dubious neighbourliness to which she was habitually subjected by Druscilla.

The object of these uncharitable speculations returned a few minutes later with two cups, which she set down on the pinewood bird table that formed the centrepiece of her own contrastingly ordered front garden. 'And here's some change for the children.' She pressed two warm fifty-pence pieces into Isobel's hand. 'I know it's not much these days . . .'

'Really, Druscilla, you shouldn't.' Isobel tried to hand the coins back, but to no avail.

'They're lovely girls and they deserve it.'

'Well, thank you, they'll be thrilled,' replied Isobel, staring at the money, while she struggled to reconcile the small confusions of distaste and gratitude caused by such unexpected and inappropriate generosity. She offered Druscilla the first genuine smile since their exchange had begun, wishing she could bring herself to like the woman more, wishing she could feel warmth rather than distrust at all her prying conversational ways. She appeared well intentioned enough, though there was something sinister about the scaffolding of dyed black hair, back-combed to such an unnaturally high distance from its roots that there were visible gaps between each strand, like spaces in a wood of trees. Her eyebrows were starkly blackened too, thick grimaces, half an inch or so above the faint mousey line where nature had clearly destined the original articles to be. But then there was no crime in heavy make-up, Isobel quickly reminded herself, thinking fondly of Juliet cursing into a matchbox-sized mirror on the wall of a caravan the summer before. Juliet refused to approach even a swimming pool without lipstick and lashings of non-drip mascara.

'I expect you miss that friend of yours, don't you,' commented Druscilla with quite unwitting perspicacity a few moments later. 'The one that did those adverts for that butter spread?' She hummed the tune as a reminder, heedless of the fact that Isobel was more than familiar with the main commercial triumph of Juliet Howard's career. 'Where's it they've gone?'

'Ilcombe.'

'That's right – lovely. Pity for you, though . . .'

'Not at all. It's not far. The children still go to St Leonards and next year Eddie will start at Crofton, where Ben teaches, so I'm sure we'll still see lots of each other.'

'Should have had boys really, shouldn't you,' Druscilla exclaimed with a sudden cackle, only just struck by the irony of which the Tarrants themselves had long been aware, that the generous discount offered to children of teachers at Crofton College was quite irrelevant for a family of female offspring.

'We should,' replied Isobel, biting her lip, glad that her delightful neighbour had arrived after the birth of Megan rather than before. 'Careless of us, wasn't it,' she added with a light laugh, while inwardly she quailed at the thought of the conversational possibilities Druscilla would have found in a subject so inviting as a miscarriage.

'Well, I can't stand here chatting,' declared Druscilla abruptly, seizing Isobel's mug and flinging the dregs on to her lawn. 'Some of us have work to do.'

'Don't let me keep you,' murmured Isobel, trying not to feel indignant at the insinuated reprimand. Quite what such work was supposed to comprise remained a mystery, since the woman was clearly well into her fifties and seldom left the house except to buy tins from the mini-market two streets away, or to walk one of her cats round the cathedral close. The religious atmosphere was good for their souls, she said.

After her neighbour had gone back inside, Isobel dawdled in the front garden for a few moments longer, taking deep breaths of the fresh sun-filled air and marvelling at how bound to the seasons human moods still were. Perhaps Ben would call that night, she thought, her spirits lifting still further, buoyed both by the weather and the ease of loving someone at a distance. She wondered what he would have made of her reading till the small hours, as she had the night before, drawn in by the quite unexpected pleasure of encountering Jane Austen first hand. Having opted for *Pride and Prejudice* for the shamefully simplistic reason that it looked a more manageable length than some of the others, and because, thanks to the TV, she was at least familiar with the cast of characters, the enjoyment had come as something of a shock. Even the Mrs Bennet character, whom she had found so grating on-screen, made her laugh out loud. What struck her most forcefully, however, were the social constraints endured by the characters, the painful infrequency with which anyone could truly speak their mind. Thank God for telephones and liberality, she had thought, turning out her bedside light at last and hugging generous wadges of the double duvet round her chin. Whereupon it occurred to her that even without nineteenth-century codes of behaviour to bind them, most humans were still busy performing daily social rituals that did little to illuminate the machinations going on inside their heads.

The character of Darcy accompanied Isobel on the gentle slide towards sleep. Not because she found the literary version any more appealing than his soaked-shirt screen counterpart, but because it vexed her that a fictional hero could get away with appearing romantic by saying practically nothing at all; when in real life such emotional reticence and simmering silences felt only worrying and unkind.

8

'I've put the tickets in an envelope on the hall table. The plate covered in tinfoil is some old bits of lettuce and carrot for Eddie's rabbit and the bowl with clingfilm on is the stew for you. I've mashed some potatoes and left them in the saucepan ready to heat up. Add a dab of butter and milk too, remember, or it will be too lumpy and dry. And a sprinkle of nutmeg is nice, if you can be bothered, which I expect you can't. The microwave is still being funny, but if you press the button twice it usually works. If the children demand waffles for breakfast there are some in the deep-freeze, between the fish fingers and the pizza with the olives on top. I've put out a cheque for the milkman and given the children their pocket money. If Eddie asks to let that creature of his loose in the house again, by the way, the answer is no. I'm still finding those horrid little pellets from the last time, when he *promised* it wouldn't happen.'

'Eddie's rabbit broke a promise?' murmured James absently, his attention more engrossed by the local paper than his wife's instructions. He would muddle through somehow. At least, being a weekend there were no challenges relating to urgent time-keeping or the mysterious intricacies of school uniform and lunch boxes. 'Perhaps we could skin the rabbit and grill it instead of the waffles,' he went on, warming to his theme. 'That way no rabbit dropping could ever darken our doors – or should I say floors – again.'

'James, don't be vile.' Juliet planted an affectionate kiss on the top of his head and took a bite from the piece of toast on his plate. 'Are you going to miss me?'

'Dreadfully.'

'You're not, are you? You're going to be a slob and enjoy every moment.'

He winked at her for a reply before returning his attention to the paper. 'Someone wants to turn St Cuthbert's into an arts centre.'

'Hasn't Torbridge got enough of those?'

'It's got enough churches too, for that matter.'

'I must go.' She looped her green silk scarf round his neck and used it to pull his head close to hers. 'Now, you be good. Not too many sweeties in the theatre and be nice to Isobel.'

'I'm always nice to Isobel.'

'I know, but extra specially.' She kissed him on the lips and then lightly on the nose. 'She's got that forlorn look about her at the moment. I don't think she's eating enough.'

'I'll buy her an ice cream in the interval . . .'

'James, do try and be serious for one second.'

He held up his hands. 'I will, I will. Isobel will receive all my kindest attentions. I thought myself that she wasn't looking well – I mentioned it to Ben, as a matter of fact . . .'

Juliet snorted. 'Ben, bless his cotton underpants, wouldn't notice if Isobel was at death's door. He's an undeniably wonderful man – infinitely handsome and full of talent' – she sighed – 'but really too wrapped up in his own world sometimes . . .' She stooped to examine her appearance in the hall mirror, batting away a few corkscrew curls that had flopped below her eyebrows. 'She couldn't be brooding about the miscarriage again, do you think? . . . It's *so* hard to ask about these things . . .'

'The miscarriage?' James put down the paper. 'But that was decades ago.'

'I know, James, I know. But Isobel's the type. It was around this time of year, you know – I forget which date exactly now . . . It was only a thought,' she muttered defensively, prompted by the look of incredulity on her husband's face. She pressed her lips together and pouted at her reflection. 'I'm probably wrong. As you so rightly say, my sweet, it was a long time ago. For all I know Isobel is suffering from constipation or lack of sleep. I hardly see her these days. How do I look?'

'Ravishing.'

'I'm going to say goodbye to the children. I won't phone

tonight, in case it upsets them. I've left the hotel number by the bed.'

'Remind me exactly what you are going to be doing this weekend?' he said softly, putting his arms round the comfy spread of his wife's waist and squeezing hard.

'The Hotel Primavera near Peterford, to learn about oil and feet.' She made a face.

'And how much are we paying for this privilege?'

'Peanuts, darling, I promise,' Juliet replied hurriedly, trying to prise herself free. 'It's all part of my education. Think of all those lovely massages you're going to get,' she added impishly. 'I'll need to practise an awful lot if I'm to qualify.'

'Is that a promise?' he murmured, nuzzling her neck and enjoying the way she squirmed to get free. 'Don't go, my sparrow.'

'Got to,' she whispered, reluctantly pushing him away and disappearing off in search of the children.

Such fond farewells left James feeling more bereft than he had expected, especially since Tilly, who was usually as tough as nails, decided on an outburst of tears that took almost an entire pack of chocolate biscuits and half a video to resolve. Eddie, meanwhile, groaned antagonistically at the cartoon princesses frolicking on the screen, before shuffling up to his room in disgust. Perhaps it was going to be a long weekend after all, he mused with a sigh, checking the carriage clock on the sitting-room mantelpiece for a countdown to the theatrical extravaganza promised for the afternoon: five hours, with the small challenge of lunch to get through in between. Daunted by hazy recollections concerning the quite separate roles required of Tupperware and pudding basins, James found himself toying with the idea of eating out instead. Pizza Hut maybe. The prospect raised his spirits sufficiently for him to treat himself to a biscuit and to embark on one of the many unread medical journals piled on the coffee table beside him. He had got as far as '*Craniosynostosis – premature closure of different cranial joints may . . .*' before being interrupted by the observation that his daughter was feeding biscuit to a rabbit, and that his son was hanging over the banisters bellowing something incoherent about a missing piece of Meccano.

* * *

They had reached the far side of Ilcombe Woods before James realised that the theatre tickets remained in the silver saucer on the hall table; at which point not even the thought of a lifetime's supply of aromatic massages could appease his attitude as regards his wife's absence. Juliet, as his son took pleasure in reminding him, would not have forgotten the tickets, nor indeed the whereabouts of a Meccano spanner. Their mother had turned domestic organisation into an art form, agreed James acidly, as they doubled back into the busy traffic from which they had just emerged. To intensify their father's suffering still further, the children responded to this additional postponement of lunch by groaning for food. A packet of extra strong mints, unearthed with some triumph from the dusty recesses of the glove compartment, offered little consolation. Were they behaving badly, or was he simply too old to be a father? brooded James, reversing out of their drive after their unscheduled return home with such aggression that he only just managed to avoid collision with a passing cyclist.

'Wicked, Dad,' gasped Eddie, in ill-judged appreciation of the brake screech that accompanied this manoeuvre.

It was unusual for James Howard to harbour any misgivings at all about his suitability and skills as a parent. The relative lateness of his acquaintance with the delights of fatherhood had been quite deliberate, stemming not only from a wise caution about being the author of such lifelong ties, but also from a hearty enjoyment of bachelordom. In his heyday as a young doctor he had experimented with partners like a lover of exotic food, trying out new colours and flavours in an endless quest for surprise and gratification. With several London hospitals and hordes of pretty nurses on which to feed, such appetites were richly served. It was only when Juliet crossed his path, a delectably curvaceous package of good humour and sensuality, then shackled to a nearly famous actor with a bald head and short legs, that James became convinced he had finally encountered a creature who could satisfy his tastes and needs on a long-term scale. That he had been forced to work for her attentions only sharpened this conviction. His capacity for jealousy had been tremendous, both on account of the actor – who took some time to absorb any scenario that did not include himself – and the demands of Juliet's career as a whole, then bird-hopping along between disappointment and relative success. In his more honest moments, James recognised that such jealousy had probably been far more instrumental in his agreement to whisk his wife away to premature retirement in Torbridge than any serious concern for his own career path. Sometimes, he even caught himself missing the emotional trauma of the early days, when the mere sight of her strutting her stuff on stage had been enough to fill him with paroxysms of possessive envy and pride. More prosaically, James was also beginning to feel some nostalgia for the repeat fees and other haphazard payments which had constituted his wife's income at that time. Endearing though it was, Juliet's enthusiasm for channelling her creative energies into courses on basket weaving and body massage was beginning to tell on the family expenses. Even the sight of the prices printed on the theatre tickets prompted James to embark on a quick mental recap of what they had spent on the house and what Eddie's fees at Crofton would add to their outgoings over the coming year.

9

The package had been placed, somewhat unimaginatively, in a litter bin between the multistorey carpark and the start of the cobbled shopping precinct that led down towards the theatre. More imaginative were its contents, which contained enough explosives to kill the homeless old man who had the misfortune to be poking round the contents of the bin when the bomb went off, and to injure all those strolling past within a radius of twenty yards. It was a small device by modern terrorist standards, but nonetheless shocking for that.

Isobel and James, sitting amongst hundreds of other families enjoying the sight of Toad disguising himself as a washerwoman, gasped in unison as the noise and tremors shook the theatre. It was so loud, but over so fast. For a few moments there was complete silence. The actor playing the part of Toad stopped in mid-speech, his lacy bonnet flopping comically over one half of his face, his white dress barely concealing the checked plus-fours underneath. In the next instant, no doubt compelled by ancient adages about shows and going on, he attempted to rediscover his lines. But his voice was quickly drowned by the murmurs of fear and speculation, which rose to a crescendo as the unmistakable sound of Torbridge's emergency services could be heard, whining into action outside.

Toad pulled off his hat and looked to the wings for inspiration. All about them children were asking questions in breathy, high-pitched voices while their adult escorts grabbed hats and coats and began herding them along the rows towards the aisles. An atmosphere of contained panic prevailed. Just as the murmurings reached a fever pitch all the lights on the stage were flicked on and the theatre manager, looking somehow noble in his black tie and shiny patent shoes, appeared before them clutching a microphone.

'Ladies and gentlemen . . . children . . . please stay in your seats. It appears that some kind of explosive device has gone off in the arcade outside. The police are dealing with the situation and have appealed for calm. They are arranging an orderly evacuation of the town centre and have asked all of us to await their instructions. Please refrain from crowding the exits and return to your seats. The police are trying to clear the area outside and will be here shortly.'

'There could be another,' shouted one man.

'We're sitting ducks,' yelled a woman two rows further on.

These discouraging comments were greeted by swelling murmurs of assent.

For the first few minutes Isobel was too busy stonewalling Megan and Sophie's frightened questions to take stock of her own responses. Beside her, James was doing the same with his two. Not wanting to alarm their charges more than necessary by appearing to hurry, they had only just risen to their feet when the manager appeared on stage. At his words most people were obediently returning to their seats, though a shameless few stayed where they were, guarding their proximity to exit signs with defiant eyes. An unnatural hush descended then, while the audience waited for the cavalry – in the unlikely form of Torbridge's local police force – to appear on the scene. Isobel got out a bag of toffees she had been saving to quell any restlessness during the second half and offered them down the line of children occupying the four seats between her and James. Having thus brokered a temporary silence, the two of them exchanged a look of deep concern, a sense of mutual responsibility preventing them from voicing their thoughts out loud. Everyone was talking in whispers. A woman in the front row started her children off in a shrill chorus of 'Ten Green Bottles' which quickly died out for lack of support.

'Are we going to be blown up?' enquired Sophie at length, sucking noisily on her sweet.

'Shut up, stupid,' retorted Megan, digging her in the ribs and prompting a howl.

'No, Sophie, I don't think so. We've just got to wait a little bit until the police come and tell us we can leave.'

'Where are the police anyway?'

'Coming,' Isobel whispered, listening, as most of them now were, to the muffled sounds emanating from the street outside and imagining the worst. She glanced across at James, who appeared grim-faced but calm. He turned and caught her stare, his grey eyes full of reassurance.

'We'll be out in a jiffy,' he said quietly, giving Eddie's flat head a pat and then reaching his arm along the backs of the children's seats, towards Isobel. Still holding her gaze, he held out his hand for hers. Without a word they linked fingers tightly. A cordon to protect the children, thought Isobel, shifting her eyes to the row of subdued heads between them and feeling the physical strength of the hand that held hers. But she felt something else too, something not protective at all. His thumb was stroking her palm, lightly and gently, soothingly, under cover of their knotted fingers.

A man in one of the circle seats stood up and asked loudly if there was a doctor in the house, because his wife had fainted.

James got to his feet at once, dropping Isobel's hand, ready to declare himself; but a woman seated nearer got there first.

'Perhaps I ought to volunteer my services outside,' he whispered. 'God knows how bad it is.'

'But you might be needed in here. Anything could happen—'

A buzz of relieved approval travelled round the room as a policeman at last strode on to the stage, the smart cut of his uniform bringing a much-needed sense of order and control. A few hearty souls clapped. They were thanked for their patience and reassured of their safety. The bomb had resulted in one fatality and a score of injuries. A helpline had been set up for those anxious to enquire about relatives. They were instructed to leave the theatre in an orderly fashion by the main exit and turn right into King Street instead of left towards the mall. Those with cars trapped in the affected area were warned they would have to be patient. Reassured by both the calmness and clarity of this address, the audience formed tidy lines and filed out of the theatre like lambs. Outside, several police personnel, aided by bollards and fences of orange tape, steered them down King

Street, away from the pedestrian precinct. Thanks to James's earlier reluctance to cater for lunch, they were able to make their way to his car, which he had left down a small alleyway that ran between the back entrances of Pizza Hut and a department store. Isobel's car remained imprisoned but unharmed, on the lower ground floor of the multistorey carpark, just a couple of hundred yards from the scene of the explosion. She asked to be dropped home, but James would not hear of it. Not till they knew exactly what was happening, he argued, driving right past the end of Fox's Crescent and heading for the short cut to the ring road south. Inwardly, Isobel was relieved. After putting on such a brave front to the girls, she was aware of her own fears bubbling unexpressed inside. Her hand trembled as she tried to pull the seat belt across her and Sophie, who had insisted on sitting on her lap.

'Here, let me help – it's devilishly stiff.' James reached across her and tugged hard. 'All right?' he asked, touching her arm lightly as he straightened himself.

By the time they reached Ilcombe the car radio had informed them that the bomb was suspected to have been the inspiration of the IRA, though the only warning call received had been an uncoded message to a local newspaper a couple of minutes before. Much was made of the merciful safety of the cathedral and several other buildings of antiquity which had remained intact. It was a miracle too that more people had not been wounded or killed, said the report several times, given that the bomb had been planted on a busy spring Saturday afternoon.

'Bastards,' muttered James, winding down his window and scowling at the chalky green landscape flying by. Isobel stared out too, clasping Sophie's bony ribcage and thinking that the brightness of the day had been somehow deceiving.

With Isobel's help, the four children were fed rounds of sandwiches and mugfuls of hot chocolate. Afterwards, they were granted the unprecedented treat of sucking lollies in front of the television, while James and Isobel retreated to the kitchen.

'A drink, I think.' James tipped the dregs of his tea into the sink and reached for two tumblers from the dishwasher. 'Speaking as a doctor, I would recommend brandy. Sound OK to you?' He turned to check on Isobel, who was sitting at the kitchen table with her head in her hands. 'Hey, are you all right over there?'

She nodded, but kept her face down to hide the fact that she wasn't all right at all.

James, torn between appropriate and inappropriate responses to such distress, gave her time to collect herself. He poured two generous brandies and flicked on the small radio that lived on the shelf above the microwave, so as to be sure not to miss any of the evening news.

'Do you want to call Ben?' he asked, lowering the volume and approaching with a glass held in each hand. A telephone call to Juliet during tea had met with a few gratifying expostulations of horror, before she reverted to a detailed account of the riveting events that had filled her own afternoon.

Isobel lifted her face and took a deep breath. The skin around her eyes looked tight and drawn, accentuating the striking darkness of the lashes and the clear pools of green inside. She must have had a haircut, James realised, registering for what felt like the first time the startling colours of the features usually left skulking under a fringe.

'Oh dear . . . I feel quite shaken up.' She smiled apologetically and took a sip of the brandy, closing her eyes as she swallowed.

'So do I,' he confessed, though he knew his own inner trembling stemmed not so much from terrorist activities as the peculiarly charged atmosphere that seemed to be forming in his kitchen.

'Do you want to call Ben?' he asked again, more quietly.

'Yes, yes of course.' Isobel cleared her throat. 'I've got the number here somewhere . . .' She pulled a small brown diary out of her bag and went to the phone which lived on the wall beside a framed watercolour of Torbridge cathedral.

Ben was not at the hostel, and the manager, who sounded unfriendly, claimed no knowledge as to when the party might return. When Isobel explained the reason for her call he grew marginally more co-operative.

'Could you just pass the message on that I'm all right – that his wife is all right . . . oh, and that I am at the Howards'.'

She had to repeat the name and spell it out several times.

James, watching from across the room, smiled and rolled his eyes.

After she had put the receiver down the shakes came back again, together with a sudden urge to cry. She took a sip of brandy and swallowed hard.

'You, my dear, are in shock,' said James gently, steering her by the elbow to the battered two-seater sofa that lived where Juliet eventually planned to have a Shaker dresser installed. He sat next to her and after a couple of minutes lifted her spare hand and pressed it between his. They remained side by side in silence, each absorbing the unmentionable fact that their shock extended to matters other than bombs and wondering what, if anything, to do about it.

10

Ben picked up a smooth flat stone and hurled it at the water. It flew fast, bouncing three times with small elegant splashes before finally sinking into the sea. Behind him, six boys, clad in windbreakers and hiking boots, were sketching the textured lines of the cliffs that towered over the shingle. Limestone and shale in cross-section. A geological snapshot of history, Ben liked to call it, a glib enough phrase that had served him well for several years in succession now, but which did nothing to communicate the awesome power of the place, the way the stone thrust itself out of the ground, how it seemed to breathe through the cuts and fissures of its craggy face.

Grey and huge, the sea boiled with energy, the waves slopping round the jagged edges of the coastline like dull soup. A band of brilliant blue stretched across the far line of the horizon, but immediately overhead the sky remained overcast and leaden. Ben, more than familiar with Welsh coastal predilections for rain, did not mind unduly. There was a drama to the place that warranted such elemental accompaniments. Besides, it was good for the boys to get their necks wet, he thought with a chuckle, hurling one last stone before turning back to check on the artistic progress of his charges.

'Come on, you lot,' he shouted cheerfully, 'we're not here for a picnic.' He stopped behind one boy and nodded approvingly at his drawing. 'Got your inclines and anticlines nicely under control, Lewis, well done. Don't worry about every limestone fragment lying on the beach, though.' He gestured at the cliff-face. 'It's that lot we're worried about for the time being. We've got an intraformational clast in turbidite to delight us before tea, remember, so don't put your brains or your pencils away just yet. Not entirely necessary to the curriculum, but tremendously interesting and only half a mile down the coast, so we couldn't miss it, could we, Harrison?'

'No, sir, absolutely not.'

'And how's the headache?'

'Headache, sir?'

'Anyone who requires Coca-Cola for breakfast has a headache. Next time you decide to smuggle bottles of beer under your bedclothes, consult me first, there's a good lad. I was extremely disappointed not to be invited along too.'

Harrison nodded eagerly, his regard for the geography master soaring to new heights.

'And what does intraformational mean, by the way?' added Ben slyly.

'It's all about the stuff coming from the rock in which it's found.'

'Not the most eloquent of answers, but it will do. Yes. If by stuff, as you so inspiringly put it, you refer to pebbles and other sedimentary inclusions. The one we're going to look at was eroded by a turbidity current from the sea floor, rolled up like a sausage roll and deposited on the beach. There is even some coarse sediment within the roll itself – a filling for the Swiss roll, so to speak. Dawson, if your stomach rumbles any louder I'll need a loudspeaker.' He clapped his hands. 'Right, let's go. And if you get wet socks it's your lookout.'

They set off along the shingle, the boys following the master with an enthusiasm that complimented him far better than composed classrooms or an absence of ink-blots in their work-books.

Much to the boys' delight, Ben was the one who slipped on a slimy rock and got his feet wet. Though he made a show of complaining, it was for their benefit alone, because he knew it would make them laugh. Unpleasantly chilled toes and a faint squelch to each footstep taken thereafter did nothing to dampen his energies when it came to explaining the mysteries of collapsed breccia and turbidity currents. Nor did a sizable blister on his big toe prevent him from leading the challenging climb to the cliff-top for a better view of the impressive coastline and the sea beyond.

On their way back to the minibus, which he had parked by a deserted caravan and a dilapidated billboard advertising hot dogs, Ben's eye was caught by a flash of pink amongst the clusters of grey and black stones lining the path that led up from the sea. On further investigation he discovered a stone of pale pink crystals that bore no relation he could think of to the geological rock formations in evidence around them. The mystery of its presence pleased him as much as its colour and shape. Closer inspection revealed that, if held at a certain angle, the rock could be said to resemble a heart, albeit a rather lopsided one. Ben opened his mouth to call the boys over, but then changed his mind. He dropped the stone into the deep pocket of his anorak instead, burying it under his gloves for safe-keeping and imagining how Isobel's face would light up when he gave it to her. An anniversary present, maybe, he mused, distracted for a second by the visual image of the crystal dangling on a gold chain against the freckled cream of his wife's skin.

'Mars bars all round,' he announced, hurling confectionery into laps behind him before steering the minibus on the enjoyably bumpy ride back up to the main road. Since hunger dictated a fairly lengthy pit stop for food, it was gone ten o'clock by the time they got back to the youth hostel. The boys, worn out by an early start and a day of hiking along a wind-blasted coast, meekly took themselves off to their beds, all thoughts of beer or any other rebellious activities for once far from their minds.

On account of the bottle of single malt kept hidden behind a flowerpot on the lower shelf of the reception desk, the hostel manager was not entirely lucid about the by now well-publicised events that had taken place in Torbridge that afternoon. Despite the advantage of having seen not only the early but also the late evening news, he could provide Ben with little detail beyond the fact that his wife had telephoned to say that she was all right. Ben looked at his watch, torn between phoning Isobel and waking her with unnecessary drama. She hated being woken up, he knew, never having quite mastered the art of picking up the thread of sleep once it had been interrupted.

'Did she say anything else?'

The man frowned and ran his hand over the length of his face, lingering over the grey bristles protruding from his chin.

'Ah,' he exclaimed in triumph, after a few moments, 'she said she was staying the night with friends.'

'Friends . . . which friends?'

'I'm afraid you've got me there.'

'Not the Howards, was it, by any chance?' suggested Ben, suddenly recalling his family's plans for that afternoon.

'That was it.' The man banged his hand down on the counter. 'Got it in one. Howard. Like the castle.'

Phoning so late seemed even less acceptable when it wasn't even to his own home.

'Bugger,' he muttered, seizing his room key and traipsing up the narrow stairs.

The blister, having been ignored for so long, had shed its flimsy layer of skin and started to bleed, leaving a small dark stain on his sock. Ben rinsed it in a basin of water before stepping under the inadequate tepid dribble that passed for a shower in the bathroom at the far end of his corridor. He shivered as he made his way back to his room, a towel no bigger than a dishcloth clasped round his waist, his wet feet slipping on the cold linoleum floor.

11

The Hotel Primavera had an endearingly dilapidated air about it, like a lord fallen upon hard times. Less enticing was the adjoining and sadly incongruous honeycomb of modern conference rooms in which Juliet and her fellow course members spent most of Saturday, improving their knowledge of the properties of essential oils. Having approached the weekend in something of a holiday mood, Juliet was determined not to have her spirits dampened by ugly surroundings or anything else. Shelley, on the other hand – her companion and the architect of the entire weekend – arrived in a foul temper that intensified as the day wore on. Long before the news of Torbridge's bomb had cast a shadow over the proceedings, she had found fault with most aspects of the amenities – the new wing's over-zealous heating system and the discomfort of the green plastic lecture chairs coming high on her list of complaints. It was all horribly reminiscent of school, she moaned, posting her tray of untouched dinner through a hatch before joining Juliet in the queue for the coffee dispenser. Juliet, who had only narrowly avoided the temptation to have a second plate of chicken fricassee, and who had enjoyed a healthy portion of jam sponge pudding and custard, murmured unconvincing platitudes of concurrence while wondering – for by no means the first time since their arrival – if she dared to slip away in search of brighter company.

Sunday morning brought little evidence of a change in Shelley's mood. While picking at a breakfast of grapefruit segments and natural yoghurt, she regaled Juliet with stories of her troubled night, spent, she claimed, alongside a cardboard apology of a wall listening to the mysteriously incessant gurgling of a fellow guest's lavatory cistern. Juliet, accommodated in a bed just a few feet across the same room, felt almost guilty for having slept so soundly, her dreams dimly woven with the soothing poetry of the after-dinner lecture on oils. There had been a table of samples to try afterwards, each with beautiful italicised labels, describing the powers of the fragrant liquids inside: *Myristica fragrans: oriental, rich, sensual, spicy and warm. Rosa damascena: floral, rich, rosy, sweet, tenacious. Citrus limonum: clean, fresh, lemony, light, penetrating. Jasminum officinale: exotic, exquisite, long-lasting, rich . . .*

By the time they filed out of breakfast to powder their noses before the Sunday morning introductory session on reflexology, Juliet was beginning to experience some sympathy for the husband whose faults her new young friend had found time to introduce into her catalogue of woes against life in general and the domestic arrangements of the Hotel Primavera in particular. While waiting for Shelley to complete her ablutions in their shared cubby-hole of a bathroom, she caught herself tempted by the idea of going home early. After all the fascination of the aromatherapy lectures she couldn't help thinking that learning about feet would feel like something of a comedown. Besides which, there was the awful business of the bomb, depicted in some detail on the front pages of the paper that had been slipped under their bedroom door that morning. Seeing it reported in black and white like that, with pictures of Torbridge's familiar shopping arcade covered in broken glass and people clutching hands to bleeding faces, brought home to Juliet the full enormity of what had happened. She was almost cross with James for sounding so calm over the telephone the day before, for playing it down. Prompted by such sentiments, together with the somewhat tardy realisation that she could have lost her entire family, Juliet decided to call home. She tried the number several times, turning her back with a tremor of disgust at the uninhibited view of her room-mate leering into their bathroom mirror as she sawed floss through the gaps in her large handsome teeth. When her fifth attempt still met with no answer, Juliet slammed the phone down impatiently and suggested they pack their bags.

Shelley, whose English originated from the Midlands, but who laid claim to some exotic-sounding Jamaican ancestry, tossed her beaded black hair and flashed the whites of her eyes at such a suggestion. 'No way, Juliet, no way.' She dropped her coil of floss into her make-up bag and clipped it shut. 'You and I are staying till the end. Otherwise I would have spent a sleepless night for nothing, wouldn't I?'

'It was only a thought . . . and you don't seem to be exactly enjoying yourself . . .'

'Whatever gave you that idea?' Shelley replied imperiously, flashing one of the large, gleaming smiles than had drawn Juliet to her in the first place. 'I'm away from Stuart, aren't I? That's a holiday in itself, I assure you, girl.'

Juliet, who had found a few moments in which to miss the eminently huggable, heat-radiating presence of her husband in her measly pallet of a bed, shook her head in a show of hopeless but relenting despair. It was only a few more hours after all. 'Come on, then, let's get on with it.'

Something in the weariness of Juliet's tone seemed to bring her companion to her senses. By the time they left their room to head into the rabbit-warren of corridors said to contain Lecture Room B, Shelley was cracking jokes about the eccentricities of their fellow students and confessing to an ambition to set up her own beauty therapy business. Not even the difficulty of negotiating a maze of ambivalent arrows and noticeboards soured her mood, though both women felt some embarrassment when they stumbled into a room of Japanese executives and had to be directed back the other way.

The woman in charge of the reflexology session was strikingly rotund, and encased in a long woollen tunnel of a dress that give little indication where the various sections of her ample anatomy began and ended. Before starting to speak, she pushed up the sleeves of her dress to her elbows, revealing forearms as round as pumpkins and a small tattoo of a serpent where one might have expected a watch.

'Have I got any sceptics?' she asked, flexing her hands across the impressive plateau of her chest. 'Because if I have, I can guarantee there won't be any by the end. Money back if you're not satisfied. How's that?' She beamed, taking a moment to study some of the faces among her audience. 'Now then, I want everybody to pick up their chair and make a stack of them against the wall over there. We need some space here. Right, good, that's it. Now take your shoes and socks off – or garters or stockings or whatever the hell you're wearing.' There was an outburst of embarrassed tittering, which she silenced with a clap of her hands. 'Hurry up, we haven't got all week. Good. Now, turn to the person next to you – introduce yourselves if you have to. Then sit down opposite that person – anywhere on the floor, that's it – and place your feet in each other's laps. Toes don't bite, you know.'

More embarrassed laughter; while Juliet experienced an uncharacteristic stab of modesty at having to expose her veiny white feet, thinking they looked old and positively ugly beside the creamy brown smoothness of Shelley's extremities.

'Feet are one of the miracles of the body,' continued their instructor, sorting out a few stray recruits who had not yet managed to locate partners, 'since they comprise a very small area and yet can accommodate even the most excessive weight. Their wondrous strength and mobility are achieved by the arrangement of the bones, muscles and ligaments of which they consist. In fact they contain one quarter of all the bones in the human body, not to mention nineteen muscles and one hundred and seven ligaments. Each foot is made up of twenty-six bones. Now, pick up one of your partner's feet and feel the toes. Don't be shy. Firm but gentle handling is the secret, ladies – and gentlemen,' she added, nodding and smiling at the small cluster of men working together in a group near the door. 'You will feel three bones – which are called phalanges – in each toe, apart from the big toe which has two. Leading back towards the heel we have five metatarsals – each one relating to a toe. The remaining bones are tarsals, all with names that I won't mention at this point, though if you help yourself to the literature I'll be handing out at the end of this session you'll find drawings and descriptions of them all. My object today, ladies and gentlemen, is to teach you not only some of the basic theory of reflexology – a rather misleading name, incidentally – but also to give you an inkling of the power of this treatment, through instructing you in a few basic techniques to try out on each other. The potency of this therapy is considerable and – I cannot stress this too strongly

– should be respected as such. The zones of the feet relate to different zones in your body. By over-stimulating one or the other, you could do more harm than good. Reflexology is about restoring the overall balance within our systems – chemical as well as psychological; through the correct massage we can expel toxins, restore natural equilibrium and iron out areas of stress and pain. It is essential to know what you are doing and the effect it might have. Practised wisely it is a formidable tool, a powerful form of healing, which has been responsible for helping millions of people over countless centuries . . .'

Juliet and Shelley exchanged amused grimaces of incredulity, further strengthening their new-found amity.

'I shall also be telling you of several case histories relating some quite astonishing cures to well-known and very grave diseases . . .'

Not such a bad way to spend a morning after all, mused Juliet dreamily, kneading the soft smooth ball of Shelley's right foot while enjoying similar attentions to her own. The physcial pleasure was something of a revelation; almost sexual, she decided, eyeing her partner through half-closed eyes. She and James never bothered with feet. But perhaps they should, she mused, thinking with some affection of her husband's ticklish, hairy prehensile toes and rather relishing the challenge of taming them. He would protest, of course, she thought, smiling to herself as her imagination spiralled down a sensual sidetrack of its own.

12

On Monday morning, after she had walked the girls to school, Isobel turned and set off at a brisk pace back towards home. Several loads of washing lay strewn across the girls' bedroom floor and in Ben's half-unpacked rucksack on the landing. A shopping list needed writing for her weekly trawl round the supermarket. Open University application forms sat gathering dust accusingly on the desk upstairs. A busy week beckoned, yet she felt none of her customary enthusiasm to greet it.

On reaching the beginning of Torbridge's main shopping precinct, she hesitated just for a moment before turning her back on her usual route and heading towards the shops. The orange tape cordoning off the immediate area affected by the explosion fluttered in the breeze, as if straining to be free. Though the worst of the mess had been cleared up, fragments of broken glass still littered the pavement, glinting in the spring sunshine like crystals. Shoppers were making the small detour round the flimsy fencing with barely a head-nod of acknowledgment, steering prams and buggies round the larger of the shards of glass and tugging toddlers to heel. The world had accommodated this small insult to its surface, and moved on.

Different but the same, thought Isobel, pausing to stare in wonder at the jagged hole in the pavement and the broken and boarded windows of the shopfronts immediately behind. Beyond these, it was business as usual in the multistorey. She had rescued the car on Sunday morning, dropped off by James, who sat waiting with his engine running at the exit to check that they emerged safely, before hooting his horn twice and driving off. She had tooted back, her heart quickening at the sight of him, or more accurately, at the almost forgotten sensation of being worried about at all.

Nothing had happened and yet everything had changed. Something invisible yet momentous. Isobel gazed on at the cavity in the ground, trying to recall the exact moment this alteration had taken place, trying to reconcile the James Howard of the past with the creature who had emerged over the weekend. Thrusting her hands deep into her jacket pockets, she strode away from the scene of devastation, angrily listing in her head all the components of his character that she had never liked: his intimidating self-confidence, the excluding displays of male camaraderie, not to mention his typically crude medic's sense of humour. Try as she might, however, none of these considerations could erase the peculiarly charged images of their recent encounter. A handle had been turned, a switch pressed, a door opened . . . It was flattery, Isobel told herself, increasing her stride still more as she turned down the cobbled street that led towards the cathedral: flattery in its purest, most pathetic form. Her friend's husband was flirting with her and she was enjoying it. Despicable. Unforgivable. Fantastic. She continued to scold herself as she walked, trying and failing to quash the excitement fluttering inside, the image of his grey eyes burning into hers.

Staying for the entire night had been the children's idea. They made a den of sleeping bags on the floor of Eddie's bedroom amidst toppling piles of books, torches and other provisions declared to be vital for the night. They cleaned their teeth and licked down the tangles in their hair, before appearing in the kitchen in a strange assortment of nightwear, clutching pillows to their stomachs and promising to behave; so beautifully naïve that it made Isobel argue all the more determinedly against agreeing to their request. But James had caved in almost at once, conceding with wide-eyed innocence that a Saturday night spent under the same roof could certainly do none of them any harm.

And no harm had been done, Isobel reminded herself, stopping to stare into a shop window, but seeing only her own reflection. White-faced, blurred edges, like a picture waiting to be completed. For nothing had happened. Nothing at all. They had nibbled at cheese and fruit, sipped wine and talked, seeking refuge from awkwardness in anecdotes about the children. Even the most mundane subjects seemed to burn with new meaning. Then James, for the first time in all the years she had known him, brought up the subject of her miscarriage, probing gently as he might have physically examined a wound.

'Must have been very hard.'

'Yes . . . yes, it was. But we pulled through it – I did lots of crying and so on, like you're supposed to . . .' She pulled a face, but he did not smile.

'It's soon, isn't it? The anniversary, I mean.' So distracted was James by her fingers fiddling absently with a piece of cork beside her wineglass that he had to fight the temptation to seize them in his own. There were faint freckles on the knuckles of her hands, he noticed, pretty pinpricks of ginger. It took all his self-control to command his own hands back into his lap, to return his concentration to the conversation. All his keenest instincts told him that in raising such a topic he had stumbled upon a key, an entry into the kind of emotional terrain that could lead to the intimacy which had become his goal. He wanted badly to get it right.

Isobel nodded, flashing a smile of pleased surprise at this startling feat of memory. 'The third of March.'

'Next week, then?'

She nodded. 'Some years I hope I'll forget. But I never do.'

'And you'd probably never forgive yourself if you did.'

His eyes seemed more deeply set into his face than she'd noticed before, and such a compelling, steely grey that she wondered how a careless glance had ever passed between them. I've just never looked at him properly till now, she marvelled, struggling with the urge to hold his gaze but finding it hard. Seen close to, his hair was more white than fair, and beautifully smooth, brushed back off his face in a way that flattered the strong lines of his jaw and cheeks. Even his mouth looked different, Isobel observed, not merely thin as she had always seen it before, but delicate and sensuous, the lower lip being noticeably fuller than the upper, except when stretched into a smile.

Observing how her mood had softened, James continued to

talk gently about bereavement, embarking on a moving account of the loss of his parents, who had died within a few months of each other many years before.

'The mourning doesn't end, you just learn to accommodate it.' Much to his amazement – and gratification – real tears pricked his eyes. He blinked to emphasise their presence.

'God, that's so right.' Isobel sighed, dropping her gaze to the table, unwittingly granting him the opportunity to admire the transparent delicacy of her eyelids and the dark lashes that were such an unusual complement to the glossy copper of her hair. 'My parents are alive and kicking in Suffolk, as you know.'

'Yes, yes, of course they are.' James found his attention focused on the fingers once again. Slim and papery white, like chalk. He wanted so badly to touch her, to move the situation on, to take the next stage in these extraordinary proceedings by storm. But all his antennae warned him it was still too soon. Isobel Tarrant was such a fragile thing in many ways, so delicate and complicated. Years of acquaintance had taught him that much if nothing else. He knew it wouldn't work unless she met him halfway. 'A little more wine?'

She cast a regretful eye up to the pretty hand-painted saucer of a clock on the wall behind him, wondering at the unnatural speed with which its arrows seemed to have flown past the roosting hens and grinning pigs decorating its rim.

'Better not.' She stretched her arms and opened her mouth in a display of fatigue that cheered him greatly for being so unconvincing. James played along with a yawn of his own, all the while feasting his eyes on her pale slender limbs, inwardly scolding and congratulating himself in equal measures. He had not looked for this, after all. It had just happened. A gift on a plate. Maybe even just a game, he decided, escorting her up to the spare room, talking all the while about landing lights and burglar alarms. Before Isobel closed the door, he handed her a spare toothbrush and a nightie of Juliet's, a white lacy one she never wore, as if that made the crime of imagining some other woman enfolded within it a little more forgivable.

Pulling the crisp white garment over her head a few minutes later, Isobel felt all the irony of borrowing such a thing in such circumstances. Through the wall she could hear the muffled sounds of James preparing for bed, the run of a tap, a door closing. The children were at the end of the corridor, sprawled amongst the covers of their makeshift camp, arms and legs flung out across discarded comics and games. The area occupied by the two younger ones was surrounded by soft toys, hugged and abandoned with an affection that yet knew no fear of consequences. James and Isobel had watched the sleeping four in silence for a few moments, before tiptoeing round the room, tugging covers over limbs and tucking pillows under heads. Such traditional parental rituals had helped to fortify their self-control, easing the tricky transition from corridors to beds.

'Sleep well,' he had murmured, as she closed the door, only the haste with which she did so suggesting that the action shut out emotions of an altogether more inadmissible kind.

The relief offered by sliding into the cool cocoon of the bed was brief, however, her sense of safety short-lived. Sleep was out of the question. Instead, Isobel put the light back on and lay staring at Juliet's violet wallpaper and freshly glossed skirting boards, as if by fixing upon such things she might cling on to her faltering sense of the real world. Less easily contained, was the glow of excitement burning inside, fuelled by the long-forgotten sensation of being the object of such attention. Too exhilarating to relinquish at once, she told herself, putting out the light and wishing she could click her own emotions on and off with as much ease. Alone again in the dark, with no physical distractions to get in the way, she was overpowered by a sense of her own latent wickedness and the realisation that sin could occur in the mind long before the deed.

But I love Ben, she thought bleakly, wondering if it was simply her own frailty that made the sustainability of such emotions feel so increasingly one-sided and hard. He hadn't even bothered to telephone, she reminded herself, turning on her side and pulling her knees up to her chest. It occurred to Isobel in the same instant that perhaps what she loved was not the Ben Tarrant she knew now, but the memory of the man she had once known, when his enthusiasm for life had included rather than defied her own.

Angrily, she wrenched back the bedclothes and padded over to the window. Peering through the pretty yellow curtains, which she herself had helped Juliet choose from a chic furnishings shop in Torbridge Arcade, Isobel made fresh resolutions for the days and weeks to come. Sanity would be restored by the normality of the morning, she reassured herself. James would be embarrassed and cold. Ben, returning the next night, would be refreshed and – possibly – pleased to see her. She would nurture every grain of affection; she would try harder; she would make things work between them no matter what it took.

The outskirts of Ilcombe were too far into the depths of the countryside for streetlamps. Only the silvery cuticle of the moon served to cast any light in the darkness below. A shadow passed along the furthest verge of the lane, before turning into the hedge. Something tall and grey. Isobel shivered and withdrew, scolding her imagination for seeing demons where there were none.

Back in bed, she told herself that James Howard's apparent intensity was part of a similar confusion, that it was purely a figment of her imagination, that she was a sad emotional wreck of a housewife looking for daydreams to illuminate a life dominated by domestic appliances and the preparation of meals. Such arguments buoyed her for a time. Until she was struck by the strongest sense of him lying awake and thinking of her just a few yards away. They were in each other's minds, she could feel it. The sense of intimacy was tangible. They had performed the first rituals in a game that could progress even when they were apart. She could feel his desire seeping into the room, destroying all her common sense, promising her something she had thought never to know again.

'Penny for them?'

'Oh my . . . Reverend Heston-Jones – you startled me – I—'

'It's Heighton-Jones, actually, but call me Archie, please. Enjoying the sights of the close on this fine spring morning? It really is irresistible, isn't it – everything in bud, the cathedral so spruce and majestic after its clean-up, all these gorgeous old houses. I like Lady Lacy's the best, I think. Though I wouldn't say no to this one either,' he added with a hearty laugh and a nod at the archbishop's fifteenth-century residence, glimpsed behind a handsome elm tree on their right. 'I know it's wicked, but I was so pleased to be assigned to Torbridge instead of some inner city hell-hole. Oh, don't get me wrong, I'll get to hell-holes in time, but it is a bit of a flying start to be somewhere so jolly glorious. How long have you lived here?'

'Me? Oh, let me see . . . about ten years.' Jolted from her reverie, Isobel was somewhat startled to find that she had already passed under the arch at the end of Mayers Street and into the close itself.

'Where were you before that?' Archie was not so much walking along beside her as bouncing on the rubber soles of his brown leather shoes, hands clasped behind his back, dodging shallow puddles like a child playing a private game. Instead of his habit, he was wearing ill-fitting jeans and a tweed jacket that did little to enhance the aesthetic appeal of the rather grey-looking dog-collar clinging to his neck.

'Spain,' Isobel murmured, with the surreal sensation that she was referring to the life of another person. 'Ben taught in Madrid for a year. Then he got a job at the Cathedral School. Then Crofton College.'

'And here we are,' Archie exclaimed, clapping his hands with delight.

'Well, I'm afraid I ought to be getting back,' she began, despairing of shaking him off any other way and realising that if they walked the entire circuit round the cathedral it would take at least another half an hour. 'Good to see you again.' She stopped and held out her hand.

Archie looked disappointed for a moment and then hit his head in a show of such vehement self-reprimand that Isobel flinched.

'Crumbs, silly me. What I *meant* to say was could I call round to collect my sponsor money some time?' He flushed, clearly embarrassed by the request.

'Of course . . . but look, I can pay now.' She began to unbuckle her handbag.

'Oh goodness, don't worry now, please . . . I haven't got my form or anything.' He held out his empty hands helplessly. 'And when I call I might just ask you to sign the petition too, if that's all right.'

'Petition?'

'About closing St Cuthbert's. Somebody on the council has

proposed it for an arts centre. Reverend Tully says it will probably all come to nothing, but you never know. So I've started getting signatures. Without St Cuthbert's I'd be out of a job,' he added, looking crestfallen.

'I'm sure that won't happen.' Isobel clipped her bag shut and offered her most reassuring smile. Priests, like policemen, were getting younger, she thought wryly, feeling suddenly much better, much more herself. 'Call round any time, won't you?'

'I surely will.' He grinned and waved his hand at her before hastily stuffing it in his trouser pocket as if it had misbehaved. He was a pathetically awkward sod when it came to women, but Isobel Tarrant made him worse than most. Something about the dreamy green eyes and flaming hair, he reflected, still grinning as she walked away, and thinking that even God could forgive a healthy appreciation of such assets. And who could control dreams anyway? Archie reasoned, suppressing the rather less virtuous images that hovered on the edges of his mind, trailers from various fitful nights over the preceding weeks. There had to be some compensations for a mattress with a gash down its middle and a pillow like a starched napkin. So compact was Archie's two-roomed flat that even when lying in bed he could see the edge of his small fridge and the silver curve of the kettle glinting beside it. With his first few months behind him, the novelty of such squalor was wearing a little thin. Almost worse than the lack of space were the vagaries of its ancient electrical system, which shut down in protest if called upon to supply power to more than a couple of appliances at any one time. The tactics required for a successful negotiation of the kettle, the toaster, the radio and his electric razor each morning were particularly testing. Recently, he had even fallen back on the old and much-abhorred labour of wet shaving in order to reduce the hazards.

It was altogether easier to feel tolerant about such grievances when he was at some distance from them, he realised with a sigh, pausing to admire the gargoyles ranged to one side of the cathedral's west door. He loved the ugliness of them, the suggestion of lewd humour beneath their contorted expressions. To have such portraits accommodated in something so majestic was, in his view, utterly marvellous. The church itself should be the same, he thought suddenly, able to house everything under its broad wings, ugly or beautiful, good or bad. Pleased with the idea, he burst into an ear-piercing whistle of the Magnificat sung by the choir of St Cuthbert's the previous Sunday, causing a couple of startled pigeons to retreat in alarm to the stalwart arms of a nearby oak.

13

'But Isobel, I haven't seen you for *months,*' complained Juliet, breaking off half a biscuit from the plateful left out beside the tea bags for the workmen. 'Not since my weekend away and that hideous bomb . . .'

'That was just last week,' Isobel reminded her, but thinking to herself that it did indeed feel like much longer ago.

'—If I didn't know you better, I'd say you were deliberately trying to avoid me.'

'Avoid you?' she echoed, in a small voice. 'Don't be a twit. Tell me about your course. Was it worthwhile?'

'It was fabulous – that is, once Shelley decided to start enjoying herself. I had no idea the woman could be such poison. Really – spending time with someone is such a revelation, don't you think?'

'Yes . . . indeed it is.' Isobel could feel the blood rush to her cheeks. She reached out and touched the prettily serrated petals of one of the dozen carnations that had arrived that morning. Just when she was beginning to convince herself that Saturday night had all been meaningless, a bubble of nothing, blown away as quickly as it had arrived. There was no note, just twelve tall white flowers, their simple beauty throwing Ben's contrasting forgetfulness into cruel relief. He hadn't mentioned the anniversary at all. Isobel reached out and stroked the petals again, as if seeking consolation for the expected – but nonetheless bitter – disappointment of this omission.

'So you didn't get along with Shelley,' she murmured, distracting herself from the absurd temptation to tell Juliet that James had sent her flowers, to scotch the whole terrible situation before it could advance into more dangerous terrain.

'Oh, we were bursting with mutual affection by the end. Turns out the poor girl's a slave to PMT – I just wish she'd said something earlier. The course itself was marvellous . . . I say, are you all right, Isobel? You sound a bit . . . distant.'

'Do I? Sorry. Bit of a headache . . . and the weekend did shake all of us up rather . . .'

'So it seems. James hasn't been himself at all ever since.'

Isobel felt her mouth go dry. 'Hasn't he?'

'I suspect he's punishing me for going away. Men are such babies.' She uttered a short laugh, before adding in a gloomy voice, 'So much for absence and fondness.'

The comment transported Isobel back to Sunday night and all her hopes for Ben's return from Wales. Though he looked well – wide-eyed and faintly tanned – whatever good humour the trip might have generated had clearly been sapped by a disastrous journey home. Bad traffic and several engine seizures on the part of the minibus – each requiring desperate and inexpert probing on the hard shoulder of busy motorways – had meant that he did not get back until almost midnight. When they hugged he felt stiff and reluctant. They talked about the bomb, but only briefly. Evidently exhausted, Ben had kissed each of his sleeping daughters before crawling into bed and closing his eyes. Lying tense and expectant beside him, all Isobel's penitence had shrivelled to a hard sense of injustice. She had spent all day tormenting herself with the crime of having encouraged intimacy with another man. Filled with remorse, she had washed her hair and soaked her body in a perfumed bath, feeling all the while as if she were cleansing herself at a far deeper level, preparing and wanting to love, and be loved. To find the inspiration behind such actions, the prime sandbag of her self-discipline, slumped in bed beside her, offering one dead, draping arm by way of a token caress of welcome, was not heartening. He does not love me, she thought, curling her freshly scented body away from his and thinking with new and bitter resignation that, without reciprocation of some kind, it was impossibly hard to feel love in return. And when, a few minutes later, the figure of James Howard had tiptoed into her mind, his eyes glistening with desire, his large doctor hands reaching out for hers, she welcomed him in, telling herself that such mirages of passion were the least she deserved in the circumstances.

Juliet was still talking about James. 'He's been thoroughly hateful about the course. Playing the pompous doctor. He simply refuses to admit that any good can be done beyond the boring bounds of conventional medicine. He says that alternative healing methods are mostly a load of bull, that they corrode the world's faith in real medicine, that they encourage gullible people to take silly risks and to refuse treatments that could otherwise save lives.' She paused for an indignant sigh. 'Not even the case history about multiple sclerosis – which I must tell you some time because it is *truly* amazing – would budge him. Obstinate bugger. I hate him sometimes, you know, I really do. He even had the cheek to say I was wasting money to have fun – or almost said, which was just as bad. Worse, in fact. And that got us on to money in general, which is never a good idea in our household. I told him to fuck off, too, which probably didn't help,' she added meekly.

'Oh dear,' said Isobel, wishing she could summon the wherewithal to offer help or advice.

'But still, at least we've got all that kissing and making up to look forward to, eh?' She offered an uncertain laugh.

The sensation of struggling so badly in conversation with Juliet was not a pleasant one. No matter how much Isobel reminded herself that there was nothing tangible for which to feel guilty, the guilt persisted nonetheless, and so vividly that she feared drawing attention to it simply by using the wrong tone of voice. While not exactly avoiding the Howards, she had certainly felt little inclination to encourage a meeting with either of them. Instead, she had spent the last few days concentrating so hard on being normal that even the most mundane actions were beginning to feel strange.

'Of course, we'll be coming to Ben's play,' went on Juliet, leaping with characteristic energy into new tracks of conversation, 'but that's weeks away, and I would so like to get the four of us together before then. How about dinner over here? You could all stay the night if you're worried about driving.'

'Ben's so busy,' faltered Isobel, staring hard at the carnations.

'Bollocks to that. We all need to relax sometimes – you can tell that husband of yours so from me. How does next Saturday night sound? I'll cook something really special – give us all a treat—'

'I think Ben may have a rehearsal . . .'

'Well then, tell him he can arrive afterwards. We'll eat late,' declared Juliet stoutly, determined, now that she had hit upon the plan, not to be swayed from it. 'If you're staying the night, it won't matter when the hell we finish, will it?'

'I suppose not,' Isobel admitted, squeezing the telephone flex round her fingers and telling herself that she couldn't hide away for ever. With Juliet and Ben there as well, the situation between her and James was bound to feel more normal; maybe even disappear altogether. 'But I don't know about staying the night . . .'

'But darling, it's only common sense. The children loved all sleeping in a heap – James said so – and you and Ben can push the beds together in the spare room . . . or were you horribly uncomfortable when you stayed? James should bloody well have given you our bed and slept in there himself. The smell of paint must have been awful. But it's all gone now, I promise.'

Overcome by the misguided absurdity of such speculations, Isobel almost laughed out loud.

'I'll take that pregnant pause as a yes,' declared Juliet, pleased as always to have a social event of some sort for which to shop and prepare. 'And any chance of a coffee tomorrow, after my aromatherapy class?' she added slyly, some sixth sense picking up on Isobel's reluctance to see her and pushing against it.

'No, Juliet, sorry, I . . . well, I've got this Open University stuff to plough through – I'm looking at some sample essay questions, some of the texts and so on . . .'

'I can't think why you've got it into your head to go back to school – you've got quite enough facts in your head as it is. One degree is more than enough, in my view . . . unless – I say' – she switched to her most teasing voice – 'we're not trying to recapture our lost youth or anything unwise, are we? Rose-tinted memories of all that slog in libraries and so on. It's all crap, you know. The past is usually best left to its own devices. We couldn't get it back if we wanted to and even if we could it would be a disappointment. It's *designed* to be looked back on,' Juliet concluded firmly, thinking with some pride of her own undeniably dignified exit from London life and how good she was at not missing it at all.

'I'm thinking of the future actually,' replied Isobel quietly, 'of what might lie ahead . . .'

'Well, you could fill the immediate future by agreeing to have that coffee with me for a start—'

'Oh . . . but I've also promised to visit Aunt Vi—'

'But you only just saw the wretched woman,' wailed Juliet despairingly.

'That was a while ago now—'

'You're a slave to your own conscience, Isobel, and quite put the rest of us to shame. One day you must learn the art of giving yourself a little pleasure as well as the rest of society, or you'll end up bitter and twisted and sticking hatpins in models of your friends. Let yourself go a bit, girl. There, that's Auntie Juliet's thought for the day. Now, how about agreeing to let me have a shot at your feet?'

'My feet?'

'Reflexology is the most amazing thing – you'd love it, I promise.'

'I'm far too ticklish.'

'A massage, then. I've got some lovely oils and I desperately need the practice,' Juliet added, wondering whether Isobel was being hard work or whether it was her. 'I know what, come early on Saturday and I'll do it then, before our dinner, while the children run riot in the garden. Don't argue, I've made up my mind.'

Isobel replaced the phone with a sigh and leant over to sniff the sweet scent of the flowers. After giving the matter some thought, she carried the vase through to the mantelpiece in the sitting room, telling herself that if Ben remarked on their presence she would tell the truth and face the consequences. But he probably won't even notice them, she reflected glumly, trying disconsolately to nudge the stems back into the elegant arrangement she had managed in the kitchen.

14

Ben Tarrant had always thought of himself as strong, not just physically, but deep down inside, where it counted most. That he had grown up largely on his own, at a school several thousand miles away from a father he hated, was not something to which he usually referred, either in his own mind or out loud to other people. He knew that the experience, hateful though much of it had been at the time, had helped to form him, that it lay at the heart of his inner resources. He also regarded himself as fortunate for never having doubted what he wanted to do with his life. Teaching, as well as being satisfactorily contrary to the more financially ambitious aspirations of his expatriate father, had always been the only thing that appealed. Perhaps on account of the relative turbulence of his own childhood, Ben's enthusiasm in this regard was almost a need. He knew instinctively how to get the best out of his pupils, how to nurture every precious glimmer of interest and fan it into knowledge and intelligence. He had always recognised this ability as a vocational thing, even more of a genetic gift than an athletic body and a passably handsome face.

Recently, however, he was beginning, for the first time in his thirty-five years, to wonder whether his inner strengths were quite as inexhaustible as he had always assumed. He could never recall feeling so tired. Not even the break in Wales, once an oasis of refreshment in a busy term, had worked its usual magic. Upon his return there was so much to catch up on, both inside the classroom and out, that he could barely bring himself to start. Not only did he feel as if he were drowning in paperwork, but the school play was draining every ounce of energy and patience in a way that felt worrying and new. The pleasures once inherent in committing to such enterprises were as weak as borrowed memories.

And then there was Isobel. His touchstone. His unchangeable fall-back of common sense and good humour, the one who, by her quiet, unquestioning devotion, fuelled all his conviction in himself and in what he was trying to achieve. She was shutting him out. Every time he looked at her was like having a door slammed in his face. I am unhappy, said her eyes, and I'm blaming you.

And so she probably should, reflected Ben grimly, absently running one finger along a hairline crack in the corridor wall as he traipsed down the main body of the school to answer a summons from the headmaster. He watched his feet as he walked, carefully avoiding chips and ink stains in the scuffed parquet and puzzling over the depressing fact that recognising his culpability in the curious downward spiral of his married life should offer up no starting point for remedying it. There was a fine line between relying on a wife and neglecting her, he thought wryly, nodding his head to himself in acknowledgment of the fact that he had almost certainly blundered across such boundaries, but knowing too that in his current state of mind he lacked both the energy and inspiration to atone for it.

Burdened by the lucidity of such harsh self-analysis, Ben found himself making slow and faltering progress towards the fine oak-panelled study from which Dr Peter Abbott, surrounded by auspicious photographs of his predecessors, directed operations for the successful running of Crofton College. In spite of a rather forbidding physical presence, he was a warm-hearted and open-minded man, whose habit of incorporating impromptu discussions into the busy timetables of his staff was not something that any of them usually resented. Least of all the head of his geography department, who nurtured hopes of exerting a similar style of leadership himself one day.

In a bid to shake off some of his dark mood, Ben paused to admire a colourful classroom display on the life-cycle of the tapeworm. *An invisible enemy,* said the headline, its words hugging the bulging head of a smug-looking parasite, whose multi-segmented body was sheathed within the intestines of a large, placid-faced cow. Thinking gloomily that invisible enemies took many forms, Ben nodded a brief farewell at the ruminant, whose expression he rather liked, and forced himself to hurry on his way. It was just a question of regaining mastery over his own feelings, he told himself, tightening the knot in his tie and increasing his stride; just a question of crushing all the pointless self-doubt back into its rightful, subjugated place. Isobel had not married him for his weaknesses, he reminded himself, throwing back his head and striding, jaw clenched, down the last few yards of the school's long central corridor. He would give every matter its proper attention in due course, his wife included. But both Ben's resolve and his stride faltered somewhat at the question of exactly what such attentions should involve. A hero in a book would organise a spring weekend in Paris, or tickets to the opera, he mused bitterly, thinking in the same instant that heroes in books didn't have overdrafts and a terror of appearing weak. The thought drove him on to unhappy reflections on Isobel's recent frenzied interest in literature. For, in Ben's view, this discovery of the pleasures of reading was neither a coincidence nor a cause for celebration. Whatever vocational quest Isobel claimed lay behind her visits to the library, it was painfully apparent to him that she was holding books to her face like a shield. Whenever he was around these days, she seemed to be reading, hiding behind the covers, as if to shut him out, to emphasise their separateness.

Once, a long time ago, he remembered sadly, Isobel had been proud to boast her preference for home-making as opposed to the more socially acceptable postgraduate practice of pursuing a career. Only a joint venture with him would lure her into the rat race, she used to say, or possibly sorting through stained clothes and chipped crockery in aid of a good cause. For a moment Ben wondered if he could blame Juliet – these days attending courses with the same kind of frequency that she visited the hairdresser – for his wife's recent show of self-improving zeal. But he quickly brushed the notion aside. It was impossible to compare the two women. Fond though he was of both the Howards, Ben had never doubted that Isobel was in another league. As indeed their love had been, once upon a time, he thought hopelessly. His throat tightened so much that for a moment he couldn't breathe. It took a monumental effort of self-will for him to raise a clenched fist and rap smartly on the headmaster's handsome panelled door. Two sharp orderly knocks, beating the hopelessness away.

'Ben, thank you for coming. Take a pew.' Peter Abbott gestured at the studded leather chair facing his desk.

'No, I'm fine, thanks, Peter. Slightly behind schedule, in fact.' He looked at his watch and scowled.

'Coffee?'

Ben shook his head.

'I'll come straight to the point, then.' Peter Abbott walked round to the front of his desk and leant back against it, careful to nudge a silver Victorian inkwell out of the way beforehand. 'The fact is, there's been something of a complaint from a parent. Concerning one of the boys on your field trip.'

'What sort of complaint?'

'Hard to categorise, I'm afraid.' He frowned, flexing the imposing grey bushes of his eyebrows and crossing his arms across his broad, pin-striped chest. 'Misguided infatuation probably describes it best. Nothing we can't sort out, I'm sure.'

Ben's pulse quickened. When he spoke his teeth felt as if they were sticking to the insides of his lips. 'Misguided infatuation?'

'Take a look at these. The shorter one is from the parents to me, the longer is what prompted them to write in the first place. They found it under Lewis's pillow at home.' He picked up two letters lying on the top of the correspondence in his in-tray and handed them across to Ben. 'It's got to be looked into, I'm afraid, Ben. These things always do.'

'Jesus Christ,' gasped Ben, looking up after a few moments, 'this is . . . absurd.'

'I couldn't agree more, but the parents – understandably – are anxious.'

'They actually think I would encourage this . . . this drivel?'

'I know, I know, it's unthinkable . . .' Peter Abbott sighed, but his steady brown eyes never left the face of his employee.

'Bloody hell.' Ben hit the letters with the back of his hand. 'This is the last thing I need, I can tell you.' He could feel indignation rising like panic in his chest. 'How dare they think that I would encourage improper affections from a child . . .'

'Now calm down a minute.' Only Peter Abbott's raised left eyebrow indicated his surprise and disappointment at the suggestion of hysteria in Ben's voice. The man was exceptionally talented in every respect, quite capable of running his own school before long, if he played his cards right. 'Let's keep things in perspective. I'll talk to Lewis myself first. Perhaps you would write to his parents. I've already had a word on the phone. He's an only child, as you probably know; blessed with a father who seems to spend half his time flying off to visit oil rigs in North Africa. Not so surprising that he should have latched on to you by way of a substitute.'

'Though it's hardly father–son material, is it, Peter?' muttered Ben, his face sagging with a despondence that he no longer had the energy to hide.

'No, indeed it isn't.' The head took the letters back and removed his spectacles, taking his time to fold and stow them away into the breast pocket of his jacket before speaking again. 'And Lewis seemed perfectly normal on the field trip, did he? No – er – incident that might have been a trigger for this outpouring of passion?' He smiled, to indicate his trust in the answer.

'Jesus, no.'

'Right. Good.' He rubbed his hands together. 'Let's get the matter sorted, then.' Prompted by the look on Ben's face, he added, 'There are other more pleasant aspects to being a role model for these hooligans, Ben, don't forget that.'

Ben tried to smile by way of acknowledging the compliment. But as he turned to leave the room, it occurred to him that the resilient confidence of which he had once been rather proud was in danger of seeping away, leaking out of him from the sheer force of being pulled in so many different directions.

'Steady on, there, old fellow,' exclaimed Caulder, as Ben barged into him on the other side of the door.

'Sorry. I'm late. Sorry. Always fucking late,' he growled, striding back down towards the hall.

'No matter,' humphed the elderly science master, standing back to let him pass and shaking his head in amiable despair. He was a good man, Tarrant, one of the best, in fact, but very tetchy lately; very tetchy indeed.

15

Guilt could make one do strange things, Isobel reflected, pulling up outside the newsagent's in order to buy her husband's aunt a packet of peppermints. As well as the sweets, she bought a large print paperback entitled *Mistress of Destiny*, whose cover featured a full-breasted woman nose to nose with one of the chiselled-faced heroes which had proved such a success on previous occasions. If I bump into Juliet, she thought, then she will see that I am telling the truth, that I am too busy visiting decrepit relatives for idle chat in Royles over cappuccinos and wedges of gateau.

The fact that another bouquet of flowers had been delivered to Fox's Crescent that morning had greatly aided this drive towards virtue. They were more ostentatious than the first lot, all crimson and pink, with fat speckled stamens and wide silky leaves. Overtly sexual, in fact, decided Isobel, telling herself she should be appalled, but managing only to feel secretly thrilled instead. But such flowers definitely needed hiding, she had realised, her heart skipping a beat. Even Ben couldn't fail to notice the flamboyance of their lush red curves and fat green stems. So she put them on the wide window ledge in their little box of a spare room, taking the precaution to pull the curtain half across so that, should anyone open the door, the only evidence of their presence would be a pungent aroma, as unsuspicious as the sickly sweetness of a newly opened air-freshener. Only as Isobel closed the door behind her was she struck by the potentially awesome significance behind such a simple act of deception. It was almost interesting that such a very small – and ostensibly harmless – deed could feel so very wicked.

It wasn't Juliet she bumped into, however, but James. James, whom she had spent all week dreading but hoping to see, by scurrying round Torbridge like a nervous thief, steeling herself for chance encounters round every corner, and then sighing with gratitude and dismay when none occurred.

They caught sight of each other just as Isobel had returned to her car. James, *en route* for a meeting at Torbridge General Hospital, had parked a few yards further up the road in order to post a letter. There was no avoiding each other. He waved at once and began to walk towards her. Torn between beating an unseemly retreat into the safety of her vehicle and yet wanting to appear attractively unflustered, Isobel found herself leaning against the passenger door in the most unnatural of poses, the pages of Aunt Violet's book flapping unhelpfully in the gusty breeze.

'Isobel, how are you?' He was all warmth and confidence, even kissing her on the cheek. He was wearing a grey double-breasted suit flecked with blue and a light pink shirt. His tie was a daring swirl of pink and grey; a tie that Ben would have consigned to the bin, observed Isobel wryly, but which for James was the perfect finishing touch. He would look just as clean-cut and dashing at sixty, she realised, self-consciously putting her fingers to where his lips had touched her skin and offering him a nervous smile in return.

'I'm fine. How are you?' Her voice was unnaturally bright, while her eyes surreptitiously searched his face for signposts as to how they should proceed.

'The Open University has a broader curriculum than I thought.' He winked, gesturing at the paperback with his chin.

'You mean . . . oh this? Oh no, it doesn't – I mean, this is for Ben's aunt. I'm on my way to visit her.'

'Sounds grim.' He made a face.

'She's OK,' replied Isobel quickly, unsure as to whether she was defending Aunt Violet or herself.

'Did you get the flowers?' he whispered suddenly.

'Oh God – I mean, yes, I did, thank you so much, James – they were lovely, but no more I think, don't you? I just feel . . .'

'No more.' He smiled gravely, casting glances between the polished tips of his shoes and her face. 'I can't stop thinking about you, Isobel,' he whispered. 'It's hell.'

'Oh dear.' Though it was what a part of her had been waiting to hear, the disclosure of such intimate information threw Isobel into fresh confusion. 'We're coming to dinner next weekend. Juliet wants us to stay the night. Did she tell you?'

'She most certainly did.' James threw back his head and laughed, pushing his hands deeper into the pockets of his trousers and showing two impressive archways of teeth.

'Don't laugh,' she urged, glancing nervously about them. 'It's awful – I mean, I feel awful. Well, to be honest, I don't know what I feel . . .'

'I know what I feel,' he interrupted with sudden and sober urgency, every trace of amusement wiped from his expression. 'I know what the hell I feel and it's driving me mad. I know you feel it too, Isobel, I know you do.' He slapped the roof of her car, taking a step towards her. 'I can't carry on like this . . . thinking about you all damned day . . .' He was speaking through clenched teeth. '. . . imagining . . . you and me.' He swallowed hard.

'Don't,' she whispered, steering her shaking fingers towards the door handle. 'Don't . . . there's nothing . . .'

'There's everything,' he said hoarsely, touching her shoulder, moulding his hand round its hard curve.

Compelled mostly by a terror of being observed, Isobel somehow wriggled free and levered herself into the car. She did not look up again until she was safely ensconced behind the steering wheel, key ready in the lock, her left hand gripping the handbrake.

James remained on the pavement watching her, feet planted squarely apart, both hands still thrust into his trouser pockets, a look of shameless intensity on his face. If anything her obvious nervousness made him more determined, more excited. It felt like a long time since he had wielded such power over his wife. A long time since he had wielded power over anything.

'Isobel!' exclaimed Aunt Violet, throwing wide her mottled, bangled arms and pressing soft jagged pink lips to her forehead. 'How lovely – how absolutely divine. My dear girl, sit down, sit down and tell me all your news.'

The nurse, who had warned Isobel that her patient was

having something of a good day, winked briefly as she closed the door.

'I brought you these.' Isobel held out the book and peppermints.

'But how kind,' exclaimed Aunt Violet in the high tremulous voice she reserved for special occasions. Making no attempt to examine the gifts, she fixed her eyes upon her visitor's face instead. 'But my dear girl, you look exhausted and so terribly . . . *worried*. I do hope it's not on my account. I love being here – quite the right thing to do. The North was never my *thing*. I should have left years ago . . . but change takes such courage, don't you find? But I always loved my visits to England,' she continued merrily, throwing back her head and pressing her hands together. '—I used to take Ben out on weekends, you know, whisk him off to London and the theatre . . . Ah, but those were gay times . . .' She fanned the air in front of her face, flapping both hands, while her habitual head-nod ran wild, as if keen to offer its own independent support of such enthusiastic emotions.

'And you also left Scotland to visit your brother sometimes, didn't you?' put in Isobel, in a bid to appear interested, wanting, if only for conscience's sake, to see this charitable chore through to the best of her ability. For a moment it seemed as though the question had snapped the chain of lucidity. 'Your brother Albert, the one who settled abroad,' she prompted gently.

Violet's crinkled eyes darkened and then grew dreamy. 'Once or twice . . . such a journey. But blood is thicker . . .' She sighed and started to fidget at the hem of her dress. As the material jerked in her hands, Isobel glimpsed a wide ladder in the thick brown tights; a terrible staircase of veiny white flesh that made her swallow hard and look away.

'Such a fool, Albert was, such a dear fool . . .' She was muttering to herself now, her voice reduced to a series of sniffs and tut-tuts. 'Falling for that Louisa . . . just a girl herself . . . and a foreigner too. Leaving us all like that . . . without a thought for anyone else.' She snorted, before adding more matter-of-factly, 'She couldn't cope when the baby arrived, of course, which was why Albert asked me to visit.'

'That was nice of you,' murmured Isobel, trying and failing to conjure an image of her husband in a pram.

'He was the spitting image of his father. But had his mother's eyes.' Aunt Violet continued, her tongue darting out to retrieve the saliva that had a habit of collecting in the creases round the corners of her mouth. 'Dark Latin eyes . . .'

'So sad that Louisa died,' said Isobel softly, concerned now by the look on her companion's face, the way her jaw was sagging. 'They sound like such a perfect couple—'

'Perfect? They were a disaster,' retorted the old lady indignantly. 'She broke Albert's heart, you know, not once, but many times.'

'Did she?' responded Isobel, mildly intrigued by these disjointed revelations in spite of herself. Ben's own memories, infrequently though they were raised, had always begun with the fatal crash and his father's decision to send him away to England.

'May I have a peppermint now?'

'Of course, they are for you – to eat whenever you want.' Isobel pressed the cool, liver-spotted hand in hers, inadvertently moved by the childishness of the request. 'I brought them for you, remember? And the book.' She patted the cover on the window seat beside them. 'Would you like me to read to you for a while?'

At this, some of the haughty bitterness with which Isobel was more familiar flooded back into the old lady's face. 'Certainly not. Stupid as children, most women. Dressing up and flirting when they shouldn't. Like that one.' She shot an arch look at the provocative image on the book cover. 'In my day we were gay, but never . . . wicked.'

'Is it wicked to flirt?' asked Isobel with studied innocence.

'Louisa was the one to answer that question.'

'Why, what did Louisa do?'

'She was Ben's mother.'

'I know . . . I was just wondering what she was like—'

'So many questions – it's rude, you know, to ask so many personal questions. You should mind your own business, young lady. Who let you in? This is my bedroom . . . my bedroom.' Aunt Violet gripped the arms of her chair and struggled to lever herself upright. Isobel got up to help, but was pushed rudely away. 'I'll ring if I need assistance, thank you. I have servants, you know.'

Isobel remained standing, debating how best to take her leave when her identity had so obviously been mislaid and suppressing the impulse to take offence.

'Could you bring cigarettes next time?' The thread of hostility had been lost. She was all chiming bangles and fluttering smiles again. 'Those pretty cocktail ones – colours like rainbows with heavenly gold tips on the end. Perfect for parties, don't you find?'

Isobel nodded and smiled, though she was sure a no-smoking policy reigned throughout the home. 'I'll see what I can do.'

Once outside, a reluctance to return to the tensions awaiting her in Torbridge made Isobel stroll away from the driveway towards the sloping grass viewed from Aunt Violet's bedroom window. While much of the grounds surrounding the home was rambling and overgrown, the central lawn was kept trimmed and spruce for those still hardy enough to venture beyond the confines of their rooms. Though mowed to a tidy half-inch, the grass proved to be riddled with moss and weeds, a kaleidoscope of different greens that closed round the edges of her shoes like the pile of a soft carpet. After a few minutes she sat down on one of the many benches parked within easy walking distance of the house. A few yards to her left, two peacocks were fanning their tails at each other round a laurel bush, jerking their velveteen necks and looking indignant every time a gust of wind threatened to bowl them over from behind. An old lady swaddled in scarves and furs as protection against the light spring breeze appeared from round the other side of the house. She paused unsteadily, watching the birds' comical courtship for a few minutes before edging her way back along the gravel path by which she had come.

Ben could bring cigarettes if he wanted, decided Isobel crossly, suddenly furious at herself for not having had the courage to tell Juliet outright that she did not wish to meet, for having succumbed to the base and pathetic impulse of manufacturing excuses to account for her time. A screech from one of the peacocks made her jump. The old woman had unnerved her, she realised, leaving the bench and hurrying back towards her car. Those faded eyes could look so horribly beady at times, so disconcertingly knowing. It was almost as if she had recognised her confused state of mind, and had wanted to punish her further with a few timely revelations about the past. Isobel kicked angrily at a pebble on the lawn. Whereas the very last thing she needed was to be furnished with details of the apparently sad subject of her husband's parents' marriage. To feel any curiosity on the subject was irritating beyond belief. She could feel it blocking her mind, preventing her from quite cutting off the tendon of emotion that still bound her to the man she had married. A man who no longer loved her, Isobel reminded herself, opening the car door and throwing her bag inside. The least – the best – thing she could do for all their sakes was to learn not to feel anything in return.

16

Virtue was no good unless it extended to the head as well as the deed, Archie told himself, as the sight of Fox's Crescent induced a frenzy of butterfly wings to beat against the walls of his stomach. In one hand he held a folder of papers relating to both his sponsored walk and the on-going threat to St Cuthbert's. In the other he clenched a Biro which, every few minutes or so, he ran round the inside of his dog-collar to ease the itching. The skin there was a mass of red bumps; not spots exactly, more like a rash, but painful as hell. It did not help that the day was turning out to be curiously warm for early-March; a flagship for summer glories ahead, perhaps, thought Archie grimly, consigning the Biro to his mouth and resorting to his nails.

Archie had spent a dispiriting morning knocking on doors and pressing bell buttons. Many parishioners had not been in and those that had had not exactly greeted him with the warmth he had hoped his smiling, well-intentioned presence might inspire. Anything overtly connected to the Church seemed to make people feel guilty, he had discovered, especially if money was involved. Though the sums relating to his sponsored walk could hardly be described as bankrupting. Thirty-four pounds was an almost embarrassing total compared to the amounts raised by some of the other volunteers. The walk itself – once he had managed to shake off the cloying attentions of the irrepressible Flora Dobbs – had not been too bad at all. The rain held off for the first couple of hours and by the time the drizzle did set in, he was enjoying some lively conversation with a group of Macmillan nurses who had driven from a hospital a hundred miles away to participate. They had insisted on him accompanying them for a celebration drink in a pub afterwards, where they quaffed pints of beer and cracked increasingly risqué jokes through screens of low-tar cigarette smoke. Archie, somewhat alarmed by the force of personalities and ribald humour emerging from the staid mackintoshes and wellingtons that had kept him company through the afternoon, had speedily finished his own pint and slipped away.

Getting close to people was unbelievably hard, he mused sadly, thinking not only of his ineptitude with the nurses, but also of his experiences on doorsteps throughout the morning. Humans were so wary, so painfully suspicious of hidden agendas; when all he was after – all that he longed for – was not to make converts or hear penitent excuses about church attendance, but to be taken on as a friend and confidant. Someone to be trusted. Was it nineties cynicism or was it him? he wondered glumly, running his Biro with a satisfying click along a set of railings to his left. Perhaps he just didn't have the right personality. A cat, roused from a snooze on a dustbin lid, arched its back in disapproval at the noise. As Archie reached out a hand to soothe it, the animal sprang away, disappearing through a gap in a hedge.

Being so hatefully baby-faced and freckled didn't exactly help, Archie reflected with a sigh, catching sight of his reflection in a car wing mirror and glancing quickly away. Nor did having two parts to his surname. Heighton-Jones somehow didn't sound humble enough for a priest. Yet it was a name to which he felt greatly attached, both on account of a generous affection for his parents and the interesting eccentricities of the ancestors from which it derived. Abandoning any part of it would be tantamount to an admission of defeat.

People could take him as he was or not at all, he thought with a surge of defiance, his expression lightening at the sight of Isobel Tarrant's front door. Three Easter chicks made from pipe-cleaners and cotton wool dangled precariously from the door knocker. So precariously that he took the precaution of rapping on the wood beside them instead. When there were no sounds of response from inside he submitted to the temptation of peeking through the letterbox. A couple of envelopes on the doormat reinforced his disappointment. Though it did justify another visit, he thought slyly, straining his neck to see down the hall.

'I'm afraid she's out, Reverend. Shopping, I think. She usually goes to the supermarket on the ring road.'

'Oh, hello there.' The blood rushed to Archie's cheeks as he hastily straightened himself and turned to face Druscilla Carew. 'Yes, yes, I'm afraid that does appear to be the case.' Only the knowledge that all members of the Lord's flock were equally deserving provided Archie with the resources to smile. Mrs Carew had not been on his calling list. Not even for saving St Cuthbert's. There was something alarmingly voracious about the woman, a sense of unappeasable appetites behind the sticky lips and pillar-box smile.

'Anything I can help with?' Her dark eyes alighted upon the papers in his left hand.

'A signature would be marvellous.' He trotted over to the low fence with studied jollity and a heavy heart. 'We're trying to save St Cuthbert's from the arts people.'

'I've just made some macaroons. Would you like one?' She took a step back from the fence and crossed her arms.

Archie patted his stomach, which had a tendency to cave inwards no matter the quantity or density of anything fed into it, and shook his head in a show of regret. 'That's very kind but I'd better not . . .'

'Fiddlesticks. You're all skin and bone. If you eat one of my macaroons I'll sign anything. I forbid you to refuse.' Her eyes blazed from under their heavy canopies of purple and blue eyeshadow. 'And we'll have a coffee,' she commanded, waving a heavily ringed hand at him by way of an instruction to follow her to her front door. 'It'll have to be instant as my percolator's broken. Clogged, I think. Perhaps you would have a little look at it for me?'

'But I'm useless with machines,' protested Archie meekly as she disappeared inside. Muttering expletives to himself, he looked round for a way out. But the street was empty. Apart from a small sparrow with its eye on a crumb at the base of Druscilla's bird table. Though tempted, the sight of the priest's tall figure striding in that direction himself made the creature judge the risk too great. By the time the front door had closed and silence had descended once more, a fat magpie had got there first, alighting upon the morsel with a croak of triumph that set the sparrow hopping in dismay.

Isobel put down her book and brushed the flaky crumbs from her chest. Though a double-sized croissant filled with cheese and bacon had seemed like an inspired subsitute for her usual apology for a lunch – picking at leftovers from the fridge on most days – it had left her feeling faintly sick. She had stopped in a roadside café on her return journey from the supermarket, driven both by genuine hunger and a lingering reluctance to return home. Being between places had suddenly felt potentially liberating; like a pause between sentences, time just to be. The café was new and smelt of chip fat mixed with fresh paint. The only other customers were two lorry drivers and a motorcyclist with a purple birthmark splashed across his left eye and down one side of his nose. The tray of croissants had looked sorely neglected, as had the spinach quiche beside them and a full tureen of orange liquid, which the girl said was carrot and mandarin soup, made fresh the day before.

Having recently progressed from the sedate drawing-room dramas of Jane Austen to the altogether more tempestuous world of *Anna Karenina*, Isobel had at first found some trouble in adjusting. Especially since Anna was clearly one of those infuriating women bent upon a course towards self-destruction, no matter how friends or fate tried to intervene. Yet after a few chapters she had nonetheless become intrigued by the woman's avalanches of passion, towards her lover, Vronsky, in particular. The eroticism of it was breathtaking. It made everything they did forgivable. It made the jealous, vicious rages of her husband despicable. Though wronged, the husband had so far gained the least of Isobel's sympathies. In her view, Anna deserved to keep her child and to have her lover as well. It was obvious that she should, yet equally obvious that such an outcome was not to be. Isobel, wiping the grease off her fingers with a tissue, found herself wondering whether it was just a trick of art that adultery could seem justifiable. Or whether it was the certainty of doom that made it so redeeming.

She sighed and dropped the tissue into her empty coffee cup.

Ben, continuing in the acerbic vein with which he had taken to delivering most remarks, had recently commented that if she read any more she might consider running an Open University course instead of applying to join one. Suppressing the faint hope that such reactions might evince a husbandly jealousy of some kind, Isobel had managed to contain herself to a pursed-lip silence of a response. She did not feel able to stop reading. As well as granting some genuine enjoyment, she was aware that the self-absorption it required presented a legitimate distraction from the failure going on around her, and from the hateful and unrewarding business of trying to prevent it.

She pressed the tissue with the back of her teaspoon, squeezing it into a soggy brown ball, while dwelling on how increasingly incapable her husband seemed of loving anything, except perhaps his work. He had agreed to dinner with the Howards, but only after considerable debate. In fact, so reluctant had he been, so contortedly hesitant, that Isobel had found herself urging the invitation upon him without any of the reserve she had originally felt herself. He didn't even want to spend time with friends now, she thought miserably, let alone with her.

As she brushed a few remaining crumbs off the ripped cellophane cover of her library book and got up to return to her car, it was the recollection of her chance meeting with James that Isobel found the most sustaining. Remembering the pleasure and interest written so plainly across his face during their encounter outside the newsagent's, she smiled and felt stronger. There was someone who would appreciate her all right. Even if he wasn't supposed to.

The difficult, the impossible question of what to do next remained unanswered. As she drove slowly back towards Torbridge, Isobel's gaze kept leaving the road and scanning the hills and tree clumps on either side of her, as if their chalky faces might hold decipherable answers to such a dilemma. On the skyline to her left a lone skeletal tree crouched like a human begging for forgiveness. With a shiver of apprehension Isobel averted her eyes. There was always prettiness too, she assured herself, heaps of it, if only one looked hard enough. All around her spring was unfolding with fairytale perfection; lambs were finding their feet; fields were lush with sprouting tufts of grass; clusters of bobbing flowers lined the roadside. Though summer was many months off yet, the countryside already seemed enveloped by its promise; all its tight, bright colours throbbing with the ripeness contained inside. Like an unwrapped present, she mused. Like her and James: poised for fulfilment. Erotic images began to seep into the tangle inside her head. Images that took all her common sense and self-discipline to force aside. In a way, the situation was perfect as it was, Isobel realised, and a part of her longed to keep it that way. Unwrapped parcels had a horrible tendency to lose their allure, the shapes inside never turning out quite as one had dreamed. It was wonderful being wanted without having given in to it. It was wonderful too to feel such things and yet still be able to say, hand on heart, I have done nothing wrong. Except perhaps to hide a bunch of flowers. It meant she could enjoy the consolation of desire – of being desired – with none of the sin. Isobel gripped the wheel, telling herself that any woman in her shoes would feel the same, that any human would nurture these pleasures as some compensation for the coldness now endured within the sanctuary of her own home.

17

On the Saturday of the Howards' invitation to dinner Ben woke early, his head aching from a fitful sleep. Through bleary eyes he studied the sleeping figure of his wife, his heart filling with a sort of sad longing, as if she were some priceless thing he desired but could not touch. Her lips were relaxed and slightly open, as though ready for a kiss; one thick tress of auburn hair was flung to one side across the pillow; copper on white. Ben stroked the wisps near his face with the back of his hand. She opened her eyes and for a moment their gazes connected. Then reality broke through, bringing with it an awareness of where they were, of unsolved problems, of distance.

'Have you got to go into school?'

'I told you, I've got the first run-through in costume this afternoon.'

'I meant this morning . . .'

'It's my turn to invigilate prep for the boarders.'

'Could you drop Megan at her flute lesson on the way?'

'I mustn't be late—'

'Don't bother, then. We'll manage.'

She kicked off the bedcovers and stretched, reaching her arms up towards the bedstead and screwing up her eyes as she yawned. Her green nightshirt rode up over her shins, revealing bony knees and a slim, creamy portion of thigh. Beside her Ben closed his eyes, leaden with sleepiness now that the day had arrived, and hugged the covers round his face like a child with a comforter. All Isobel could see was a small segment of one cheek, darkly unshaven against the white sheet, and the solid curve of his right arm now clutching the area of duvet she had vacated. The hairs lay flat and dark along his forearm, save for the smoother, lighter band of skin left by his wristwatch. She could see the exaggerated lump of his wrist bone, a famous family trait which he had pointed out to her himself, shyly, on the first night they spent in the same bed. 'If that's your greatest fault then I'm on to a good thing,' she had teased, tracing the shape with the tip of her finger and loving it already because it was a part of him. How uncritical they had been then, how forgiving, how generous. Staring at the lump now, she was struck by the incongruity of it, the curiously inelegant start it made to the long, strong hand; a hand, she thought grimly, which once would have chosen to caress her in preference to a padded bedspread. Tentatively, she reached out to touch him; so tentatively that the moment her fingers made contact with his arm he twitched away, imagining in his sleepiness that he was shaking off a single stray hair or a nervous shiver within the layered mysteries of his own skin.

Ben left the house some twenty minutes later, his face still puffy with fatigue, his hair ironed into odd shapes through nocturnal tussles with his pillow. The girls danced in circles round him, while he grappled with chain locks and bike wheels. They leapt on his back and hung on his arms, squealing with threats never to let go. Somehow Ben seized them both at the same time, spinning them round in a carousel of flaying limbs and laughter till they begged for release. Isobel, watching from inside the hall, hugged herself against the stream of chill morning air, while a terrible envy welled inside. That he could be so unchanged for their children only heightened her own sense of alienation and loss. By the time Ben looked up to wave, she had retreated into the bathroom to wash and plait her hair.

Her fingers worked deftly with the thick wet strands, while her eyes gazed defiantly at her reflection in the mirror. Her mood hardened still further as she rummaged through shelves and cupboards for clothes. Aware that she should not mind what she wore – that it would be wrong to mind what she wore – only increased Isobel's mounting concern for her appearance. She wanted to compose an outfit that would do for the day as well as the evening. I am going to dress for James, she realised with a start, discarding a handsome but dull brown dress in favour of a calf-length bottle-green skirt and a creamy cotton shirt. It had a wide lacy collar and crisp broad cuffs, fed by billowing sleeves that were pleated attractively at the shoulder. Shoes were harder. It wouldn't do to look too dressy. Having settled on a pair of low-heeled old black favourites, she looked up to see her youngest daughter, indignant and pink-faced, surfacing from amongst the heap of bedclothes.

'I was hiding and you didn't even notice,' she wailed.

'But Sophie, darling, you were so terribly good and still, how could I possibly have known you were there?'

Partially mollifed, Sophie flung herself across the bed on to her elbows and stared sulkily at her mother. 'Are you going to a party?'

For a moment Isobel felt caught out. 'Don't be silly . . . I mean, we're going to Eddie and Tilly's house, remember?' she added, recovering herself. 'The grown-ups are having a special dinner and we're all staying the night. Mummy thought she would look a little smart for once.' She tossed her plait over her shoulder and began punching air into pillows. 'Off the bed now, or I can't make it.'

'I think you always look smart – and *very* pretty,' announced Megan, bounding in barefoot through the doorway and slipping into a dusty pair of court shoes, which Isobel had excavated from the back of the wardrobe. 'Why don't you wear these?' she enquired, balancing with difficulty on the high heels. 'They're beautiful.'

Surveying her eldest parading Lolita-like round the bedroom made Isobel laugh in spite of herself. 'Because nowadays if Mummy wears those for more than ten minutes at a time the circulation stops in in all her toes.'

'What's circulation?' asked Megan, now eyeing her dramatic footwear more doubtfully.

'It's the blood going round our bodies. Every little finger and toe needs it otherwise it falls off . . .'

'Falls off?'

'But only if the blood can't get to them for quite a long time,' explained her mother quickly, suppressing a smile.

Megan kicked off the shoes and began a worried inspection of her extremities, before being distracted by the more rewarding pastime of studying her hair for split ends and seeing if any might be encouraged to split a little further. Behind her, Sophie, endeavouring to do a headstand in the middle of the bed, yowled with frustration each time her skinny legs toppled out of control.

Watching the pair of them, Isobel experienced a rush of sentimental love. Were the girls really all that kept Ben with her now? she wondered, reaching out to stop Sophie's knees from a collision with her sister's head. The idea prompted a motherly hug of such inappropriate intensity that Sophie, sensing an emotion that made her afraid, scowled and squirmed away. Long after her daughters had chased each other out of the room, Isobel stayed where she was, twisting a fold of sheet between her fingers and wondering how long they could all go on as they were.

Ben cycled fast, barely pausing to check for traffic at the end of Fox's Crescent before swerving left in the direction of the town centre. A small detour took him past Torbridge's famously irresistible Old Bakery where he bought a large Danish pastry by way of breakfast. As he left the shop, already chewing hungrily, he was confronted by James, looking spruce and clean-shaven in a padded green vest of a coat and rust-coloured corduroy trousers. He clicked his heels and saluted when he saw Ben, who, for no explicable reason, felt his heart sink ungratefully in return. He hastily raked his fingers through his hair and wiped the crumbs from his cheek with the back of his hand.

'James . . . on Saturday duty are you?'

'Only in the domestic sense.' James grinned and waved an empty shopping basket at him by way of an explanation. 'On a mission in aid of our revels tonight. Fresh rolls – some of this establishment's finest – half a dozen eggs and . . . buggeration . . . what was the other thing?' He began patting his pockets in search of a list. 'Wrote it down somewhere . . .'

'Milk?' suggested Ben, for no reason other than the fact that it popped with enticing coherence into the fog of his head.

'Milk. That's it, exactly. You're a genius, Ben. Four pints. Three semi-skimmed, one completely skimmed. Juliet's trying to keep us all fat-free,' he added, rolling his eyes at the sky in a show of amused tolerance that bore little relation to the real state of affairs at home. Juliet was on her high horse and would not get down. It did not help that he was aware he had put her there, through irritation at all the absurd hocus-pocus about feet and flower oils, and – rather less complicatedly – because of Isobel. Unfortunately, the tentacles of such unresolved conflicts seemed to have probed every other aspect of their existence too, instilling a general negativity about domestic life, which was for James quite unprecedented and highly unsettling. The approaching evening with the Tarrants had been the only shaft of light in what would otherwise have been a very dark tunnel indeed.

'How was Wales?'

'Wales?' For a moment Ben's mind refused to move on from milk. Then he remembered all the problems connected with the boy Lewis and frowned. The child had been removed from the school; behaviour that suggested the parents remained suspicious in spite of all Peter Abbott's reassurances to the contrary. Without such unfaltering support from his headmaster, Ben was not sure how he would have coped with the situation at all.

Another customer leaving the bakery murmured an 'excuse me' and stepped between them. The interruption gave Ben a moment to collect his thoughts. 'More to the point, how are you . . . ?' he burst out heartily. 'I mean . . . Christ, I haven't seen you since the damned bomb – haven't thanked you properly for fielding Isobel and the children – that was very kind, James, very kind indeed . . . it will be months before the girls are properly over it . . . hope they catch the bastards.'

'Got a couple of Irishmen in custody apparently – heard it on the news this morning.'

'Really? Well, that's marvellous . . . look here, James, I've got to go – late as usual.' Ben smiled weakly. Remembering his half-eaten pastry, he took a large bite. 'See you tonight, of course,' he muttered, ineptly fielding crumbs with his tongue.

'Absolutely.' James gave Ben an affectionate pat on the shoulder, declaring, 'I'm looking forward to it enormously,' and thinking to himself that this was true, even if the prime cause for such zest remained as wholly inappropriate fodder for conversation with Isobel's husband. 'Look like you could do with a night off, mate, to be honest,' he added, on a spurt of sincerity that may well have derived from the uncomfortable duplicity of such notions.

'I'm fine. Only a few weeks till the Easter break – I'll catch up on myself then.'

'Lucky sod,' growled James cheerfully before disappearing inside the shop. He chose a selection of brown and white bread rolls and a sesame-seed baguette for good measure. By the time he re-emerged, Ben and his bicycle were at the far end of the street. Raising his arm in salute, though there was little chance of the gesture being received, James was struck by how small and curiously vulnerable Ben Tarrant looked. The thought was at once novel and vaguely disturbing. A weak man was harder to respect, easier to beat. Not just on the squash court, but in other areas too. A small, unforgivable sense of power tightened in the pit of the doctor's stomach as he embarked on a deliberately unhurried drive back to Ilcombe. A power that thrilled as much as it disconcerted. Of course it was wrong to lust after another man's wife, but it was exciting too. Especially if the wife concerned responded with such charming and eager perturbation. James slapped the steering wheel hard several times, inwardly riling against the social constraints of his immediate situation, and more deep-seated, less easily defined disappointments to do with the pattern of his life in general.

18

'Do you ever miss that first flush of being in love?' The question slipped out of its own accord, oiled by the smooth pummelling of Juliet's hands across her back. The entire length of Isobel's body felt drowsy and warm. The heavy scent of roses, which had at first struck her as merely cloying, now tasted like the sweetest air; each inhalation seemed to drug her mind with fresh colour and depth.

Having expected only the unease of guilt, Isobel had been somewhat overcome by the pleasure she had experienced upon seeing Juliet again. Their friendship came into its own, fuelled by the separate but related difficulties each had endured during the preceding weeks. While the children stampeded upstairs to begin constructing dens for the night, Juliet had shooed Isobel into the spare room for her promised introduction to the delights of aromatherapy.

'All that brooding over one sentence, one word, one inflection? All that navel-searching over which feelings one should have and how intensely?' Juliet snorted. 'Not bloody likely.' She ran her thumbs down Isobel's spine, from the nape of her neck to the small of her back, pushing hard. 'I'm a bit off love in general at the moment, to be honest.' She brushed a few stray zigzags of hair out of her eyes, using the back of her hand so as to avoid the oil gleaming in her palms, and gave a dismissive sniff. 'And lust for that matter.'

'What, even with that Adonis bricklayer of yours?' teased Isobel lazily, her mind cruising soft, insouciant seas of crimson and orange.

'*Especially* with him.' Juliet paused to sprinkle a few more drops of oil on to her hands. 'Not even that scrubbing board of a stomach moves me now.'

Isobel giggled. 'Harsh words indeed. What crime has he committed?'

'You mean apart from leaving a superglue-like trail of cement and filth through the house when I specifically told them all to use the side door? Oh God, and the downstairs loo . . . by the time that lot have finished with it in the morning . . .' She groaned. 'Cigarette stubs floating in the bowl, half a roll of paper gone . . .'

'I get the picture,' interjected Isobel, feeling, as she so often did with Juliet these days, that she was being entertained rather than spoken to. 'Reality strikes again.'

'You're telling me. But listen to this, you haven't heard the worst of it.' She lowered her voice. 'I was standing in my bedroom the other day, doing my face in the mirror by the window. Still in my petticoat. One eye done, hair its usual morning haystack, when suddenly there he was, standing in the doorway behind, staring at me . . .'

'There who was?' enquired Isobel, incredulous.

'The handsome one. The workman with the ponytail. Only suddenly he didn't look handsome at all. He looked greedy and hopeful. And in the same moment I saw myself as he must: a plump middle-aged woman looking for a bit of young stuff on the side . . .'

'Oh, come on now . . .' Isobel tried to lever herself up off the bed, but Juliet pressed her down.

'Stay where you are or the effect will be ruined. I knew at once that it was entirely my fault. I batted my eyelashes once too often and he thought he really stood a chance. But it was quite a shock, I can tell you.'

'So what did you do?'

'I told him to get the hell out of my bedroom, that's what I did. And he scampered off like a naughty schoolboy. I haven't managed to feel the same about him since.'

'I'm not surprised.' Isobel couldn't help laughing.

'Now you see, I couldn't tell James about that.'

At the mention of James, Isobel felt the breath snag in her throat. 'And why not?'

'Not in his present mood. He'd get angry – with me and that silly boy, probably. That is, if he could get angrier than he is at the moment.'

'What's he angry about?' asked Isobel in a small voice.

'Oh, nothing much.' Juliet's tone was airily dismissive. 'Me. Aromatherapy. Reflexology and any other perfectly good healing practice which is not scrupulously itemised in medical textbooks. I've decided that eventually I want to train in reflexology as well, you see. It's just too fascinating for words. We've had some fearful rows about it,' she added ruefully. 'Personally, I think it's a gender thing. We women believe in the mystical stuff – healings and happenings that cannot necessarily be explained – and men don't. The darlings are just so hopelessly calculating and analytical . . .' She sighed again. 'What does Ben think about things like that? Could I convert him with a massage or two, do you think?' She karate-chopped her way across Isobel's shoulder blades to emphasise the point.

'Ben? I'm not sure,' faltered Isobel, thinking that she was in fact more certain of her husband's views on Juliet's penchant for creative hobbies than she was of most things.

'I'll ask him tonight.' Juliet studied her palms, which were looking warm and very red. 'And you see if you can cheer James up a bit for me, will you? This is quite the sulkiest I've ever known him.' She clapped her hands together, clearly ready to move on to other subjects. 'Now . . . I want you with your forehead down so I can get at your neck. And let's keep this beautiful plait safely out of the way – God, this mane of yours is glorious . . . that's it. I need you centralised. There we are. How are you feeling, by the way?'

'Wonderful,' mumbled Isobel, wondering quite how she was supposed to continue breathing with the flat of her face buried ear-deep in pillow.

'Rose oil is by far the best, in my opinion,' went on Juliet from behind. 'The most expensive too, mind you. The Egyptians swore by it. It's supposed to be a mild sedative, an antidepressant, a soother, a spirit-lifter and – oh yes – an aphrodisiac, especially for women. Isn't that incredible? Should I warn Ben?' she enquired slyly. 'Or don't you do it in other people's houses?'

'Mind your own bloody business,' retorted Isobel, managing a brief muffled laugh before burrowing deeper and more gratefully into her pillow. A white lake with grey specks floated into view. She squeezed her lids tightly but the image remained. Cold and empty. My husband flinches at the touch of me, she remembered, the misery of it connecting somehow to the drab screen fixed like a mask before her eyes. She pressed her head deeper still into the bed, wishing she could stifle such knowledge away.

'Keep still, for God's sake,' scolded Juliet. 'This last bit is so important.' She began kneading authoritatively along the slender ridge of Isobel's neck, pushing up under the base of the skull in a way that felt curiously wholesome and yet unpleasant. Then she took hold of Isobel's head in both hands and gently stretched it towards the bedstead, as if trying to lengthen the spine itself. The sensation was so unsettling that Isobel opened her mouth to protest. In the same instant Juliet released her head and lightly scraped her nails down her back and legs, stopping at the tips of her toes. 'There,' she whispered, tucking the towel back round Isobel's shoulders and ankles. 'You mustn't get cold. Stay like that for a bit while I clear up.'

Isobel kept her eyes closed, floating again in a pinky darkness of her own, while Juliet bustled softly between the bedroom and adjoining bathroom. 'You're looking fabulous, by the way, Isobel,' she announced, drying her hands on a small yellow hand towel. 'I've been meaning to say . . . I was quite worried about you a couple of weeks ago, but now you're all lit up. I love that shirt too. Heavenly sleeves. You haven't acquired a lover by any chance, have you?' She held the garment against herself for size and did a small twirl round the end of the bed.

'A lover?' Isobel turned over slowly, keeping the towel up round her chin.

Juliet carefully hung the shirt on the back of a chair. 'Or is it this Open University lark that's giving your cheeks such a glow?'

Isobel groaned, despising the relief that flooded through her on being so swiftly diverted to safer ground. 'Hardly. I can't decide whether to make a formal application or not. To be honest, I dread the thought of having to write essays again, when I suppose all I really want to do is read the books.'

'Well, read books, then. Bugger the course. Cup of tea?'

'Time for a drink, Tarrant?'

Ben looked up from his desk to find Dick Caulder peering at him over the rims of his half-moon spectacles.

'I don't think so, Dick. Sorry.' He shot him an apologetic smile before returning his attention to the pile of rehearsal notes in front of him. He was marking the lighting cues – each one of which had been disastrous – with angry slashes of red felt pen. 'I should have left already,' he added, since his colleague showed no signs of moving away. 'We're out to dinner in Ilcombe tonight. Old friends. I was going to cycle but' – he frowned at his watch – 'on second thoughts I'll call a cab.'

'I could drop you. Ilcombe's on my way.'

'No it isn't.'

'Well, not far off.' Dick jangled the change in his pockets. 'I'd like to, Ben.'

Ben sighed, threw down his pen and leant back in his chair. 'You're an obstinate sod, aren't you?'

Dick Caulder grinned. 'I'll get my coat, then, shall I?'

Some twenty minutes later they were standing elbow to elbow in front of two pints of toffee-coloured real ale, sharing a bag of bacon-flavoured crisps.

'I haven't eaten since this morning,' Ben confessed, tearing the bag apart and pressing out the last of the salty crumbs inside.

'How'd the rehearsal go?'

'Middling to bloody awful. Though I suppose some of the little buggers know their words now. And most of the costumes worked, after a fashion. Julius Caesar – the infamous Giles Turner – is finally coming good too. In fact, it looks as if he'll end up carrying the whole show. There's a sort of atmosphere when he's on, a feeling of suspense, a sense of danger even . . . or maybe desperation is starting to play tricks on my imagination.' He laughed uncertainly and took a large mouthful of beer.

'Sounds most promising to me.'

A comfortable silence ensued, during which the two men sipped their drinks and contemplated the colourful array of bottles and labels on the wall behind the bar.

'I've been seeing one of those what-do-you-call-thems . . . a counsellor,' announced Caulder, just as Ben was on the point of draining his glass and suggesting they leave. 'Therapy.' He scowled and pressed the bridge of his nose.

'Because of . . .'

'Agnes – the wife – dying. Yes, because of that. Thought I could cope, but I coudn't. Anxiety attacks started. Saw my GP, got referred. Simple, really.'

'And has it helped?' Steered by compassion for the unimaginable effort of making such an admission, not wanting to make it any harder than it was already, Ben began an engrossed inspection of his wedding ring, pulling it to the hump of his knuckle and back again.

'Do you know, it has. Can't think why, really. Just someone to talk to. Used to talk to Agnes all the time, I suppose . . . kept ourselves very much to ourselves. Too much probably. Not great ones for friends or socialising. Find myself talking to the shrubbery these days – are you into gardening, Tarrant?'

Ben shook his head, smiling apologetically.

'Neither was I at your age. Agnes did the lot. Now I spend half my spare time out there. Roses are my speciality. I've planted a whole bed of Rugosas called "Agnes" in her honour. Sentimental, I know, but I can't tell you how it's helped. Big flowers, thorny stems – just like her,' he chuckled quietly, 'all heart and bark . . .' He clamped his teeth together to hide a momentary tremble in his jaw. 'They'll look a treat in May.'

'Dick . . .'

'Oh, I'm not saying I don't get down – I miss her like hell most days – most nights too . . . but it's' – he hesitated, searching for the right word – '*manageable* now. I know I can live with it. Nice lady counsellor I got. Kind without going overboard. No pressure either, to say anything really. Or even to keep going. Unshockable too, which was nice. When I think of some of the things . . .'

They were on their second pints now. A couple more empty crisp packets had joined the heap of old cigarette stubs in the massive pewter ashtray in front of them.

'All I'm saying is, it gets such a knocking – all this business of people seeing shrinks instead of talking to each other – but it can really help. Anybody. It can help anybody.'

It took a while for Ben to realise that instead of being in the role of sympathetic listener, as he had, perhaps arrogantly, assumed, he was himself being given some veiled advice. The realisation shocked him so much that he could think of nothing appropriate to say at all. It was like being found guilty of a secret crime. And for his accuser to be a man towards whom he had grown accustomed to feeling nothing but pity was at once humiliating and deeply humbling.

Caulder was still talking, more quietly and more directly now. '. . . the Lewis business hasn't helped, I know, though believe me it will blow over. Has already. The boy's a twit and his parents no better. But coming on top of everything else . . . I've been watching you for a while now, Ben, seeing how much you've taken on, the extra hours you give to every damn project, every ass of a boy . . . not spending enough time at home . . .'

Inside, Ben felt as if one single remaining thread was holding him together, that if Caulder said anything else that was either true or kind, he would collapse into a state of total incoherence.

'I've got her card, if you're interested.' He put something in the nearest pocket of Ben's anorak. 'Or just throw it away, of course. No more said on the matter, if you don't want to. Entirely up to you.' He slipped off his stool and dangled his car keys in front of Ben's still-unregistering expression. 'Better get you to this dinner, mate, or you'll be in the dog-house in no uncertain terms. Mind you, I even miss that,' he added, leading the way to his car, 'damn fool that I am.'

19

Walking into the Howards' sitting room that night reminded Ben of walking on stage. Except the audience was closer and participating volubly. Their chorus of reassurances that being late did not matter at all only served to convince him that it in fact mattered very deeply. Juliet, kissing the air beside his ears with theatrical noises of welcome, looked the most obviously flustered of the three. 'Isobel warned me from the start that you'd have a horrid rehearsal to get through first. Was it ghastly? You look quite washed out,' she chattered, not looking at Ben at all, before hurrying into the kitchen to put the starters in the microwave. 'I warn you,' she called gaily through the open hatch connecting the rooms, 'I take no responsibility for the state of the meal.'

'Ben's a good cook, he can take over,' quipped James, winking over the top of his glass.

Isobel, beaming to make up for the disheartening look of bewilderment on her husband's face, the dishevelled state of his hair and clothes, shrugged hopelessly, as one might shrug at the endearing misbehaviour of an errant child. 'He is a good cook, you're right, James,' she declared firmly and falsely, crossing the room to bestow a kiss on Ben's cheek. As she did so she smelt the beer on his breath, the unpleasant aroma of smoke in his clothes.

'Good rehearsal, was it?' she murmured, all her loyalty crushed by this evidence of duplicity.

'Fine.' He switched his attention to James, who was now offering him a flute of champagne.

'We're at least a bottle ahead of you, old friend, so drink up.' As James handed the drink over, his eyes found time to flick to Isobel's face. Her expression was unreadable, disappointingly so. 'How's your glass, Isobel?' he urged, wanting to draw her gaze to his.

'It's OK, thanks.' She offered him a flutter of a look, an embarrassed, reluctant acknowledgment that made the hairs on the back of his neck stand up. James took a step nearer. He could smell her perfume; sweet musky roses. Anything could happen, he thought breathlessly, a heady sense of freedom exploding in his mind. He had quite forgotten how acutely attractive the perception of such possibilities could be, how bloody intoxicating. His present life seemed positively deprived in comparison, all his existing relationships nothing but uninspiring cul-de-sacs of familiarity.

'I thought about inviting some other people, but decided it was so long since the four of us had got together that I'd keep it cosy.' Juliet, revived by the pretty sight of her dinner table and the benevolent smile fixed on her husband's face, raised a glass in toast to them all. 'Welcome. To friendship.'

'To friendship,' they echoed, while each in his heart questioned the meaning of the word.

Ben found his stomach quailing at the sight of the milky flesh of the scallops that formed the centrepiece of their first course, the humps of their brilliant orange tails swelling somehow obscenely out of the generous lakes of Juliet's heavy cream sauce.

'Freshly caught this morning,' she whispered, tracing the line of his gaze and misinterpreting its cause. 'They're a bit like oysters, you know,' she continued, raising her voice so as to include James and Isobel. 'That is, they are said to have aphrodisiac properties . . . like rose oil.' She gave Isobel a pointed look.

Isobel dutifully opened her mouth to pronounce upon the delights of aromatherapy massage, but James got there first with a good-humoured groan.

'Not those bloody oils again. Juliet's obsessed by the damn subject. Thinks she can cure the ills of the world . . . I'm not saying a good massage isn't relaxing – whatever part of the body is involved' – he paused to chuckle and dab his lower lip with his napkin – 'but as to actually healing, in the sense that an antibiotic goes about its work . . .' He stabbed a scallop with his fork. 'Well, frankly, it's ridiculous. Don't you think, Ben?'

'Probably.' Ben, fighting an overwhelming sense of alienation, of not belonging or knowing anybody in the room, had to force his attention to the subject. 'Though my Aunt Violet used to swear by lavender oil for cuts and bruises.'

'There. See?' Juliet pointed across the table with her fish knife. 'I told you, it's been going on for generations.'

'And how is your aunt?' asked James, ignoring his wife and turning to Ben, still smiling but with an icy edge to his voice. 'I'm sometimes grateful that all our own dear ancients are pushing up the proverbial daisies. Such a worry, old people, aren't they? Especially when they're not even immediate family. So time-consuming, all those visits . . .' As he spoke, his knee brushed against Isobel's. The movement was so swift and subtle that a moment later she was wondering if she had imagined it.

'Aunt Violet is family,' replied Ben slowly, managing to fuel his irritation into the grip on his wineglass.

'So, no regrets about taking her on, then?'

'Taking her on?'

'The move to the home.' James chewed lazily on a crust of sesame seeds, unaware of the latent hostility in Ben's tone. Only Isobel recognised it.

'Aunt Violet's a dear old thing,' she interjected hastily, 'no trouble at all.'

'As a matter of fact, she did more for me than most parents,' said Ben, his emotions back under control and his spirits lifting at the smell emanting from the casserole dish Juliet had set down on the place mat in front of her. The dizziness in his head told him that he was badly in need of food, real food. 'Isobel is marvellous about visiting her. It's harder for me to find the time. And to be frank, it's bloody depressing.'

'But not depressing for Isobel?' chirruped Juliet, thinking she was being clever, thinking that it was high time one of them made a show of sisterly support.

'Of course.' Ben swallowed. 'Though Isobel didn't know her before, when she was still . . .' To his horror, he felt a lump block his throat. Images of Aunt Violet, gusting into school occasions, decked in embarrassingly flamboyant hats and trailing cigarette smoke, her voice zigzagging shrilly across crowded rooms, flooded his mind, bringing with it an absurd sadness. He had hated her. Partly for being so conspicuous. Mostly for not being his mother. 'As I said,' he resumed, in normal tones, 'Isobel is marvellous. I am deeply grateful to her, in many ways, but especially with regard to the burden of my aged and cranky aunt.' He lifted his wineglass, his dark eyes glittering at his wife across the table. Though the ostensible subject of this tribute, Isobel sensed only a coldness at the heart of it. While their hosts cheered in support, she realised with fresh force that her husband was a stranger to her, that he had been for some considerable time.

Several stories of Juliet's about an ancient acting acquaintance with four miniature poodles and a penchant for vodka saw them through to the cheese. By which time all four members of the party were, to varying degrees, enjoying the peculiar lack of inhibition generated by the consumption of alcohol. Shielded by an increasing sense of unreality, Isobel found herself waiting for the by now regular contacts from the warm knee beside her, each more prolonged than the last. Nor did it come as any surprise when James's hand sought hers under the generous canopy of Juliet's treasured damask tablecloth. His fingers felt cool and very sure of themselves. It's only holding hands, she reassured herself, while the squeezing and stroking to which her fingers were being treated blatantly suggested intimacies on a far grander scale. Whilst not exactly unpleasant, it was the absurd audacity of such behaviour that struck Isobel more forcefully than anything. Across the table, the glazed look in Ben's eyes seemed merely neglectful. While beside him Juliet was drooping visibly, dry squirls of her hair trailing amongst abandoned crumbs of cheese and wholemeal crackers.

A little later, while Juliet clawed ineffectually at the cellophane on a box of mint chocolate sticks presented to her by Isobel that afternoon, James found the wherewithal to produce a jug of coffee. Back in the dining room a sense of disintegration prevailed. Juliet's half-hearted plea for Ben and Isobel to entertain them at the piano was quickly swept aside by her husband. Much to the relief of the Tarrants themselves. Never had Isobel felt less capable of steering her clear but subdued soprano through their limited repertoire of theme tunes. While Ben, too, felt quite unequal to the challenge of justifying his reputation for ingenious improvisation at the keyboard. So great was the weight of sleepiness now pressing upon him, that he only managed to keep his eyes open with the accompanying facial support of a frown. He reached an elbow towards the table, but found only empty space. Inside, melancholy pressed like a need for air.

'Funny how the past always looks so much better,' he said quietly, snapping his stick of chocolate in half and laying the pieces side by side. His head was full of Aunt Violet again, of her dogged loyalty to his father, of a guardianship bestowed not for love of a child so much as an obstinate family duty. 'No matter what you felt at the time.'

'Oh, I don't know,' murmured James, 'the future can look pretty rosy too.'

Isobel fixed her eyes upon the candle sputtering low amongst a flower arrangement in the centre of the table. There was yellow and green at its heart, she noticed, and a small core of blackness. It never occurred to her that Ben could be referring to his childhood. He means to hurt me, was all she thought. He is trying to tell me that we have nowhere to go. With what felt like enormous courage, she forced her eyes to leave the flame and meet her husband's, to face the rejection that awaited her there. But all that greeted her were the scruffy dark curls of Ben's head. With the grateful closing of his eyes, his chin had tipped down on to his chest; his cheeks sagged visibly with the relief of release.

'Poor love,' crooned Juliet, nearly asleep herself. 'Let's get him upstairs.'

'I'm fine,' retorted Ben, jolting awake and looking round the table with a kind of rage, his eyes bloodshot and heavy-lidded.

'But we're all going to bed, Ben, my sweet,' cooed Juliet, patting his hand. 'We're all in a hopeless state . . .' She levered herself out of her chair, yawning deeply and shaking her head. 'Just clear this lot . . .'

'I'll do it, my love,' offered James slyly, adrenalin inspiring sobriety. 'Isobel will help, won't you, Isobel?'

She nodded meekly, not trusting herself to speak. It felt suddenly as if events were in control of her, and that only by submitting to them would a resolution ever be found.

20

Druscilla was watching television in the dark. A group of men with shaved heads and earrings were talking about parenthood and the rights of homosexuals to adopt a child. A woman waved a microphone between them, interjecting questions which seemed to have little effect upon the general course of the conversation. Druscilla was studying the woman's scarlet bubble of a mouth, intrigued both by its vibrancy and elasticity, when she heard the noise outside. A cross between a clang and a thud that made her jump. Driven more by curiosity than concern, she edged her way to the front window and peered into the night. The row of terraced houses across the street huddled shoulder to shoulder, like dark sleeping giants. With what moon there was veiled in cloud, only the streetlamps cast any light on the scene. There was no sign of movement or life outside; only the sense of it. One of Druscilla's cats hopped on to the window sill and ran its tail across her face.

'Did you hear it too, my pet? Did you? Clever girl. Yes, she is. Mummy is going to see.' She scratched the smudged white face with the tips of her scarlet nails. 'You stay here and watch these lovely people,' she instructed, lifting the cat on to the armchair in front of the television and pulling a rug off the back of the sofa to wrap around her bare shoulders. Though it was well into the small hours of an evening that she had spent entirely alone, Druscilla was wearing her best frock, a long pinky silk affair which she had rescued from a charity shop a few years before. A floppy cotton rose was stitched at the centrepoint of its plunging neckline, while remnants of lace trimmings hung like streamers from its arms and hem. Druscilla found it impossible not to feel glorious in such a thing. Marvellous tonic for a sleepless night, or a pick-me-up for one of those rare low spots, when the past came at her like a dark avalanche, when even the cats seemed to embody spirits of people she longed only to forget.

Outside, the cold paving stones sent icy charges through the slim soles of her pumps. The scrape of a dustbin lid made her start and spin round. 'Come out!' she shrieked, waving the umbrella that she had taken the precaution of bringing with her like a sword. A small fox scurried away across the road. I am fearless, she thought excitedly, jigging on her frozen feet and la-la-ing in celebration. She was dancing towards the Tarrants' front door, conducting herself with the umbrella, when the sudden grating of an opening sash window momentarily stole some of the valour from her heart.

'Who is it?' called an angry voice which she recognised as belonging to Mr Coombes, head of the impossibly hostile family who were her neighbours on the other side.

'Only me. Druscilla Carew,' she trilled back. 'I heard a noise.'

'Do you have any idea what time it is . . . ?'

'I think it was a fox . . . but the Tarrants are away tonight, so I'm taking a little look . . .'

'Bloody woman,' muttered the man, yanking his window shut and wondering, not for the first time, what had to happen before a citizen could be locked away for being certifiably insane.

'Silly, silly bugger,' whispered Druscilla to herself, pushing open the Tarrants' front gate and scowling at the rusty squeak of its hinge. Having got this far, it seemed only right to make a proper investigation. It was just her poor toes that were really starting to suffer from the cold. The rest of her was tingling almost pleasantly, adding to the delightful sensation of being exaggeratedly alive, of being ready for any foe, invisible or otherwise. What if I did scare away a burglar? she thought, skipping through wet leaves up to the front doorstep, imagining how pleased Isobel would be, how wonderfully grateful. The notion was so sustaining that she extended her exploration to both sides of the house, even peering through the crack in the side door across the alley that led round the back. But there was nothing to see, save for the faint dark outline of the tree swing and the small garden shed beyond. After a few moments

Druscilla made her way, with a little less exuberance, back round to the front gate. She had almost reached it when her eye was caught by something white, half hidden by earth and twigs. She stopped at once, thinking it might be an item belonging to one of the girls, a mitten maybe, or one of Megan's pretty white socks. Instead, she found herself retrieving a small calling card, with a tiny pink rose embossed on the top left-hand corner and a couple of lines of writing – smudged and muddied almost to the point of illegibility – across its middle. Curiously consoled, feeling that she had found at least some kind of a memento of her night's adventure, Druscilla tucked it into the deep cleft between her breasts before hurrying back to her open front door.

She would tell Isobel about her vigilance anyway, she decided, stirring large quantities of sugar into hot milk as she returned to her armchair in the sitting room. Not to blow her own trumpet, but just because it would be neighbourly to do so. Burglars were everywhere these days, like those horrid bombers. Nobody could be too careful. Pleased to see the earringed men had been replaced by James Stewart in a bow tie, Druscilla curled up happily under a blanket, pulling a cat inside it for added warmth. She placed the card on the arm of the chair beside her. *For Isobel. My darling, no words can say what I feel,* it said, which was nice, Druscilla decided, giving the card a little pat. Very nice indeed.

Archie slid two more pieces of bread under the grill and poured himself a second glass of milk. While inconceivably hard for a sandwich, the bread made fine, if slightly brittle, toast; more than adequate as a vehicle for the unsurpassable luxury of his mother's home-made damson jam. Since the heat control on the grill functioned only in the sense that it moved rapidly to a blinding maximum, Archie kept a close guard. Turning away for just a second too long had, on countless occasions, proved fatal for many a promising sausage and fishcake, not to mention loaves' worth of healthy bread. Scraping out every last blob from under the lip of the jar, he spread the red jelly thickly across both pieces of toast, swirling his knife around in small circular motions so as to mix in as much as possible of the melting butter.

He ate very quickly, taking enormous mouthfuls, oblivious of the specks of yellowy pink dotting his chin. As soon as he had finished Archie felt sad, partly because of the empty jar, and partly because of the half-written letter awaiting his attention on the small lumpy Formica table in front of him. There was nothing to do but return to it now. He would not be able to sleep until it was done. It was already two o'clock. He had to be up before daylight to help Reverend Tully at the early Sunday service, a prospect for which he was struggling to experience any enthusiasm at all. There had been the grand total of eight communicants attending the previous week, and that included old Terry, whose reasons for huddling by church radiators were rarely spiritual and who smacked his lips shamelessly after receiving the sacraments. In a few years there would be no one at all, thought Archie grimly, visualising the grey bent heads of this early congregation with a new cynicism that he hated but could not dispel.

Taking his milk, he slumped back down at the table and glowered at his attempts to end the only serious relationship he had ever had – or had expected to have – in his life.

Dear Bridget,

You're probably wondering why I have not been in touch for a while. I am very busy here, as you know, but I'm afraid there are other reasons too. No, I have not met someone else, if that is what you are thinking. But I have decided that you should not 'wait' for me any more. I don't think I'm going to be ready to settle down – with anybody – for a long time to come, if ever. Knowing how much you want to start a family and so on, I think it only fair that you should feel free to see other people.

The worst thing about all this is the thought of hurting you, Bridget. You are the most perfectly good and kind person I have ever met – I mean that – and deserve to be really happy. It's just that I no longer believe I am the right person to bring you that happiness . . .

Which was the gentlest way he could think of saying precisely the opposite, acknowledged Archie wearily, rolling the pen between his palms as he agonised over how to start another sentence. He had known Bridget Evans since his teens, had shared with her the awkwardness of first kisses, of holding moist hands in cinemas, between whispered promises of inexhaustible love. While many friends of the time had been enjoying similar experiments, Archie and Bridget differed in that they did not move on to fresh partners and oaths, but remained a pair. They had – with only a trace of smugness – shaken their heads at the fickle emotions of their peers, secure in the knowledge that they were working towards something infinitely more long-lasting and worthwhile. By the time Archie left Cheshire for theological college, leaving Bridget to embark on training as a speech therapist, marriage had been openly discussed and postponed for the next stage of their respective careers. During the ensuing few years they had seen each other when they could, often with months passing in between. Their loyalty in the face of such absence – not to mention abstinence – was something of which Archie had once been fiercely proud. He felt a great well of gratitude too, for the early inflaming zeal of Bridget's support, especially early on, when so many acquaintances had scoffed at his choice of career.

Archie dropped the pen and clasped his head in his hands, recalling with despair the sweet naïvety of all their promises. The jewel of her virginity for his. Not a jewel now, he reflected grimly, but a deadly weight, a millstone of unignorable preoccupation and guilty desire. Sex had never been allowed to be the focus of their relationship. Sometimes Bridget allowed his trembling fingers to explore the soft pointy contents of her bra. She would keep her eyes closed while he probed and stroked, assuming a look of serene forbearance that made him anxious not to linger over such activities for unseemly periods of time. Where such sacrifices had once seemed inspiring, Archie had recently been confronting the growing realisation that there was another kind of love he wanted more; a love fired by a passion that could not have waited as they had, a love that embraced the sort of searing sexual images that fuelled his shame-ridden nightly fumblings with the flies of his pyjamas and a box of tissues. Confessing such habits to Bridget was unimaginable; far, far more frightening than facing – as he did on each occasion – the wrathful disappointment of the Lord. Even less admissible, to himself or anyone else, was the way the long red hair of Isobel Tarrant seemed to weave its way through his private mental library of erotica, at once strangling the life from him and quickening the pulse of his desire.

> *Please try and accept what I say,* he wrote desperately, his Biro skidding across the page. *I am not worthy of you. God, more than anyone, knows this to be true. Show the same faith in me you always have. Trust me.*
>
> *As I have told you many times, you will make the most wonderful healer – and mother. Good luck, Bridget, and be happy.*
>
> *Please do not reply to this letter. Nothing you say or do could possibly change my mind. But I'll always treasure what we had.*

Signing the letter presented fresh dilemmas. While 'Best wishes' sounded false and cold, Archie feared that anything to do with 'love' might be misinterpreted as reason to hope. After sucking the tip of his pen for quite some considerable time, he simply wrote his name in the middle of the space below the last paragraph. As an afterthought he drew a thick line underneath his signature, pleased with the air of finality that it gave the page.

21

It was almost dawn when Isobel crept into the Howards' spare room. Ben lay sprawled half in and half out of the covers, one arm flung out across her side of the bed, as if inviting an embrace. All trace of rose scent had vanished. Instead, the faint, sweet smell of alcohol lingered on the stuffy air, mingled with the garlic that had formed the mainstay of Juliet's venison casserole. Mechanically, without making any attempt to be particularly quiet, Isobel peeled off her clothes and slipped into her nightie before going into the small adjoining bathroom to clean her teeth. Her eyes, framed by smudgy lines of mascara, looked unnaturally wide and still, as if shocked into a state of inexpression. Great straggles of hair had worked their way loose from the plait and hung limply down her neck and cheeks. In spite of the clammy efficacy of the Howards' central heating system, so unlike the haphazard – and strictly pre-midnight – warmth of their own home, Isobel's face looked cool and pale. Only her lips glowed. Scarlet mouth for a scarlet woman, she thought, working the toothbrush with slow but vigorous strokes, until the white froth streamed down her chin.

They had waited a long time, attending to abandoned lumps of meat and stale breadcrumbs, wiping gravy droplets off place mats and rinsing wineglasses. They worked efficiently and in a silence filled with the strain of listening for evidence of movement upstairs. Though she had felt steady and sober, Isobel knew she must be drunk. The drudgery of their work dissolved in the dizzying significance of each moment. James, gliding from chore to chore, stepping round chair legs and through doorways with all the self-conscious precision of a dancer, did not seem like James at all, but a partner in an elaborate game. With every circuit between kitchen and table he came nearer. As the silence from upstairs drummed in their ears, so the tension grew, hardening the possibility of what lay ahead into the unavoidable. With only one more plate to go in the dishwasher, Isobel found herself clinging on to it, staring at the green-and-gold diamonds edging its rim until their bright points zigzagged before her eyes. She was trying to tie a rubbish bag, her fingers slipping on the greasy overstretched plastic, when James stepped, for the first time that night, into the full frame of her gaze. 'Let me,' he murmured, his eyes holding hers while he deftly knotted it shut and reached for the handle of the back door. 'Come,' he said simply, carrying the bag in one hand and three of her fingers in the other. 'Come with me.'

They kissed standing next to the Howards' tall handsome black wheely bin, the icy night air pressing through their clothes, their lips dry with cold. His intensity was at once frightening and irresistible. All teeth and tongue and hot breath. Alien and ravenous. When she tried to arch away he pressed his hands into her lower back and pulled her closer, bending the curve of his body into hers. While a part of Isobel's mind floated free, shaking its head in horrifed incredulity at their imprudence, another infinitely less cerebral part luxuriated in the unabashed greed of his embrace. She had forgotten the sensation of being desired, how intoxicating it could feel, how deeply empowering. After a few moments, disjointed and distracting images from the past bird-hopped in and out of her consciousness: echoes of similar emotions experienced during happier times. Isobel redoubled the passion of her responses in an effort to dispel them, angry that not even betrayal could set her free from the blind alley of such retrospective longing.

James, struggling with the vagaries of an unfamiliar bra strap, had his sights set on rather more immediate preoccupations. And when thoughts of his own spouse did at last break through, it was to savour the tantalising comparisons between one woman's body and another's. What he had forgotten was the rich diversity of such terrain, the hidden secrets in every store. More than the childlike slimness, her sweet flowery scent, the cool, tight texture of her skin, it was the sheer unfamiliarity of Isobel that excited

James the most. In the instant the clasp of the strap gave way a hot rush of excitement charged his veins as powerfully as any drug. And like any addict at last succumbing to his vice, he found himself marvelling at the self-restraint than had allowed him to forgo such delights for so long.

Shaking her hair free of the green slide that had controlled the bulk of the plait, Isobel bent over to brush out the tangles. She worked with almost brutal insistence, barely flinching as knots were caught and pulled. And even when every thick rusty strand was smooth and clear, she brushed on, as if trying to smooth out the last of the ridged markings left by the plait, keeping her head bent towards the floor till the blood rang in her ears. When she finally crawled into bed the steely light of the March dawn was already visible through the central chink in Juliet's fresh yellow curtains. Gently, she tugged the covers from Ben's clenched hands and tucked them round herself with exaggerated care. She lay on her side and watched his sleeping face, the dark handsome curl of his eyelashes, the soft full line of his mouth, and remembered a time when she had been naïve enough to believe that the tenderness reflected in such loved and loving features was a possession she could rely on. Instead of being something that could be withdrawn, a gift snatched back, leaving her bereft and alone and uncomprehending. Isobel caught her breath, panic at what had happened to them, at what it was driving her to do, punching her lungs.

Yet, in spite of James's at times frenzied persistence, they had not made love, not quite. It was too much for Isobel, even in her befuddled, peculiarly sensitised state of mind, to commit adultery either up against an icy wall next to a dustbin, or on the cosy sofa where she had nibbled peanuts and reassured Juliet about the resilience of game casseroles just a few hours before. Instead, James had cajoled her into a pledge to meet during the coming week, at a time and place to be arranged round the non-negotiable commitments of school runs and surgery hours.

'I'll sort something out and let you know. Promise me, Isobel, promise me you'll be there.'

'But where?' she had asked faintly, playing for time.

'I don't know yet – like I said, I'll sort something out. I'll call you.'

'I don't know, James, I don't know . . .' She prised herself free and sat up on the sofa, hugging her knees. 'This can only lead to . . . to harm . . .'

'And pleasure,' he interjected gruffly, reaching out to stroke her hair. 'And not necessarily to harm . . . no one need ever know, Isobel.'

She shook her head. 'People always know . . . in the end.'

'Look, let's just meet once,' he pleaded gently, his hand moving down to the nape of her neck. 'Let's just treat ourselves to a few wonderful hours . . .' For a moment a lump of emotion blocked his throat. 'And then it need never happen again. We could simply . . . treasure it . . . keep it as our secret. You never know,' he added with a soft, confident laugh, 'it might be an unmitigated disaster.'

'I suppose we could . . .'

'Of course we could,' he interjected softly. 'It would settle what we've started – give it a natural end – see it through . . .'

'It'll change everything—'

'Everything's changed already, Isobel, whether we make love or not. Everything changed from that one extraordinary afternoon, when I looked at you and realised—'

She pressed her hand to his mouth. 'Don't say any more. I'll wait to hear from you. I'll meet you if I can. Just once.'

'Just once,' he echoed, smiling at her, deafening and quite unutterable celebrations exploding in the privacy of his head. 'Christ, Isobel, I don't know how I'm going to wait . . .'

'We'd better go upstairs. The children will be awake soon.'

'Oh God, what an awful thought.' He rolled his eyes and grinned, unable to hide the boyish jubilance bubbling inside. While Isobel, following him upstairs, had felt only a deep stillness, the slow-motion calm of surrender.

The next morning old patterns of amiability dictated that the Tarrants, instead of rushing home, as they both secretly would have wished, stayed for an hour or two after the mêlée of breakfast. While Ben, gaunt and black-eyed, retreated behind the Sunday papers, Juliet put on a display of unnatural perkiness before subsiding, quite suddenly, into a deep chair in the sitting room, slumped vacantly over a colour supplement article on breast implants. James remained with Isobel and Ben in the kitchen, refilling coffee cups and quizzing Isobel in a self-consciously interested way about the literary textual choices offered by the Open University. The four children meanwhile, clearly sensing that some level of adult responsibility had been withdrawn for the morning, grazed freely on prohibited snacks from the larder, in between constructing an elaborate system of corridors and walls using all the Howards' smartest cushions and chairs.

'Juliet said you've agreed we'll go to Greece with them this summer.' Ben wound down his window, ignoring the chorus of protest from the back seat, and tipped his face towards the rush of cold air.

'No, I haven't.' Isobel curled both hands into fists, emptying the fingers of her gloves.

'Well, she's under the impression that you have.'

'I agreed to think about it, that's all.'

'You'd hate Greece.'

'I know. That's why I agreed to think about it.'

'Why didn't you just say no?'

She shrugged, wondering herself why the simplest answers were sometimes so hard.

'We can't afford it anyway.'

'No, I know.' Isobel slid her fingers back into their slots and folded her hands. 'Shall we go to Suffolk, then?'

Ben scowled. 'I suppose so.'

'They'll need fair warning . . .'

'It's March, for Christ's sake. Are you telling me your parents need to know things five months in advance?'

'You know what they're like,' she murmured, reminding herself of James in a bid to feel strong. He had squeezed her arm when they performed the ritual of goodbye pecks on the doorstep. Only the merest hint of pressure, but with an effect not dissimilar to that of a small electric shock. She wondered how he would contact her, what he would say, whether she would be brave enough to carry out her promise. It took a certain courage to give in to temptation, Isobel thought suddenly; it wasn't just about selfishness and being unhappy.

'I need a proper holiday,' Ben was saying. He had wound the window back up and leant back against the headrest, his eyes barely open, only one hand on a central spoke of the steering wheel.

'Yes, of course,' she replied automatically, not concentrating. 'It'll be the Easter holidays before we know it.'

'Can we have an egg hunt?' piped a voice from the back.

'I expect so.'

'Chocolate is bad for you,' declared Megan with a pout. 'It makes you spotty.'

'Does not.'

'Does.'

'For Christ's sake shut up you two, just shut up, shut up . . .' Shocked at the pitch of his own voice, Ben swallowed the anger away. The girls, crushed into immediate silence by the volume and rage of such an uncharacteristic outburst, exchanged looks and shrank into their coats. Only by the greatest effort of self-restraint did Isobel allow herself to show no flicker of reaction at all. Instead she stared, unblinking, at the dots of moisture just beginning to fleck the windscreen. It was clear to her that the anger, though ostensibly aimed at their children, was all for her. He hates me, she thought, feeling lucid and brave. Nothing I do matters. Nothing could make it any worse.

22

A service in the cathedral never failed to cheer Archie up. It was so much easier to feel sure of God beneath the vaulting beauty of its ceilings and with the cherubic-faced choir's fluting trebles spinning their way through Tallis or Byrd. Sitting in the splendour of one of the ornately carved choirstalls, Archie attended to each note and word with grateful wonderment, feeling his spirit soar heavenward on the echoing clouds of sound. Though well aware that religious faith should stand on firmer ground than the sensual spectacles of ceremonial beauty, Archie consoled himself with the argument that every career needed a little inspiration at times. God understood, he was sure. A cathedral was like the Rolls-Royce of religion, he mused happily, but better because it was available to everyone. The thought led him on to a series of absorbing analogies between other, less dramatic places of worship and equivalent vehicles. St Cuthbert's was a Volkswagen Beetle, he decided, rusting round the edges but endearing to the last. So engrossed was Archie by this theme that he quite forgot to listen to the Bishop's ennobling address on the importance of spiritual pilgrimage and opening windows on to the soul. He was juggling, a little sleepily, with a confused carpark's worth of cars and associated buildings when a pointedly loud amen from a more attentive neighbour alerted him to the fact that the service had moved on and that small snoring sounds might possibly have been emanating from the recesses of his nose.

'Thanks be to God,' he muttered to himself, groping for the fat tapestried hassock at his feet and clasping his hands for added effort in prayer.

'A prayer for unity,' began the Bishop, using the dignified vibrato which Archie had been dismayed to observe overtook most of God's servants when called upon to cope with the cavernous acoustics of the cathedral. At least his own tremulous tones – unsteady still before the smallest of congregations – could never be accused of sounding false or insincere. He squeezed his eyes shut to narrow the focus of his concentration. The carpark shrank into a black dot. Unity. Archie mouthed the word, wishing the black dot would allow itself to be superseded by something more appropriate, or at least charitable. Instead he saw his letter to Bridget, felt again how it had fallen from his fingertips into the postbox, so quiet and weightless for such a loaded thing.

After the service he skipped tea in the chapter house and found himself instead hovering in front of the noticeboard by the main entrance. The new Canon Residentiary had put up a notice about a breakfast project for the homeless, to be served out of the cathedral hall on weekday mornings. A pencil hung on a piece of string beside a large empty piece of paper inviting names of volunteers. Archie ran his finger round the inside of his dog-collar and sighed. It was a good idea. A great idea. But so hideously early. The only decent sleep he got these days was in the couple of hours before the shrill dawn chorus of his two alarm clocks.

Someone approached the other end of the board and set about pinning a small yellow poster into a space beside a faded notice about donations for Rwandan refugees.

Glad of the interruption to the ever-faltering engine of his conscience, Archie strolled over for a better look.

Crofton College presents:

JULIUS CAESAR
by William Shakespeare

Saturday 6th April

Seats: £5.00

Tickets available from School Secretary or call 01867 422091

It was only when the man turned round that Archie recognised him as Ben Tarrant. He was quite imposing when seen close to, with his tall figure and hooded black-browed eyes. He was wearing a shapeless grey sweater and a blue scarf wrapped several times round his neck and chin. That his face clearly had not seen a razor that morning only struck Archie as adding to the impressively casual and rugged look of the man. Of course Isobel would love such a person, he thought miserably, taking a step backwards and feeling suddenly gauche and pitifully young.

'Hope that's all right there,' growled Ben, responding only to the clerical dress of the young person hovering next to him and nodding his head at the board. 'I believe the school secretary has cleared it with whatever powers have to be consulted about such things.'

'Oh no – I mean yes, I'm sure it's fine there. Absolutely fine.' Archie nodded hard and approached the poster for a better look. '*Julius Caesar*, eh? Never seen that one. Or read it for that matter. Is it the one where everybody dies?'

'Quite a few people do,' replied Ben, smiling, 'but I think you may have *Titus Andronicus* in mind. That's the play where you really can't move for bodies by the end.'

'Ah yes, probably.' Oh no, and he's nice, thought Archie miserably, torn between lovelorn curiosity and a violent urge to run away. Instead, he found himself saying, 'I think I know your wife,' which he hadn't meant to at all.

'Isobel? And how is that?' Gripping his bunch of papers more tightly to his chest, Ben plunged his left hand deep into his coat pocket where, beneath two used hankies and several sweet wrappers, he felt the cold bobbled edge of something hard. His fingers closed around it. The pink stone from Wales. He had forgotten all about it.

'I've been bothering her for money, I'm afraid. Sponsorship – a charity walk thing. You might tell her I'll be calling again soon,' added Archie eagerly, as if such openness could somehow atone for the other less innocent enthusiasms firing his heart. 'I'm after signatures too at the moment. Fighting the good fight for St Cuthbert's. Some people on the council want to turn it into an arts centre.'

'I thought it was one already,' murmured Ben, squeezing the stone so hard that he could feel it cutting into his skin.

'Well, it's used for the odd concert and so on . . .'

'Oh, I see. Well, good luck. Are you coming this way?' Ben gestured with an inviting smile at the massive oak door behind them, something in the troubled expression on the young curate's face compelling him to be kind.

Once outside, they fell into step on the narrow tarmacked path that cut through the cathedral's manicured carpet of grass towards the cobblestones of the main gateway. Though a quick walker, Archie found himself hurrying to keep up with the long strides of his companion, the panels of his black tunic catching irritatingly round his ankles.

'So you're based at St Cuthbert's?'

'First posting, so to speak.'

'I thought of going into the ministry once.'

'Did you really?'

Ben flashed a self-deprecating smile. 'Only briefly . . . hard to believe, eh?'

'No, I didn't mean that at all . . .' Archie stammered, cursing himself for having sounded so surprised.

'It was only a teenage phase. I chose teaching instead . . .'

'Yes, I know. Geography, isn't it?'

'Yes.' Ben nodded, worrying suddenly about the tinderbox of rumour, whether the Lewis story had, after all, spread beyond the padded safety of Peter Abbott's study. 'That's right. And drama too. Do you think you might come to the play, then?'

'I'll certainly try. I say, have you got loads more of those to stick up?' Archie pointed at the wodge of yellow notices under Ben's arm. 'I'd be glad to help. I'm sure I could get rid of a few for you.'

Ben stopped walking for a moment. 'If I wasn't hung over and if it didn't look as if it was going to rain any minute' – he cast a rueful glance at the sky – 'I might just have been able to refuse such a generous offer . . . but as it is, I should be delighted.' He took a few pieces of paper off the top of his pile and handed them over.

'Oh, heavens, I can do better than that.' Archie helped himself to a generous sheaf. More generous than he had intended, as it happened, though having taken them it felt impossible to hand any back.

'Oh, really . . . thank you . . . er . . . Reverend.'

'Heighton-Jones – Archie.' He held out his hand. 'It will be a pleasure, honestly. I could do with a walk – wear me out for bedtime,' he added, darting off while Ben was still formulating a suitable reply.

'I'll warn Isobel you'll be round, then, shall I?' he called after a few moments.

'Absolutely. Thank you,' Archie shouted back, waving his stack of yellow notices in salute and making fresh vows of purity and penitence in his hopelessly wayward heart.

23

A quarter of a mile down Chapel Street, beyond the butcher's where they made vegetable sausages, was a small boutique which Juliet usually did her best to avoid. It was run by two beautiful, long-haired women, with permanent honeyed suntans and long pearly nails. The window of their shop never contained more than one mannequin, its implausibly sculpted body decked in one simple dress or suit, often barefooted, with perhaps only a string of pearls for decoration. The attraction for Juliet was not simply the sartorial elegance offered by such classical, understated styles, but the treatment that went with it. It was a charade, she knew, the two assistants purring round customers like cats, stroking the soft natural fabrics of the wares with their pretty talons and innocently batting their almond eyes at prices that would feed ten starving families for a month; but she loved it nonetheless. It was how shopping ought to be, she had enthused to James, when he ventured into the place with her to watch the investment of a generous birthday cheque (and a little bit more) a couple of years before. He had sat in an armchair shaking his head or nodding as she paraded in and out of the one fitting room, like some kind of indulgent lord overseeing purchases for his mistress. Afterwards, Juliet had skipped out of the shop with all the glee of a spoilt teenager, bags flapping against her legs as she danced on tiptoes to plant smudgy kisses of gratitude on her husband's benevolently smiling face.

It was an altogether less carefree frame of mind, however, which drew Juliet to Chapel Street mid-morning on the Tuesday following their dinner party with the Tarrants. She had spent the previous hour and a half at the hairdresser's, having her roots done, with a quick trim for good measure. Consultation with the stylist, Sylvie, had resulted in the joint view that the growing-out look of the latest perm in fact suited her rather well – all smooth on top with long tumbling curls lower down. It was quite Sarah Miles-like, Juliet decided, cocking her head at her reflection and trying to recall the exact film she had in mind. She had rather modelled herself on Sarah Miles at one stage – during her English Rose phase, when she'd gone all out for an Ophelia with a wonderfully inspiring director called Michael Jacobs, who had drunk himself to death a few months after the production ended. The memory was not a happy one. Not simply because of her failure to land the role and the subsequent demise of the charismatic Mr Jacobs, but because – as the hairdresser's mirrored walls reminded her – any passing resemblance she bore to Hamlet's luckless girlfriend was being cruelly and inexorably buried by the passage of time. Juliet scowled at herself and gave an extra pound to the girl who had washed her hair.

'I've got all morning,' she confided, as the sleeker of the two assistants in the boutique offered to take her coat amidst apologetic murmurings about the temperature of the room. 'It's lovely,' Juliet reassured her, rubbing her hands at the greenhouse warmth and beginning a slow tour of the largest of the circular rails. She ran the back of her left hand across the clothes as she walked, not yet really looking. The quiet swish of the materials was somehow thrilling, as was the sense of barely having begun. It was like standing on the edge of pleasure, brimming with the bliss of anticipation. She pulled idly at a panel of a long beige skirt on a small rack in the corner.

'Now that *is* special,' crooned the girl, deftly slipping the hanger off the rail and holding the skirt against her own enviably slim frame for her customer to admire. 'It's loose, but so smart. Stunning with one of those jackets over there, especially the darker blue. Though Miriam swears by the brown, don't you, Mirry?' Her colleague obligingly groaned her concurrence.

'Which jackets?' murmured Juliet, turning her head slowly, savouring every moment. The girl seemed to glide across the carpet ahead of her.

'With your eyes you'd want the blue, I think.' She held up a long smart navy jacket, with large pockets and wide lapels.

'Though you've got the sort of colouring to get away with either. It's a sort of chocolate brown, see?' The other jacket was in her hand now. 'More of a county look, you might say. Whereas the blue somehow has more of the town about it, don't you think?'

'Doesn't it just.' Juliet stood back and folded her arms. 'I'll try on both, shall I? Size fourteen, if you've got it.'

The girl drew in a breath of disbelief. 'I'd have sworn you were a twelve. Are you sure?'

Not even the knowledge that such doe-eyed incredulity constituted flattery of the most despicably calculating kind marred Juliet's determination to enjoy the compliment. Everyone needed lying to sometimes. 'I'll try both sizes, then, shall I? Oh, and I'll need a shirt or two, size fourteen,' she added, patting her chest with a rueful smile. 'Something in silk would be nice.'

'Is madam buying for any particular occasion?'

'Not really.' Juliet pushed all ten fingers up through the curly mop of her hair, before dropping her arms to her sides with a theatrically wistful sigh. 'I just felt I needed to clear out a few cobwebs. Spring does that to one, don't you find?'

'Oh God, yes.' The girl led the way into the compact, brightly lit changing room and hung the clothes on the line of hooks beside a full-length, gold-framed mirror with sunflowers painted in each of its corners. 'Shout if you need any help, won't you. I'll be just outside.'

Juliet needed a lot of help, as it turned out. Not just with skirts and jackets, but with trousers and shirts too. Being unable to choose between colours planted the alluring idea of covering all options by buying more than one of each. Though all size twelves had, discreetly, to be withdrawn from the running, the teeth of each zip on their replacements slid into place with such sweet, snug smoothness, while their buttons slotted so easily into their respective holes, that Juliet began to feel like a gambler on a roll. Everything looked perfect. When some billowing pantaloon-style trousers – not her usual thing at all – proved an inch or two too long, a pair of high-heeled Italian leather shoes were deftly slipped under the door of the fitting room. With their assistance, the wide hems of the trousers floated as prettily as their designer had intended, just an inch or so from the ground; most of the soft creamy leather of the shoes was denied the possibility of public admiration as a result, but with the happy side effect of adding greatly to the perceived length of the wearer's legs.

'I look yards taller,' exclaimed Juliet happily, wriggling her toes in celebration, 'and these darlings are as comfy as slippers. Who would have thought it with such a heel?'

Her assistant, now on her knees at Juliet's feet with a shoehorn, sat back on her ankles and shook her glossy head in wonder. As well she might. For just a few feet to her right, the pile of this unusually amenable customer's 'probables' had swelled to dramatic proportions; price tags dangled like Christmas tree decorations from amongst its multicoloured folds. The shoes were added to the heap, together with the pantaloon trousers and the last-minute addition of an irresistible suede waistcoat with a string of gold buttons down its front and two pretty finger pockets in its sides.

At the till Juliet almost faltered. But only for a second or two. While the girl unsnagged tags and totted up prices, she slipped her credit card out of her purse and gripped its hard edges tightly between her fingers. When the final numbers appeared in the small window facing her, she did not even blink, though her heart raced for an instant or two. She handed across her card in a kind of trance that lasted all the way home.

Strangely, having unloaded all her bags from the car, she felt little inclination to examine her purchases further. Instead, she pushed them under the bed, feeling suddenly hollow inside. Kicking off her shoes, she flopped on to the bed, still unmade from the night before, and lay on her back staring up at the ceiling. A hairline crack ran from the corner of one window right across to the lintel above the door. Had it been there all along or had she simply not noticed it before? All was quiet outside. The workmen had not been for a day or two, even though piles of bricks and sand still defaced the once immaculate lawn of the garden. They were doubling up on another job, she was sure. The floor of crazy paving was laid, but the low wall that was to surround it still awaited construction, as did the pathway destined to run round the side of the house and up through the middle of the lawn to the attractive log cabin of a garden house at the far end. She ought to phone the men on one of their mobiles, find out exactly what was going on, put some pressure on, remind them who was in charge. James might be cross if there was still no sign of further progress by the weekend. At the thought of James the trance-like feeling came back again. The ceiling crack melted into a faint blur. Then she remembered the bags of new clothes packed beneath her under the bed and allowed herself a small smile of terror. He would go mad.

For a few minutes Juliet toyed with the notion of ringing up the shop and grovelling for a refund. On the grounds of diminished responsibility. Or foolhardiness. Or an impending war with her spouse. But there's a war anyway, she reminded herself, shrugging away the idea and getting off the bed. Started deliberately by James, she was sure, though quite why remained a mystery. Juliet crossed to the window and frowned at the half-finished state of the garden below. Time would sort it all out, no doubt, as it always did. Meanwhile, since all her attempts at reconciliation had been so hurtfully rejected or ignored, she resolved to fight her corner as hard as she could, with every weapon at her disposal. Juliet gripped her elbows with her hands as tears pricked her eyes. Including money. For a moment the realisation of her own strength burst into the hollowness inside, before dissolving into disappointment. How absurd, she thought, that loving someone could impel such an overpowering need to defeat them.

24

As the last and latest addition to an already overcrowded list, James could not help regarding the presence of Archie Heighton-Jones in his consulting room as something of an inconvenience. In less than an hour he was due to meet Isobel in the carpark of a roadside hotel in which he had already taken the liberty of booking a double room. It was a large and impersonal-looking hostelry on the stretch of the Drayford Road beyond Ilcombe, of the kind whose prime source of income was tourists and itinerant executives with small expense accounts. A venue, in other words, of the safest kind. He had a bottle of champagne concealed in a thermal bag under the driving seat of his car, together with a small box of Black Magic chocolates, which he had bought along with his paper *en route* to work that morning.

'How can I help?' he began briskly, tweaking the crease of his trousers as he sat down and uttering a brief, silent prayer of gratitude for not having been born with the affliction of the springy, carrot-coloured hair smothering the head of the young man seated opposite him.

Archie, whose nervousness had been greatly enhanced by a considerable stay in the waiting room, glanced at the doctor's sharp grey eyes for just a moment before reverting to a keen examination of his knuckle-bones. A recently acquired twitch, an annoying blip of a pulse just below his right eye, doubled in ferocity under the bold, enquiring gaze of the doctor. Though outwardly friendly, James Howard was not – as Archie sensed at once – empathetic. He frowned hard in an attempt to swallow the facial convulsions above his right cheekbone, which, though barely detectable to a casual observer, felt grotesque to Archie himself.

'I'm not sleeping very well . . .'

'Since when?' James was already punching the keyboard of his computer.

'I don't know . . . I suppose for a month or so.'

'Ever happened before?'

'No . . . no, not like this.'

'Got anything on your mind?'

Archie let out a nervous laugh at the utter inadequacy of the question. 'This and that . . . you know.'

James dropped his hands to his lap and turned back to face the young man, in the same instant flexing his mouth into the most avuncular of smiles. So stretched were his lips that they almost disappeared into the skin surrounding them.

'Are you – I hope you don't mind my asking – are you employed?'

Archie hesitated. He had changed out of his cassock before coming to the surgery. An absence of obvious symptoms made him wary of drawing attention to himself. After filling out the various forms required of new patients, he had hovered behind a large rubber plant, planning fictitious aches and pains in his defence, should the need arise. For a clergyman to admit to an inability to sleep seemed to Archie's exhausted mind to be tantamount to admitting that he had lost touch with his God, or, worse still, that he was being punished by him. The nature of many of the feverish thoughts peppering his periods of insomnia did little to dispel such notions.

'Yes,' he ventured at length, 'I'm a member of the Church . . . a curate.'

James raised his eyebrows. 'Really? How interesting. Been in Torbridge long?'

'Six months. It's a two-year job.'

James increased his smile. 'And are you finding it a particularly stressful one?'

Archie shook his head miserably. 'No. It's not like that at all. Everything like that is fine.' He wrung his hands and clenched his teeth, fighting the urge to confess to the extent of his misery. 'I've recently split up with my girlfriend,' he stammered at length. 'I suppose that might have something to do with it.'

James let out a long, knowing 'ah' and leant back in his chair, in the same moment pulling up the sleeve of his jacket so as to get a clear view of his watch. 'These things pass, you know, with time.'

'It's just that I feel so tired – I can't think straight – nothing feels normal – I mean, it – that is, the tiredness – it's just really beginning to get me down.'

'Of course it is.' With the end of the consultation in sight, James was fired with new energy to be kind. 'Insomnia can be devilish.' He swivelled his chair back round to face his desk and reached for a prescription pad. 'A couple of these a night should help. Just to see you through. Stop the moment you want. If you run out, come back. They are addictive but only if used unwisely.'

'Addictive?' Archie looked up, his tic fluttering like mad, a little creature trapped inside the skin below his eye.

'Don't look so worried,' said James, now at his most jovial. 'Your body has lost some of its natural rhythm, that's all. These—' he held out the paper for Archie to take – 'will help get you back into the swing of things again. Until the next girlfriend maybe . . .' James winked as he stood up, though in his heart he felt nothing but pity for the evident gaucheness of the young priest. Sexual naïvety was such a burden, he reflected with some complacency, holding wide his door and nodding Archie through. The thought led on to a few moments of indulgent speculation about the afternoon ahead. Though many problems might beset his meeting with Isobel, the sexual side of things, he felt sure, would not count among them. He would see that she was not disappointed; and since giving physical pleasure had always – in James's considerable experience – been the most efficient route to enjoying similar sensations oneself, he had high hopes on his own account. Such was the intensity of these musings that his fingers actually trembled as he set about tidying the papers on his desk. Isobel Tarrant, of all people. He whistled softly to himself. There would be guilt, of course. He could feel it already, crouching just around the corner, ready to pounce. But Christ, it would take a lot more than that to deter him now, James realised, giving his computer a companionable parting pat and heading for the door.

* * *

Archie, who, in spite of all his apprehensions, had been secretly hoping for more of a heart-to-heart with whichever of the Stanton Street practice's various GPs was allocated to him, trailed out of the surgery and across the road to the chemist with little sense of relief. To be a twenty-two-year-old servant of God, tortured by an unforgivable obsession with another man's wife and with a dependency on sleeping tablets, was not exactly an ideal condition for fuelling faith or self-esteem. As he pushed open the chiming door of the chemist, tears of self-pity pricked his eyes, blurring his vision and sense of balance so badly that he tripped on the step down and almost collided with a laden display stand of bath caps and corn pads.

Later, as he waited his turn to be served, a little girl with a chalky face and a thunderous cough began playing peek-a-boo behind the tails of her mother's raincoat. Using his prescription paper as a mask, Archie found himself returning the compliment, until the mother was smiling too, while a lilac-haired old lady, sitting on a stool beside a hedgehog of lollipops, silently clapped her delight. And when the pharmacist handed him his prescription, the pills looked so small and innocuous – taking up barely a third of the tiny brown bottle – that Archie found some of his misgivings evaporate. A good night's sleep would be a hell of a treat after all, he thought to himself, however unnatural the method of obtaining it.

All morning Isobel looked for a sign that she should not keep her appointment with James. If Ben is nice to me, then I won't go, she told herself. But Ben, for whom the emotional effort of getting through each day had now reduced his conversational skills to a series of monosyllables, showed no indication of being nice to her or any other object in his path. Fire-fighting invisible terrors inside his head, he pedalled off to school with his forehead creased against the wind, his hands white on the handlebars. In the briefcase strapped to the rack behind him was, among other things, Dick Caulder's card with the counsellor's name on it. Throughout the ride Ben's head throbbed with the pulse of this new dilemma. At every other lamppost he changed his mind. It felt too desperate for words even to be tempted to pick up the phone to such a person. Worse still, it felt like failure.

Men like him – educated, sensible, able men – should be able to sort their own lives out, he scolded himself. They should not need to pay someone to listen and nod at their problems. Whereas the wretched Caulder had at least had good reason, Ben felt all the awkwardness of possessing nothing solid to lay at a therapist's door beyond a general, debilitating feeling that control over all quarters of his life was slipping away, that the once clear waters of his future had turned to mud. If it wasn't so sad it would be laughable, Ben mused bitterly, slowing down at the sight of a phone box, but then pedalling past it twice as hard. How long, he wondered, before other people started to notice that his once unquenchable well of energy and confidence had become nothing but a sham? And Isobel . . . Ben clenched his face, as if gripped by a sudden spasm of pain. For he feared for her opinion of him most keenly of all. That such fear had already produced the most painful alienation they had suffered to date was bad enough. Their marriage was on hold, he knew, waiting for such a time as he had the energy to attend to it. And attend to it he would, he promised himself, for by no means the first time; just as soon as he felt a little better, just as soon as some of his inner strength had returned. When he was more like his old self again; the one that his wife had loved.

The steepening gradient of Crofton Hill forced fresh reservoirs of energy from his legs. On meeting this by now familiar physical challenge, Ben found himself wishing that he could flex a comparable muscle over other elements in his life. It was almost comical, he thought grimly, flicking up the gear switch to make himself work still harder, some part of him relishing the pain, that a creature of such apparent physical resources could be the vehicle of so much weakness inside.

Throughout the walk to school, meanwhile, Isobel remained fully prepared for one of the children to develop a sudden illness which would require hospitalisation or bedside vigilance at the very least. Given the approaching tryst with James, it seemed only right that God or sod's law should intervene to remind her of her rightful duties as a wife and mother. But both Sophie and Megan skipped along pavements and zebra crossings with uncanny zeal, pigtails and satchels flying, as if their sole desire in life that morning was to get into their classrooms and release their parent to her fate. They were so early that the playground was virtually empty. Isobel hung around for several minutes, half hoping to catch the arrival of the school bus and the Howard infants, as if the sight of them might act as an emotional deterrent for what lay ahead. In the end her own children shooed her away, rolling their eyes in embarrassment at such an unnecessary and uncharacteristic show of solicitude on their behalf.

Rain, Isobel told herself, as she turned on her heel for the walk home; if it rains then it means I'm not supposed to go. But, even as the thought entered her mind, the grey scudding clouds which had shrouded the early disc of a sun were being tugged away by a friendly spring breeze. By mid-morning Torbridge was basking in its first truly yellow sunshine of the year, to a backdrop of magnificent, unqualified blue.

After a frenzy of domestic chores, Isobel decided to pass what remained of the time by embarking on an examination of an arts study pack that had arrived from the Open University the day before. It was entitled *Words* and came with a cassette tape and a cheery introductory leaflet that promised access to academic material without the burden of exams or having to submit written work to tutors. Though Isobel read and reread the sentences, their significance eluded her. In the last few days she had been too distracted even for fiction. *Anna Karenina* and several other worthy works sat gathering dust on the table in the hall, waiting for her to have the spurt of energy required to return them to the library. It felt as if she were now too caught up in the tangled thread of her own life to expend the emotion necessary to the enjoyment of reading about anybody else's.

Isobel was also beginning to see that all her indecision over the Open University was linked to issues of a far more fundamental kind. So many years had passed without having to confront the muddle of her own ambitions. Ben's needs had always led the way in that regard, not because he had been a bully, but because she had wanted them to; because, if she was honest, she had been only too grateful to seize upon the abdication of self – of responsibility for the wavering course of her own life – that marriage to him had involved. Looking back, Isobel saw more clearly than ever that their union had only ever worked because of the mutual devotion that had empowered it. Without that there was no point or logic to their relationship at all. Without that she had nothing, except the children, already beginning to be baffled by a breakdown of something they could not understand, something that was only beginning to be tangible now that it had ceased to function.

Abandoning the desk, Isobel retreated back downstairs for her umpteenth trip to the bathroom. If I'm pink and blotchy I won't go, she told herself, casting a sly glance at her reflection in the mirror as she washed her hands. But her face was its usual pallid self, set off particularly that morning by the bright auburn tumble of her freshly washed hair. The pupils of her eyes looked particularly wide and black, dark holes in the usually predominant green. I'll go, but only to talk, she promised herself, retreating into the bedroom where she struggled to avoid the lure of the full-length mirror in the corner. She had forgotten the torture of feeling so self-conscious; the concentrated deviousness of dressing to please while aiming to look as if one had barely tried at all. Not that Ben would have noticed, she thought grimly, taking James's hastily scribbled note from the drawer of her bedside table and tearing it into long strips: *The Cobbler's Inn*, it said, *Drayford Road, 1 o'clock Wednesday. Please be there. I think I love you*. The pieces of paper fluttered from her hand and into the tin wastepaper bin behind the bedroom door. Quickly she set about camouflaging them with various discarded tissues and old envelopes, telling herself as she did so that deceit was not really so very difficult, but that it needed to be worked at, like any other activity that felt new and strange. But after a few moments she fell to her knees, removed the old tissues and placed the torn pieces of James's note back on top again. It would be easier to be found out, she thought desperately, for an instant wanting only to fast-forward this terrible, leisurely crumbling of her life to a point where the worst had happened instead of being yet to come.

25

A tiny spider was making its way down the steep white rock-face of Aunt Violet's hair, dangling precariously between one flat curl and the flabby lower section of an earlobe. Did ears grow bigger with age? Isobel wondered, unconsciously fiddling with the pearl studs in her own small, neat lobes and trying not to stare at the minute creature's daring acrobatics. Whether to mention the spider or not had been bothering her for some minutes. Like a snowfall of dandruff, or a rebellious bra strap defying the confines of a sleeveless shirt, it was not a matter easily raised. The thought did occur to her of reaching across the distance separating their two chairs – one deft sweep of her hand and it would be gone. But bridging such distances was a challenge at the best of times, especially with someone like Aunt Violet, whose hands fluttered like wings as she talked, as if to beat people back, warning them to give her space.

Instead, Isobel tried to concentrate on the old lady's face, quite animated that afternoon and flushed with genuine colour beneath the dusty beige dunes of her face powder. As on her previous visit, Aunt Violet was talking a lot, spilling snatches of anecdotes about ancient friends and places, leading herself in circles that were almost charming but mostly nonsensical. Sitting in the chair opposite her, conducting an unconvincing charade of reactive interest, Isobel grew increasingly aware of the fraudulence of her position and the suspect motives that had impelled her to make the visit at all. As the old lady talked on, she could feel her own thoughts slipping the safe moorings of her surroundings and drifting into the more treacherous current of the events that had preceded her arrival;

events connected to the clean but dingy hotel room in which she had found herself undressing before the admiring eyes of a man married to a woman who was supposed to be her friend.

To begin with, it was the thought of Juliet that had given Isobel the courage to say no, to back into the room with her hands like shields in front of her, keeping James at bay while she muttered apologies for having come at all. In spite of being so eager to touch her in the corridor, he had merely folded his arms and watched her retreat. Kicking the door shut behind him, he stood quite still, studying her in intent and unhurried silence until her withdrawl was halted by the wall on the other side of the room. Isobel pressed her palms and back up against it, as if willing the busy floral patterns to swallow her from sight. Between them stretched the bed, its crisp white bedspread yawning like a blank page.

'It's all right, Isobel, I know what you're feeling.' His voice was gravelly and sure. It soothed her. 'I feel it too. It's all right. Don't be worried. Don't – for heaven's sake – be scared, about anything. We're both in the dark here. We're both struggling to know what to do; whether to follow our hearts or our heads. I'm not in the habit of this either,' he added, rolling his eyes in distaste at their surroundings and shrugging helplessly. 'If I had my way we'd be alone on a desert island . . .'

'But we're not on an island, are we, James? We're here . . . in real life . . . in this vile, poky room. Oh God, I shouldn't have come, I feel so dreadful.' She turned her back on him and leant against the wall, resting her head on her arms.

'Hey, take it easy. Nothing has happened, remember? And nothing has to happen, Isobel, if you don't want it to. Let's just talk. I brought this.' He produced the bottle of champagne and the chocolates, his face a picture of apology. 'For you . . . I had to bring you something,' he stuttered, while his heart hammered at the thought of the condom in the small back pocket of his trousers.

'Thank you,' she whispered, managing to smile, marvelling now at the dubious strength that had empowered her this far. She watched as James nimbly uncoiled the wire from the top of the bottle and began easing the cork out with his thumbs. She noticed for the first time how beautifully manicured his nails were, trim white tips and tidy white crescents.

'Oh Christ, we're going to need some glasses. Could you look in the bathroom?'

The sight of the cork edging its way towards explosion urged Isobel to hurry obediently across the room. The bathroom was green and tightly packed. Barely an inch separated the shower curtain from the lavatory cistern, while the curve of the basin rim only just allowed a clean opening of the door. On a shelf beneath a small square mirror were two beakers sheathed in transparent plastic. Isobel took them at once, not daring to look up, not wanting to see her reflection for fear of what it might reveal.

'I found these.'

'Well done . . . closer – come closer, quick.' James laughed and held the bottle at arm's length. 'We're almost there. Are you ready? There we go.' He whooped with satisfaction as the cork flew across the room and the champagne spilled into the plastic cups. He took one from her and raised it high, staring her in the face until she met his gaze. 'Not so troubled, please, my lovely Isobel. We're here. That's all that matters for now . . .'

'If only it was.' She sipped the champagne and sighed, closing her eyes. 'I can't . . . go through with this after all, James, I'm so sorry.' She sat down on the bed next to him, stretching out her legs in front of her and staring at her shoes. A last-minute change from trousers to a skirt had resulted in faint sock lines round her ankles, just visible through her tights. Instead of minding, she felt brought down to earth by the sight of so humdrum and inelegant a physical detail. It made her feel unalluring and quite safe. 'I think I've only just realised the full enormity of what's been going on,' she continued matter-of-factly, wiggling her toes, 'of what it would do – to Juliet especially—'

An imperceptible tightening of James's jaw preceded his response to this confession. 'Of course, of course,' he interrupted. 'Though, for what it's worth, I don't think Juliet would spill too many tears . . . I mean, she's no stranger to, er . . . how shall I put this . . . ?' He took a swig of his drink, scowling as the bubbles filled his nose. '. . . marital transgressions?' He swallowed hard. 'Yes, I think that just about sums it up.'

'Juliet?' Isobel was genuinely astonished.

'The actress in her, I suppose,' continued James, now affecting a pained nonchalance which a less vulnerable or confused observer might have judged as being a little overdone. 'Needs attention. Misses the limelight,' he added, thinking to himself that the lie was so good – so plausible – that it almost had a right to be true. 'I've tried to analyse – to understand it – a thousand times.' He shook his head. 'I only wish I could lump my feelings for you in the same bracket. But Isobel . . .' Slowly he reached his hand to her face, stroking her cheeks and lips with the tips of his fingers. Isobel watched the hand approach as if it were an object quite beyond her control. When his skin touched hers, she closed her eyes, unexpectedly reassured by the simple pleasure of the contact. 'What I feel for you,' he murmured, 'I never thought to experience again. You light up my life . . . just the thought of you . . .' He stopped touching her face and picked up her hand, slotting his fingers through hers.

'But Juliet . . .' she whispered. 'I can't believe . . . I mean, she always seemed so . . .'

'I probably shouldn't have told you. It's not relevant,' he continued earnestly, 'it's got nothing to do with my feelings for you . . . I want . . . oh Christ . . .' He dropped her hand and turned abruptly away, his voice cracking with emotion. With hunched shoulders he gripped his plastic cup in both palms, staring dejectedly into the lemony bubbles.

For a moment Isobel thought he was going to cry. The notion that she had reduced him to so vulnerable a state made her feel both culpable and tender. 'I am so sorry,' she whispered, putting her cup down on the thinning carpet and reaching an arm across his back.

'I think we need each other,' he murmured, responding to the touch of her arm with an embrace that was far more fervent than anything she had anticipated and which tipped the precarious balance of control entirely, and finally, his way.

She let the weight of his body press her back on to the soft lumpy mattress of the bed, while the wallpaper trellises of flowers surrounding them danced before her half-closed eyes like the twisting spirals of a pretty cage.

'You don't seem yourself,' snapped Aunt Violet, the edge in her voice bringing Isobel back to the present. The old woman cocked her head quizzically. 'You're not listening,' she accused with a sniff.

'I'm sorry . . . I'm . . . a little tired today. Sorry . . . please forgive me.' Isobel reached out to pat the veiny hand nearest to her, but found it withdrawn before she got there. A trivial rejection which somehow sharpened her sense of wrongdoing; not just about seeing James, but for not having driven straight home afterwards; for yet again complicating her duplicity by drawing Aunt Violet into the tightening circle of deceit. She folded her hands back in her lap, wondering if the old lady sensed her lack of affection, whether she somehow intuited that she was being used as an unwitting alibi for the whereabouts of an ineptly adulterous housewife.

'Too many parties, I expect.'

'I beg your pardon?'

'Being tired – too many parties.'

Isobel managed a weak laugh. 'No – no such luck, I'm afraid.'

'Ben's mother was a great one for parties. Oh Lord, yes. How that girl could dance.' She clapped her crooked hands. 'And the dresses . . . my dear, you should have seen the dresses – thirty or forty at least . . . and hatboxes too . . .'

'Really,' murmured Isobel, working harder to be polite, longing now to get away, especially from the possibility of any more intriguing tidbits about the Tarrants' family history. It only brought the sense of Ben closer, and she wasn't ready for that. By deceiving him she had quite destroyed her curiosity.

'One for every lover, Albert used to say – though he wouldn't throw them out, you know . . .'

'I really think—' Isobel stood up.

'One for every lover,' repeated Aunt Violet more harshly. 'Louisa was a tart.' Her head was doing its nodding trick, jerking in crazed agreement with itself. 'Deserved everything she got. I say, would you like to see some photographs?' With the invitation her voice switched to the sweet, silky tones that had greeted Isobel's arrival, while the rheumy eyes flickered with traces of a disturbingly girlish pleading, each one like a glimpse of the person lost inside.

'Perhaps we could ask for a cup of tea?' suggested Isobel faintly, wondering suddenly at the maze of subterranean motives that had impelled her to make the visit, whether it was an alibi she had sought, or some kind of self-inflicted punishment. It did not help that James's champagne was now wreaking its revenge, enhanced by the stuffy temperature of Aunt Violet's bedroom. Her tongue and gums felt sticky with thirst, while a painful pulse was gathering speed and intensity in her temples.

'Tea?' Aunt Violet's voice was scathing. 'The servants are instructed to bring tea at four o' clock.'

Isobel picked up her bag. 'Well, in that case, perhaps I'd better—'

'My albums are up there, on the shelf. Right behind you.' She waggled a finger at some high point behind Isobel's head. 'I want the red one.'

'Ah yes, the photos.' Isobel, feeling hysteria threaten, rubbed the palms of her hands together in a desperate parody of enthusiasm.

Aunt Violet's twisted fingers twitched with painful inefficiency at the edges of grey tissue paper interleaved between the pages of the old album. The fact that countless photographs had come loose did not make the task of studying them any easier. Unstuck corners fluttered to the carpet like confetti. Isobel, standing silently at her shoulder, gripped the edge of the chair in a bid to control both her impatience and dismay. The pictures were all from days prior to Albert Tarrant's posting to South America, prior to his encounter with Louisa da Costa and subsequent decision to make his life and living permanently overseas. Most of the images were too smudged or faded to be appreciated for any reason beyond sentiment; private ghosts from a private past.

'Here we are,' trumpeted the old lady suddenly, stabbing at a photograph of a woman posing with a baby in front of the broad, sweeping feathers of some pampas grass. She let out a humph of satisfaction. 'The tart herself.' Isobel recognised Louisa at once, from the one picture Ben displayed of his parents, a formal shot of their wedding day, which lived on top of the crowded bookshelf in the hall. She was undeniably beautiful, with raven hair and wide, challenging black eyes that stood out despite the blurred and browning look of everything around them.

'And is that Ben?' she asked in a final bid to appear appreciative, pointing to the moon-faced infant propped, rather stiffly, in Louisa's arms.

'Ben? Good heavens, no. That's the other child, the one that died.'

'Whose child?'

'Louisa's. Though whether poor Albert was the father . . .' Violet sniffed and closed the book.

Isobel knelt down beside her. 'So Ben had a . . .'

'Shh.' A spray of saliva accompanied the reprimand. 'Family secrets, my dear.' She glanced nervously at the door, before whispering, 'Baby girl – died in the crash and a good thing too.' Pressing her lips together, she tilted her head back and closed her eyes. 'We might ask for tea now, don't you think?'

'Tea?'

'Got to go, have you? Always rushing off.'

'Yes, yes, I must.' Isobel's voice had shrunk to a monotone, an instrument for saying anything that would allow her to leave. 'I have to collect my children from school,' she lied, reaching for her bag. Sophie and Megan were both at friends' houses and required nothing from her for several more hours. 'They hate it if I'm late.' Quickly she brushed her lips across one soft, shrunken cheek.

'My cigarettes – where are they? You said you'd bring some, remember?' The accusation exploded out of her with such force that for a moment Isobel was almost afraid.

'Next time,' she faltered, moving towards the door.

'Don't bother – I haven't smoked for years.'

She was rescued from the incongruities of these farewells by a buxom, steely-haired nurse who bustled in carrying a tray. 'It's tea and tablets, Mrs T, and I won't take no for an answer . . . I heard all about what happened yesterday, you naughty girl . . .' She winked at Isobel, who managed an unconvincing smile before hurrying down the stairs.

The confusion of emotions that accompanied Isobel on her drive back to Torbridge was quite unlike anything she had ever experienced before. To have discovered on that day – of all days – that the fateful crash had deprived her husband of a sibling as well as a mother was ironic to the point of farce. It didn't matter, she told herself. It was no longer her business – or her right – to care about such things. That Ben had never told her himself clearly meant that he didn't think so either.

It was almost a relief when fresh surges of guilt began to override the finer points of such sentiments. Isobel clenched her teeth together and drove faster than felt either safe or normal, inwardly cursing the fact that a spouse's neglect should turn out to be no proof against the emotional consequences of seeking solace from other quarters.

The only redeeming feature of her circumstances was that she was beginning to feel, not love exactly, but certainly a great well of tenderness towards James Howard. And he loves me, she reminded herself, clinging, with unconscious desperation, to the padded leather of the steering wheel, as more intimate details of their recent encounter flooded into her mind.

As she turned off the Drayford Road towards Torbridge, the spire of the cathedral rose into view on the skyline, pushing up from amongst the chalky hills like the blade of a knife. In the same instant Isobel remembered that, in spite of all her resolutions, she had promised to meet James again. Her eyes glazed over from staring at the view ahead; the tarmac seethed like a black river, the cathedral blurred and divided. The car seemed to hurtle forwards of its own accord, gobbling up the old Roman road like a creature bent upon destruction.

26

A couple of weeks later it was the turn of Druscilla Carew, returning from an excursion to Drayford's celebrated Roman ruins, to admire the view of Torbridge cathedral afforded by the most ancient of its approach roads. Though she sighed with delight as the familiar prospect came into sight, it was out of satisfaction with life in general rather than from any appreciation of Gothic architecture. In fact Druscilla could not remember when she had last spent a more exciting few hours. The remains themselves had been a bit of a disappointment. She had only signed up for the trip because the nice young priest who failed to fix her percolator had mentioned it, and because she fancied getting out of Torbridge for a change. She had been meaning to visit the place for years, just as she had always fancied booking herself on one of the guided tours they did round the cathedral. It was the tourists who put her off, as well as laziness about paying attention to the countless historical things within her daily reach.

There had been three Americans in the group and a large herd of Japanese, whose rendering of English seemed to Druscilla to be quite indistinguishable from whichever oriental dialect they used to communicate amongst themselves. Having accepted the small disappointment that Archie Heighton-Jones was not to be among the party after all, she resolved to keep herself to herself. A resolution to which she managed to remain loyal, even when the American with the big moustache smiled in a way that showed he wanted to talk. She bought a *Daily Mail* at the bus station and kept her nose buried in it all the way to the Drayford Road, by which time she felt so sick that only by an intense study of the passing scenery did she manage to persuade the contents of her stomach to remain where they were.

Though their guide boasted that very little restoration work had been done on the site, Druscilla, surveying the faded, incomplete maps of mosaic flooring, separated only by knobbly knee-high divisions for walls, could not help thinking that a proper rebuilding of the place would have made the visit far more worth everybody's while. As soon as the guide released them, she retreated into the café for an early lunch and then spent the rest of their allotted time browsing through boxes of trinkets in the gift shop. Unenticed by key-rings of Roman generals and posters showing aerial views of crumbling stones, she treated herself to a cat calendar and a small bag of potpourri that smelt of lilac and roses. By the time the rest of the group had got to the shop, Druscilla was already back in the coach, doing the coffee-break page of her paper and sucking, rather noisily, on the liquorice straw of a sherbet lemon.

On the return journey it was one of the American trio, a wide-hipped lady with braces and bleached hair, who confessed, loudly, to feeling ill. Shortly after one roadside stop, during which she gulped air from the open door of the coach, she began retching into a plastic carrier bag held, rather gingerly, by the man with the bike-handle moustache. Druscilla, having so narrowly avoided a similar affliction herself earlier on, could not help feeling rather smug, and somewhat entertained. I ought to get out more, she thought happily, while the woman sobbed for access to a bathroom and the guide entered into frantic whispered consultations with the driver. A few minutes later they pulled up on the grass verge opposite an ugly roadside hotel, where several vehicles were already packed on to the adjoining piece of fenced tarmac that served as a carpark. The coach driver grudgingly flicked on his hazard lights and lit a cigarette, while the guide ushered the two Americans over the road. The rest of them, who had been asked to contain any urges relating to basins and lavatories until their arrival at Torbridge bus terminal, sat and waited.

Idly chewing the last coil of her liquorice, Druscilla stared after the hobbling American lady and her two escorts. The woman looked ugly and stupid in her view, and the man unhappy. Probably why he had smiled so invitingly at her, she decided, with a small pout of satisfaction; though she had never liked moustaches, or Americans either for that matter. She was on the point of dismissing the pair from her thoughts completely and returning to the testing top left-hand corner of the coffee-break crossword when her eye was caught by two figures emerging from a side door of the hotel. For a moment she could not believe her eyes. But the auburn hair, streaking out behind in the whip of the wind, was unmistakable. As was the well-groomed figure of the man whose arm was round the woman's waist, his fingers curled protectively round her hip bone. At the sight of them Druscilla experienced a profound and quite unexpected stab of jealousy. Dr Howard was undeniably handsome; well preserved and distinguished-looking with sleek dusty grey hair and wonderfully penetrating eyes. Just the kind of man, she thought wistfully, whom she might have gone for herself, once upon a time. After one hurried farewell kiss – lips on lips, Druscilla noted, with mounting excitement – they got into their respective cars and drove away in opposite directions; for camouflage, no doubt, she decided, swallowing the last speck of her liquorice and dabbing her lips with a tissue.

Upon getting home, Druscilla positioned herself – and a full box of After Eights – in a comfortable chair by the bay window of her front room. Every few minutes she dipped one of the slim chocolates into her mug of coffee before sucking it, relishing the way the sweet minty juices slid between her teeth and on to her tongue. Untouched envelopes of chocolate lay in several saucers scattered round her feet, awaiting the arrival of the other members of her household, currently occupied with more obviously feline pursuits outside.

She had suspected the existence of an admirer for some time. Husbands like Ben Tarrant didn't send bouquets – at least, not two such large ones – in the space of one week. And then there was the note too, Druscilla remembered with a heart-flutter of excitement, the tiny trophy she had unearthed from the damp ground inside the Tarrants' front gate. Abandoning her vigil by the front window, she fetched the old biscuit tin from the middle shelf of her small kitchen dresser and tipped its contents on on the carpet. Amongst the heap was a ball of rubber bands, her wedding ring, a set of miniature screwdrivers, a broken but favourite earring, four curtain hooks, a tube of hand cream and several business cards advertising the services of taxi firms and carpet-cleaning companies. But no sign of the flower note. Druscilla frowned and sat back on her heels. It was unlike her to lose track of something so intriguing. She tried pressing the tips of her fingers to her temples and concentrating hard with her eyes closed, taking herself back to the small hours of the night when she had been so disturbed by a noise outside; but beyond images of Cary Grant and her lovely dress she could remember barely any details at all. Cross with herself, she swept the pile of papers and trinkets back into the tin and pressed the lid shut, banging her fist impatiently at the bent edge of one corner.

Outside, a car drew up and a door slammed. On tiptoes, her spirits recharged in an instant, Druscilla stole towards her window. Isobel was walking slowly towards her front gate, hands in her coat pockets, her eyes on the pavement. There was no sign of the children. Slipping her feet into her trainers, new pink ones with purple arrows on the sides, Druscilla trotted into her kitchen to fetch a bottle of milk before returning to the hall. As soon as she heard Isobel's door slam, she carefully let herself out and scurried across the few yards separating their houses, her laces trailing in the dirt.

'I've got some extra,' she declared, waving the milk bottle, which was barely a quarter full, and pushing past Isobel the moment she opened the door. 'I know you're always short, with the girls and so on. Can't give too much to my pussies,' she continued, sidling down the hall, 'upsets their stomachs so – though chocolate doesn't, which is odd, don't you think? I'll pop it in the fridge for you, shall I?'

Isobel had been on the point of running a bath. As always, the smell of James was in her skin and hair, the taste of him in her mouth. Even the air in the car seemed to hold his scent for hours afterwards, as if breathed out by the corrupted pores of her own body. Driving home, she would wind the window right down in an effort to get rid of it, breathing in lungfuls of fresh cold air like an ex-smoker trying to destroy evidence of a relapse. The sight of Druscilla Carew on her doorstep was so unexpected, so utterly disheartening, that for a moment all sense and strength drained from her. It was only when she followed the woman into the kitchen and saw her sitting at her table, clearly bent upon staying, that some of her wits returned.

'Thank you for the milk, Druscilla, but I'm afraid I can't offer you a cup of tea. I'm *extremely* busy, as it happens . . . so if you wouldn't mind . . .' Any normal person would have understood the intention of such a politely unfinished sentence. But her neighbour merely rolled her eyes and gave a delicate pat to the hard, hairsprayed crust of her hair.

'I know you're *busy*, my dear Isobel, very *busy* indeed.' Something about Druscilla's tone sent a ripple of apprehension down Isobel's spine.

'Was there something you wanted?' she asked faintly.

'To congratulate you, my dear,' exclaimed Druscilla, with genuine warmth. She had never liked Ben Tarrant. He never had time to chat or smile. When the girls were small and still crawling, she had seen him shoo her cats from their garden, muttering about the little messes they sometimes deposited on the lawn. But never his wife. Isobel was quite different: much more tolerant and kind. Quite deserving of a lover in fact. 'I just wanted to say . . .' She beamed. '. . . that in my opinion it couldn't have happened to a nicer person.'

'What couldn't have happened?'

'You and Dr Howard. It couldn't have happened to a nicer person. There was me, wondering who the admirer was – all those heavenly flowers – but I'd never have guessed, honestly, I wouldn't, not in a million years. You dark horse, you.'

'Oh dear.' Isobel sat down and put her hands to her mouth, staring at the gleeful face opposite her in disbelief. After each tryst she found that guilt turned quickly to remorse. Regardless of the pressure of both conscience and common sense, she also continued to dread the prospect of confession, of pushing the whole pitiable state of their marriage on into its next, inevitable phase. Sometimes, between meetings with James, she would even catch herself grasping at the pathetic straw of a hope that the situation between her and Ben was in fact salvageable after all, that, with a little more patience on her part, some sort of acceptable *modus vivendi* might be found. The thought that her odious neighbour was now in a position to jeopardise such hopes

– or to make things even worse than they were already going to be – was almost more than Isobel could bear. Yet she couldn't tolerate the thought of begging to her either, of being in thrall to such a woman. 'Druscilla, I would really appreciate it if . . .'

'My dear girl, your secret is safe with me.' Clearly delighted with the situation, Druscilla hopped to her feet, and began clumsily filling the kettle from the tap. Jets of water spurted across the breadboard and on to a roll of kitchen paper on a holder attached to the wall behind. 'I think it's all heavenly. I saw you this afternoon, in case you're wondering. I went on a tour to the Drayford ruins – not worth a visit, by the way – and then was fortunate enough to catch sight of you and Dr Howard during a stopover on the journey back. Such a coincidence – I love coincidences, don't you? You were in the carpark of that inn place on the Drayford Road, saying goodbye . . .' She wriggled her shoulders. '*Very* romantic it looked too, you lucky things . . . that husband of yours never deserved you, you know . . .'

Isobel flinched. 'I think you'd better go, Druscilla.'

But her neighbour was in full flow. She pressed the switch on the kettle and took two mugs down from the cupboard. 'The only decent thing to come out of my marriage was money. Not a lot, but enough.' She dropped a tea bag into each mug. 'Mind you, I paid in other ways. Oh yes, I paid dearly . . .'

'Druscilla, please go. I want you to go.' Isobel stood up, her chair screeching on the tiled floor. 'I want you to go.'

'Goodness, you are all fizzed up, aren't you? Well, I'll leave you in peace, then. Want to freshen up, I dare say . . . but if *ever* you want to talk . . .' She nudged Isobel, who swayed against the side of the table. At the kitchen door she paused and frowned. 'I've got a little something to confess too, as it happens . . .'

Isobel gripped the edge of the table, dreading what might come out next.

'. . . that is to say, I possess something that belongs to you – a little love note, I suppose you'd call it.' She pressed her fingers to her mouth to suppress a giggle. 'Must have dropped out of one of those pretty bouquets Dr Howard sent a few weeks back. I found it by your front gate, all covered in leaves and dirt and goodness knows what. I forgot all about it until today . . . can't quite lay my hands on it at the moment, but when I do you will be the first to know. All property should be returned to its rightful owners, don't you think?' She winked, before turning and heading towards the front door. Isobel, now clinging to the merest thread of self-control, sat on the bottom stair and watched without blinking as the crack of daylight widened and Druscilla stepped into it. 'Such lovely wording it was too.' She wrinkled her nose in an effort to remember the exact phrase. 'No words can say what I feel . . . yes, that was it.' She sighed happily. '*So* nice to know that romance isn't completely dead in this unfriendly world of ours, at least not for some . . .'

She was still talking at the front gate, when Isobel finally dragged herself from the stairs in order to close the door.

27

Ben, much to his amazement, was having something of a good day. That his long-postponed phone call to Dick Caulder's counsellor – hastily made from a call-box during break that morning – might have had something to do with this turn of events did not escape his attention. In the end, it was something of a relief to have taken the plunge. Not only did it put a stop to the dreadful tug-of-war going on inside his head, but it had also been far less painful than he had feared: no probing questions, no sense of that distinctly female greed for emotional details that he felt in no position to release. Instead, the woman, whose name was Ione Brown, had suggested meeting for a preliminary session, to explain who she was and how she worked. Asking nothing about why he wanted to see her, she simply took his name in a friendly sort of way and issued directions for finding her consulting rooms. She was lucky enough to have a spare slot that evening, she said, owing to a cancellation. He could come at eight o'clock, if he liked, and they would take it from there. Without really thinking beyond the fact that he wanted the phone call to be over, Ben found himself agreeing.

After giving the matter some thought, he decided to telephone Isobel with a white lie of an explanation as to why he would be home even later than usual that night. He had no wish to tell his wife – or anyone else, for that matter – about Ione Brown. Investigating the possibility of such help was bad enough, without the added horror of advertising the fact. When, after several attempts throughout the afternoon, there was still no reply from home, Ben couldn't help feeling a little relieved. He wouldn't offer any excuses unless directly called upon to do so, he decided. One more late night could hardly make things between them any worse or better than they were already.

The run-through that lunch-time was the best yet. The lighting was more or less sorted – at last – and some final touches to the scenery had worked to marvellous effect. For the first time since the outset of the project, Ben found himself almost looking forward to the rehearsal due to take place the following night – a sort of critical preview, to be attended by Peter Abbott and a few other key members of staff. Instead of working during his free period that afternoon, he treated himself to a browse amongst the staffroom newspapers. Flicking through a weekly supplement on jobs, his eye was caught by a boxed bold-print advertisement at the very bottom of the page. A small private school called Fairlands required a headmaster. Located in Hampshire with two hundred pupils. On any other occasion in recent months Ben would have shaken his head and moved on. But thanks to the unexpectedly pleasing pattern of the day so far, he found himself scribbling down details on the back of an envelope and filing it away in his briefcase.

Upon catching sight of the boy Lewis skulking behind the headmaster's new red Volvo, this new-found and highly precarious lightness of spirit almost disappeared. Ben had to clench his fists to prevent himself from turning and scurrying away. Though it was seven thirty and quite dark, Lewis's pale face and extraordinary halo of curly yellow hair were plainly illuminated by the glare of the security light at the entrance to the school drive. It was unfortunate hair for any child, thickening as opposed ever to increasing in actual length, and retaining a colour that looked chemically enhanced on even the most sunless of days. Ben, who was heading for the metal bike rack half hidden by the bushes on the far side of the drive, paused only for a moment before quickening his pace. There was no avoiding being seen. A meeting – a chance to talk some sense into the lad – was what he had been arguing for all along, he reminded himself, striding into view with a decidedly grim expression of welcome fixed to his face.

'Evening, Lewis.'

'Oh, sir – good evening – I was hoping to catch you – I've been waiting. I recognised your bike.'

'The smart one, eh?' replied Ben, his mouth relaxing into a more genuine smile, all his apprehensions dissolving at the obviously embarrassed confusion of the boy. He was still only a child after all. 'Two gears, half a mudguard and a generous coating of rust in preference to paint.'

Lewis laughed and looked relieved. 'I've come to . . . say sorry. I mean, I know I've caused the most frightful bother . . . to you especially.'

Ben knelt down and fiddled with his bike lock. 'No harm done, in the long term. Got to keep a hold of your emotions a bit more . . .' He stopped in mid-sentence, wondering suddenly whether such advice was either true or wise.

'Yeah.' The boy looked at his boots, which were round-toed and big-soled. 'But if I feel things, they just sort of come out. But that letter – well, I'm really sorry . . . I mean, I was never going to send it or anything. The last thing I wanted was for my parents to find it . . . when they did they just flipped,' he added in a small voice.

'It's all right, Lewis. It's done with. Enjoying your new school?' Ben stood up and looped the chain and padlock round the handlebars.

He made a face. 'Not much, but we're moving to Scotland. Dad's going to work on rigs in the North Sea. Mum doesn't want to go.'

'And what about you, what do you want?'

He shrugged and shuffled his feet. 'Don't care really.' He bent down and scooped up a handful of loose stones.

'Oh, you must always care, Lewis,' Ben said gently, inwardly marvelling at the ease with which such pearls slipped out, given his hopeless management of his own emotions. He wheeled his bike up to where the boy was standing and held out his hand. 'Goodbye, Lewis, and good luck.'

'I think I'm gay,' the boy muttered, biting his bottom lip and throwing a chip of gravel at the grass verge.

Ben sighed. 'Well, it's not a crime, you know. Nothing to be ashamed of either.'

Lewis threw another stone which bounced off the security light lamppost with a resounding clang. 'I somehow don't think my dad would agree with you . . .'

'Dads can be a problem,' admitted Ben with a rueful smile, 'and mums too for that matter. Just be sure what you want in yourself and the rest will fall into place. OK? Now I'm afraid I've got to go – I've got an . . . appointment. How are you getting home?'

'Bus.'

'Well, we could walk to the bus stop together, then. Unless you've got other plans?'

Lewis beamed and shook his head. 'I could push your bike for you, sir.'

'I'll manage, thank you. I'm not a bloody geriatric, you know – at least not yet, anyway.' He shot a sideways grin to soften the rejection. Kindness, but not too much, he thought grimly, fearing for the future of his young companion.

'I don't know why I've come, actually – I mean, I'm almost certain I shall be wasting your time. It's a bit like putting off booking the doctor and the moment you get round to it your symptoms disappear like magic. Then you feel a right fool.' Ben laughed, aware that he sounded nervous.

Ione Brown smiled. 'It's the people who rush to the doctors with the slightest symptoms who are usually the malingerers. Come in and take a seat. Help yourself to water whenever you want. And I'll begin by telling you a little bit about how I work, my costs, cancellation policy and so on.'

She had one of those faces that had reached a stage of ageing beyond which it was hard to imagine anything else. Deep laugh lines radiated from the corners of her eyes and mouth, but they had the effect of softening her appearance instead of making it more severe. Though he put her at around forty, she could just as well have been thirty-five or close to fifty. Her hair, cut in a short, chic style round her ears, was very black. Apart from some pale lipstick, she appeared to be wearing no make-up at all, while her clothes, a calf-length black skirt and cream polo-neck jumper, were equally inconspicuous. Everything about her demeanour, as a person, as a female, was – Ben felt at once – wholly open and quite without expectation.

In the same soft tone of voice which she used to explain that each session would cost him twenty-five pounds and last for fifty minutes, Ione Brown proceeded to enquire whether Ben could tell her something about the events that had led him to request the appointment.

He struggled hopelessly to answer. 'Oh God, I don't really know, honestly I don't.' He ran both his hands through his hair and studied the flecks in her grey carpet. 'I mean, to tell you the truth, today has been great. A really good day. The first for a while, in fact . . . but apart from that – oh hell, it's probably just a mid-life crisis – usual cliché at my time of life, I suppose. I'm thirty-five.' He offered her a wry smile which was not reciprocated.

'Nothing's a cliché if you feel it.'

He cleared his throat. 'No, I guess it isn't.' He coughed again. 'I'm here because – well, to be frank, a friend recommended you to me. His wife died and he had trouble coping afterwards.' He clapped his hands together. 'But my wife hasn't died – I'm happy to say. In fact, everything in my life is in pretty good working order, except that recently I've felt . . . oh Christ, it's hard to put into words, but . . .' He leant forward in his chair, shamed now by his stammerings into wanting to explain properly. 'I've always been the kind of person who has coped with life. Not just coped, but done pretty well. I don't mean to sound arrogant or anything, but I was thrown into the deep end quite early on – my mother died in a car crash and I was sent to boarding school in England – we lived in Chile – and so I learnt how to get on with things. Did well at school, good at languages, drama, decided to be a teacher – never wanted anything else . . .' He paused, worried that he was boring her. But upon glancing at the counsellor's face he could identify nothing but sympathetic interest. She was leaning forward on her desk, her hands folded neatly across a pad of paper. 'And then I met Isobel.' He hesitated again, remembering with an unexpected rush of pleasure the intensity of that time, the blind, arrogant certainty of all the feelings they had shared. 'And we lived abroad together for a year – she dropped everything to come with me.' He shook his head and smiled, remembering the episode as if in wonderment. 'After getting back to England we married, moved to Torbridge – I worked as a junior master at the cathedral school for a few years, Isobel miscarried our first baby, but we went on to have two lovely girls, now nine and seven . . . the point is, nothing has gone wrong in my life. I mean, I'm now at Crofton College – head of my department – I still love my wife, I adore my children and yet recently . . . I've just been feeling that I can't . . . hold it all together like I used to . . .' He poured a glass of water, disturbed to feel his hand shaking as he did so. 'I'm so damnably busy,' he growled, holding the glass, but not drinking from it. 'I direct school plays too – I'm in the middle of one at the moment, first night this Friday – and well, I guess it's all just been getting on top of me. Too old or something, maybe. There, you see' – he took a gulp of water – 'I told you, a mid-life crisis.' He shot her a look that was meant to be challenging, though it faded fast.

'You sound as if you don't think you've any right to feel like this.'

He scowled. 'No, now you mention it, I don't think I do. I've got everything a man could want – a career, a family, a roof over my head – nothing to feel dissatisfied about at all. A charmed life. Isobel and I haven't been getting on brilliantly recently, but that's because of me . . . because of me feeling like this.' He threw up his hands. 'It's hopeless. I don't see how anyone can help, it's up to me to pull myself together.'

'I don't think that a man who has lost both his mother and his first child could be described as having led a charmed life.'

'Oh, and there was a baby sister too, by the way,' he snapped. 'Let's add that to the catalogue of woes. She was in the car crash too. Just a few months old. I was seven, so there wasn't much sibling bonding to shout about . . . but, don't tell me, I know,' he jeered, 'I feel guilty for her death, do I?'

'Do you?'

'No.' He stuck out his chin. 'Nor do I feel guilty about my mother, in case you're wondering.' Aware that he was sounding increasingly aggressive, Ben took a deep breath to calm himself before continuing. 'It was a very long time ago,' he explained patiently, using a tone of voice he might have employed for an eager but slow-witted pupil, 'at an age when a baby sister was something either to ignore or envy. And my dear mother – from what little I can recall of her – was not what you might describe as the hands-on type of parent. Hordes of servants and so forth.' He laughed quietly. 'Her company was something of a rare treat for all of us, my father included . . .' Ben paused. 'His response to being widowed was to send me to school in England. Which distressed me a little at the time; but then I got used to it – loved it in fact. The school was in Surrey, acres of grounds and all that sort of thing. A maiden aunt used to come and take me out for cream teas.' He stopped, suddenly aware of how intently she was listening to him. 'No, I did not get on with my father,' he added wearily, 'but that's not a crime, is it?'

'No, it's not.'

'I learnt self-sufficiency at an early age. It's something for which I've always been profoundly grateful.' He paused, before murmuring, 'Funny how the worst things that happen to us can also turn out to be the best.'

There was a long silence during which Ione took a sip of water from a glass beside her telephone. 'How did you feel about losing your first child?' she asked gently.

'You make it sound so dramatic. It was really only a miscarriage—' Ben stopped, realising that he sounded unfeeling. 'I'm not saying I wasn't sorry; of course it was awful, but much more so for Isobel, obviously . . .' Aware of the attention of the counsellor, he felt obliged to offer some justification for such opinions. 'I mean – hell, she was carrying the damned thing, feeling it kick and all that stuff. She had to go through the agony of giving birth to something that was barely alive.' To his amazement and horror he found he was crying. Right out of the blue, without having received any warning signs at all. Beside the jug of water was a box of tissues. 'Bloody hell. Sorry.' He blew his nose. 'Hang on a minute, that's what I'm supposed to do, isn't it?' he sneered. 'Therapy in action. Wow. Grown men weeping.'

She remained quite still and silent while he collected himself. Then she said, 'It sounds as though it was very hard for both of you.'

'Isobel was devastated, of course. She cried a lot – even after we discovered she was pregnant again. To be honest, I got . . .' He paused. 'I was going to say angry, but of course I don't mean that; but it did get to the stage where I felt that being so sad wasn't getting her anywhere . . . wasn't getting us anywhere. And it was hard for me too, I suppose, feeling the same things but in such a different way . . .' He slapped his thigh. 'We were lucky enough to have another baby on the way, for God's sake . . .' His voice softened. 'Little Meg.'

'The first pregnancy . . . was it a girl or—?'

'A boy,' he put in quickly. 'Toby. Of course, we still remember the anniversary and all that.' He offered her a tight smile. 'My dear wife has this irritating habit of starting to remind me about it weeks beforehand – like she's scared I'll forget or something. It pisses me off so much that sometimes I pretend I have . . . but not this year.' He frowned and shuffled forward to the edge of his chair, locking and unlocking his fingers. 'This year it was the other way round: her turn to say nothing at all, leaving me to wonder what kind of game she's playing, whether it's to get at me or whether it's a sign that she really wants to be allowed to let that chunk of our past go . . .' He frowned to himself and shook his head. 'She never mentioned it once this year,' he repeated absently, 'not even when I sent flowers.' He looked up. 'So I said nothing either. Funny the games people play, isn't it?' he added with a brief laugh. 'Especially the ones who've known each other a long time. But then you'd know all about that, wouldn't you?'

'Tell me more about Toby. Was there a funeral?'

'Christ, no, we thought it was a bit early for that kind of palaver. Twenty-four weeks. They took photos and so on. The hospital chaplain did a blessing. Then they took him away for cremation. Burnt in a hospital incinerator, no doubt, along with all the other medical waste that week.' He caught his breath and stopped for a moment, breathing hard. 'Oh, and there was a post-mortem.' He raised his voice a little in an effort to quell the new tremor pushing up from the back of his throat. 'Listeria, they said. We'd been on holiday to France that year. Lots of soft cheese. Baguettes and pâté and all that sort of thing . . . it was just before all those food poisoning scandals really hit the headlines. Edwina's eggs started it off, didn't they?' He chuckled quietly. 'Isobel wouldn't go near anything produced by a chicken or a cow for years afterwards – well, certainly not until after Sophie was born anyway.'

'I'm not surprised,' Ione murmured. She let out a small sigh and then raised her eyes to meet his. 'I am very much aware that some of what you have said may have been painful for you, Mr Tarrant, and that this may feel like a difficult moment to stop. But I'm afraid we're in danger of running out of time.' She paused to cast a rueful glance at the clock on the wall above the door. 'You've mentioned a lot of important things that have happened, though obviously I realise that there are many areas we haven't begun to cover. How do you feel it has gone?'

Ben was somewhat taken aback, both by the formality of this address and because his fifty minutes seemed to have sped by so fast. He couldn't help feeling a little rebuffed, offended even.

'Do you feel sufficiently encouraged to return?' As she opened her diary she offered him a warm smile. 'Naturally, it is entirely up to you to decide.'

Ben stood up, suddenly exasperated. 'Excuse me, but what's the point? I mean, what can you do for me? What can you possibly do to help?'

She remained sitting, her brown eyes steadily meeting his. 'Maybe nothing. Maybe something. From what you have said, it seems to me that ever since you were a child you have always had to be strong. Though you claim to have found this easy, it means that there may be losses in your life that you have not resolved properly. The result of that can be that smaller subsequent losses, or distress of some kind, may trigger reactions that are quite out of proportion with the events themselves.'

'You mean it's all catching up with me?'

'Something like that.'

'It sounds too simple, too pat.'

'Often the truest things are the simplest.'

'But do you think it's really worth me coming back?'

'It's up to you – whether you think you might gain anything—'

'Bloody marvellous,' he interrupted. 'I'm supposed to be the patient, aren't I? Yet I don't get told what to do.'

'Precisely.'

'Well, what do you recommend, then?' he asked, more meekly, but unable to resist adding, 'That is, if you're allowed to express an opinion.'

'Six sessions over a period of six weeks. From next week I shall have a free slot on Thursday evenings at seven o'clock.'

'I'll think about it.'

'Fine. Call me when you've decided what to do.'

Cycling home afterwards, Ben felt a mounting astonishment and dismay at the way he had behaved, not just because of the crying, but also because he had allowed his life story to sound so dramatic. Some families didn't cohere and his had been one of them. Baby Lisa, or 'the little bastard' as his father – on the infrequent occasions when he had referred to her brief existence at all – had so endearingly liked to call her, had been banned as a topic for discussion not so much out of sadness as Albert's sense of family shame. Aunt Violet, like Ben himself, had been sworn to secrecy. A pointless secrecy in Ben's view, but one that over the years had evolved into a habit rather than a challenge. Not telling Isobel had never felt like a big deal. Apart from other considerations, he had also been reluctant to stimulate any more pity from her than the details of his colourful family background had already. Ben had always hated pity, regarding it as the most belittling of responses, from loved ones or anyone else.

Instead of capitalising on his earlier good mood, the immediate effect of the counselling session therefore, was to throw him into deeper confusion. His head was buzzing with images from the past, not so much from his childhood, as from the early years of his marriage: images of little Toby in particular, what he had felt at losing him. Or rather, what he had tried not to feel. Being strong had appeared as his obvious, allotted task, he remembered, the one useful thing he could do in the circumstances; the thing he could do for Isobel. At the thought of his wife, a hand tightened around Ben's heart. Talking about her behind her back like that, pouring so much into the grey expectant silence of Ione Brown's small consulting room, felt like betrayal. It was Isobel he should be talking to, he realised hopelessly, not some empathetic stranger with a heart-warming smile.

By the time Ben got home, however, Isobel had already gone up to bed. He made himself a sandwich, which he ate along with two bananas and an overripe tomato while watching the late evening news. He started a can of beer but abandoned it after a few swigs. A pleasant exhaustion began to seep through him, relaxing his body like a warm bath. While a bespectacled weatherman pointed at cut-out rain-clouds and frothing satellite pictures, Ben's head flopped from side to side in a faltering attempt to resist sleep. In his mind he could see Isobel, but far away, a speck at the end of a tunnel. And he was running towards her, shouting at her to wait, that he was on his way. Though he ran his hardest, the speck grew ever more tiny until its existence was the merest pin-prick, something to be believed in rather than seen.

Upstairs, meanwhile, the object of Ben's dreams lay hunched in a stiff representation of sleep, listening for, yet dreading, the footfall on the stair, the creak of the loose floorboard on the landing outside their room. And when it did not come, when minutes became hours and still it did not come, something in her gave up and was replaced by the steel of resigned resolution. If James wanted her he could have her, she thought, biting the knuckles of her hand. Anything was better than not being wanted at all, than living with an absence of hope as well as love.

28

Ilcombe, Wednesday 3 April

My Dearest Isobel,

Has it really only been a matter of hours since our last meeting? How the time drags when we're apart. And yet how it flies when we're together. To say I'm missing you does not begin to do justice to the intensity of my feelings . . .

James smiled to himself as he paused to dip his fountain pen in the pot of ink. It was hard to recall when he had last felt so happy, so excited, so . . . alive. He held up the page, admiring the rich, thick squirls of his handwriting. Though it was only ten o'clock, Juliet had already gone to bed, early nights having become something of a habit of hers in recent weeks. As this was the only evidence of wifely withdrawal since the start of his affair with Isobel, and since each retirement was embarked upon with the tenderest of goodnight kisses, James had not yet allowed himself to worry over the matter. In many ways he was grateful: such behaviour generated an atmosphere of affectionate distance which suited both his mood and his capabilities perfectly. They had stopped rowing too, which was nice.

All I can see is your face, all I can feel is your body . . . James hesitated, wondering how erotic or risqué he dared to be. Matters had reached a very delicate stage. The last thing he wanted was to scare her away. *I need you,* he wrote, crushing more wildly erotic expressions of passion that flitted into his mind. Better to play it safe, he told himself, pausing again, this time to extract a minute hair from the gold nib of his pen.

As I keep saying, we need some time away together. I know your reservations. I know that, like me, you are steeling yourself for the right moment to break the news. But don't you feel it would do us both good to think through such a prospect together, in peace somewhere? What about it, Isobel? A few days away, on our own. Wouldn't that be wonderful? Could your parents perhaps look after the children? I don't mean to appear hasty or presumptuous . . . I'm just so desperate to get you away from everyone – from everything – to get you to myself. After that . . .

James stopped and frowned. For the truth was that, while implying to Isobel – because she clearly needed to hear it – that any future they chose was theirs for the asking, he had not really thought things through properly on that score at all. It was too difficult for one thing; and for another, he was enjoying himself too much. If he had one criticism of his mistress it was that she could not lose herself entirely to the moment. Their physical compatibility was unquestionable; all those weeks of fantasising and flirting had resulted in the most satisfactory of sexual relationships. Left to his own devices, James would have been happy to have let things coast for a while, to delay rocking the boat on any front until it was absolutely necessary. But Isobel's thought processes had quickly raced to a point way beyond such easy options. What would become of them? she wanted to know, almost from the start. Where would it all lead in the end? Sex had to be part of something, she said. It had to lead somewhere lasting and worthwhile. James's face softened at the recollection of the sincerity of her pleadings, how she warmed to his declarations of love. All wide-eyed and fearful. Like a child. It was impossible not to feel passionate about such a creature. With a frown he forced his attention back to the business in hand, bracing himself for the direct approach.

Since so much is at stake, I feel increasingly certain that we owe it to each other to take some time out to think things through clearly, without the pressures of time and guilt breathing down our necks. We may have a future together, Isobel, and I for one need a bit of space in order to contemplate how best to achieve that . . .

Having laboured sufficiently over the pretext for the point he was trying to make, James's handsome writing doubled in speed and flourish.

If you could escape to Suffolk for a few days, I've heard of the perfect place we could go. A wonderful country hotel; discreet and luxurious. And not at all far from where I believe your parents live. I think I shall probably be completely frank with Juliet – tell her straight out that I need some time to myself to think about our future. What you decide to tell Ben is of course your business and I would not dream of interfering. No aspect of this is remotely easy for any of us. But then of course you know that. Just as I think you know that we are very good together, Isobel, that we deserve a chance to see things through. I'm not so foolish as to make false promises about exactly what the future will hold, but I just know that everything will work out all right in the end. Because all this was meant to be.

Pleased with this last sentence, James was for a moment tempted to leave it at that. But the opportunity for a little more romance got the better of him.

This was intended as a love letter, but I'm not sure how I've done. I'd forgotten what love felt like. I don't feel hungry or tired. I don't feel anything except a burning desire to be with you. Nothing else matters. I just can't care about anything else in the world . . . I'll call you soon, my love, during a 'safe' time. I'll be delivering this by hand. I'm thinking about Suffolk already, longing for it . . . don't let me down.

Yours devotedly, James

After reading it through James wondered whether he should tear it up and do a new version that was slightly more ordered and well argued. He really had set his heart on a few days away and would be extremely disappointed if she refused. Upon a second reading, however, he convinced himself that a slight incoherence was part of the letter's charm, and that anything better structured would be in danger of seeming glib or insincere. He sealed it and addressed it by hand, before slipping it amongst some papers in his briefcase. He would deliver it the next day, at an hour when he could be sure Ben's bicycle would be absent from the tiny box of a front garden in Fox's Crescent.

At the thought of Ben, James flinched, as a twinge of something like compassion momentarily pinched his heart. It was quickly overcome by impatience. From what he could gather from Isobel – who volunteered very little on the subject – the man had been ignoring the poor girl for months. As a result James had – somewhat conveniently – decided that Ben Tarrant was one of those secret bullies, lovingly protective towards their spouses in public, but with an altogether more hostile agenda reserved for the home.

As he moved quietly around the ground floor, turning out lights and checking locks, James felt indignation mounting on his lover's behalf. He wouldn't dream of treating Juliet in such a manner, he thought, or decided to think, until the ambiguities inherent in such emotions caused him to pause, hand poised over a light switch, in order to ponder such contradictions more deeply. Although he had implied to Isobel – many times – that he wished to abandon his marriage, in his heart James was not as sure as he claimed. Juliet understood him in ways he could never imagine another woman doing. She laughed when he farted or belched. She tickled him if he snored, and rolled her palms around his shoulder blades when he was tense. Such familiarity had taken years to construct. He couldn't imagine it with Isobel. More importantly, he didn't much want to. His relationship with her seemed to exist on a purer, higher plane, quite apart from the real world. And, in spite of all protestations to the contrary to his lover, a considerable part of him wanted to keep it that way.

29

'Hello, Mum, it's me, Isobel. How are you?'

'Wait a minute, I can't hear a thing.' Betty Hitchings scowled, as she always did if her presence in the kitchen happened to coincide with the over-ebullient spin cycle of her washing machine. There was one long final vibrating whoosh followed by a relieving silence. 'Thank God for that. Your father's shirts in their final throes. The belt on the machine is about to go, I just know it. But will he look at the damn thing . . . ?' Aware that she was in danger of sounding disloyal, Betty checked herself, before rushing on with more conventional expressions of greeting. 'But how are you, darling? How are the children?'

'We're all fine,' replied Isobel carefully, wondering, now that she had got this far, how much she was actually prepared to reveal. She had never been a great one for heart-to-heart talks with her mother, as much from her own reticence as a distinct sense that neither of her parents wished to be drawn into the role of confidant, that to do so would overstep some traditional boundary line that they wished to preserve. They could be sympathetic when the need arose, but always in a brisk no-nonsense way, faintly suggestive of impatience.

'How's Dad?'

'Grumpy. He's on a diet.'

'Again?' Isobel tugged a tired grape off its stalk and squeezed it between her thumb and forefinger before placing it in her mouth. She was sitting on the edge of the kitchen table, her feet lodged between the slats of a chair.

'Doctor's orders. High blood pressure and so on. Got to cut down on his cholesterol.'

'Poor Dad.'

'He'll survive. We're eating a lot of pasta and fish. I've lost half a stone.' She laughed. 'Which is more than can be said for George. He's in the garden now, digging fiendishly round the roses in the hope of shedding a few pounds before lunch.'

Isobel laughed too, enjoying, in spite of her own preoccupations, the familiar snapshot of her parents' married existence. Was it resignation or faith, she wondered, that had kept them together for so long? What did love become after thirty-five years?

'I say, how's that university course of yours going?'

'It's not,' replied Isobel flatly, pulling at a loose thread in one of her socks until it broke.

'But you sounded so excited . . . all those books . . .'

'I've given up, actually – on the idea of literature, anyway. It was too much like . . .' She hesitated, remembering her recent frustrations with Anna Karenina and various other heroines on the reading list, how absurdly glorious their creators had made them seem, when real life was not glorious at all, but full of belittling detail and doubt. '. . . escapsim,' she ended lamely. 'I'm thinking of doing something more practical. The OU have just introduced a Spanish course – it's a new thing. Seeing as I got the hang of the basics all those centuries ago in Madrid, I'm toying with the idea of applying to start in September.' It was hard to inject any conviction into her voice. Present circumstances had deterred her from mentioning such plans to Ben. September seemed worlds away, on the other side of an abyss.

'How splendid,' exclaimed her mother in a way that Isobel knew was intended to communicate enthusiasm, but which only managed to sound patronising instead. In spite of all her efforts to the contrary, Betty Hitchings retained a fondness for the most archaic of attitudes towards the concept of women and work. Though both daughters had attended reputable universities, it remained evident that she regarded all female education as a prelude to marriage and little else. That her high-flying merchant banker of an eldest child was still showing not the remotest hint of a nesting instinct or anything related was, as the entire family knew, a growing source of secret maternal disappointment.

'I know it's very short notice,' blurted Isobel, unable to sustain small talk for a moment longer, 'but I was wondering if you and Dad were busy this weekend and next week . . . ?'

'The Birketts were due to come and stay, but they've cried off – Donald's rheumatism, Caroline says, though I suspect it's because they couldn't face the journey. It is a hell of a way for them to come and Caroline herself only has to look at a car seat and her back seizes up . . . why do you ask, dear?' she added suddenly, a note of something like suspicion edging into her voice.

'I know it's short notice—' faltered Isobel.

'Were you and Ben thinking of coming to stay?'

'Sort of . . . well, yes . . . and I was also hoping to leave the girls with you for a couple of days next week.'

'Is term about to end?' Betty squinted at a calendar of seascapes pinned to the back of the door beside her.

'Not quite. They officially break up next week . . .' Isobel cast her eyes down to James's letter which was sitting next to her on the table. With one hand she folded it back in two and pressed her fingers hard along the crease. 'But I was thinking of breaking the habit of a lifetime and pulling the girls out of school a little early . . .'

'Whatever for? Surely Ben's got to see out his term too. Has he done that play of his yet?'

Isobel, in danger of getting riled, had to remind herself that her mother was not being deliberately obtuse, that all the responsibility for the difficulty of this conversation rested entirely with her.

'No, that's this weekend. Final dress rehearsal tonight . . .' She sighed. 'Look, it's hard to explain properly, Mum, but the fact is that I need – Ben and I need – a little time apart right now.'

There was a stunned silence.

'We . . . things have not been good recently—'

'What sort of things?'

'Like I said, it's impossible to explain.' Isobel had now folded the page of James's letter into a tight, fat square. 'All I'm asking is whether I could come over with the children for a little while and perhaps take a couple of days on my own next week, to go away somewhere . . .'

'On your own?'

'To think,' put in Isobel quickly, wanting to avoid an outright lie. She wasn't ready to mention James yet, not until they knew exactly what their plans were. 'I need time to think about what to do.'

'Have you two had some sort of tiff?'

This was such a monumental understatement that for a moment Isobel was tempted to laugh out loud. A tiff sounded feisty and amusing. A tiff happened between two people who could still talk to each other, who still ate meals together. 'I'm afraid it's all much more complicated, Mum,' she replied quietly, the anguish plain in her voice.

'Of course you can come and stay,' came the barked reply, as Betty Hitchings slipped into full crisis-management mode, using a tone that transported Isobel straight back to all the landmark traumas of childhood, traumas usually associated with Angela, who had generally taken it upon herself to pioneer the reprehensible antics of adolescence. 'Where are we? Thursday afternoon. Right, then, come tomorrow if you want. We'll expect you by lunch.'

'Thank you,' Isobel whispered, despising the pang of nostalgic longing that burst inside, the brief, false relief of being a child again, of having parents to rail against instead of the inadequacies of oneself.

'Of course your father and I will do anything we can to help. But do try and sort it out in the meantime, the two of you, won't you? Running away never solved anything, you know. And think of the girls . . .'

Isobel, who had recently been thinking of little else, closed her ears to the gently scolding lecture that ensued. Telling Sophie and Megan was easily going to be the worst part of all. She dreaded their bewilderment. Though they saw too little of Ben, their devotion to him was absolute, she knew. They were fond of James, but only as a doctor who gave them lollipops for being brave, and as a grown-up with a high tolerance for tickling games and losing count of the number of biscuits consumed between meals. How they would feel about him moving into their lives on a more permanent scale was hard to imagine. As indeed it remained for Isobel herself. Try as she might, she could not picture how a reshuffled future might look, how it would feel, day to day. She was intent on pushing things that way because all her instincts told her that it was the only thing to do; the only way of redeeming anything from the situation at all. And because James, though baulking like her at the prospect of all the upheaval and hurt, seemed to be growing increasingly desperate to have her to himself. It was impossible not to be flattered by the intensity of his ardour, impossible – much as she hated to acknowledge the fact – not to be grateful for it.

'We'll come tomorrow, then,' she pressed on, swallowing her doubts and focusing on the burgeoning need to get away from the stranger who had once been her husband, away from the collapse of all that she had once held so dear. 'Be there by lunch-time,' she echoed, quailing inwardly, though her voice held firm.

'And stay the whole of next week?'

'If that's all right.'

'But you'll be going off for a couple of days on your own somewhere?'

Isobel swallowed. 'That's the idea. If it's OK with you.'

'To think.'

'Yes, to think.'

'Where?'

'Where what?'

'Where exactly is all this thinking going to take place?'

'I don't know, I've not yet sorted everything out . . . it doesn't really matter, to be honest.'

Her mother humphed. 'Well, all I can say is I'm very sorry indeed.'

'So am I, Mum, believe me.'

'I thought we might go to Granny's for a while.'

'For Easter?'

'No . . . starting tomorrow.'

'You mean miss school?'

'Just a few days . . .'

'Yippee times a million.' Sophie, who was supposed to be holding the frilly paper trim of her Easter bonnet in place until the glue dried, let go in order to clap her hands. Since a greater quantity of adhesive had found its way on to her fingertips than on to the cardboard contours of the hat, the lacy strip of paper was soon hanging in several soggy pieces between her palms.

'But why?' Megan, old enough to be more suspicious, ruled a careful line underneath the last of a set of perfectly formed fractions and closed her book. 'You don't believe in missing school. Ever.' She folded her arms. 'You made me go back when I still had all those scabs.' The recollection of this indignity deepened the pained expression on her face.

'You weren't infectious,' began Isobel, feeling diverted and hopeless.

'No, I was hideous.'

'Darling, it was years ago . . .'

'Only a little bit over two years ago. I got the first spots on Christmas Day, remember?'

Isobel smiled and reached out a hand to stroke her eldest's mop of dark hair. Even after several months of being commanded to 'grow out', Megan's fringe had still somehow only managed to reach the corners of her eyes, from where it flopped, with regular and infuriating persistence, into her long dark lashes. She was glowering from behind this new protection now, exercising a sullenness that had something to do with being almost ten and something less easily defined to do with the expression of unnatural cheeriness imprinted on her mother's face. 'I don't want to go to Suffolk. It's horrid except in the summer. All cold and windy. And Grandpa makes us help in the garden.' She scowled.

'But Granny will take you to the library and that adventure playground with the tree-house and the long curly slide—'

'And to the place with the penguins,' squealed Sophie, for whom a trip to the aquatic wonders of East Anglia's Sea World the summer before remained one of the unparalleled highlights of her existence.

'But why?' persisted Megan, unappeased.

'Because I need . . . a little holiday . . . and because I think Daddy probably needs a little holiday from me,' stammered Isobel, wringing her hands, wishing she felt more brave, wishing she could think of some acceptable way of explaining that their father no longer loved her, that not being loved had made her embark on something so imprudent and out of character that she might have to spend the rest of her life trying to make up for it.

'That's stupid.' Megan slammed her hands on the table and ran from the room, banging the door behind her.

Sophie, worried now by her sister's outburst, stared despondently at the bits of paper sticking to her fingers. 'It's all gone wrong,' she wailed, plucking furiously, and quite ineffectually, at the hardening lumps of white glue.

'We'll start again, darling. Don't cry,' said Isobel brightly, close to tears herself. 'I've got loads more paper. We'll make another edging and stick that on instead. Mum can do the glue next time and you can tell me exactly where to put it. And when it's dry we'll paint it – pink and yellow, just like you wanted.' She pulled the sobbing child on to her lap and held her tightly, while silent tears of her own trickled into the copper curls burrowing beneath her chin.

Now it's really begun, she thought grimly, clenching her jaw to steady the tremor in her lower lip. All that remained was telling Ben. She wished she could feel defiant at the prospect instead of merely afraid. Only his not loving her had made the affair with James possible. Yet even the knowledge of this truth offered little comfort. At best Ben might feel relief that she was offering him a way out of their marriage. At worst what had appeared only as cold indifference might be transformed into the most derisory form of hate. But there was nothing left for such hate to destroy anyway, she consoled herself, reaching round Sophie for the scissors and beginning to hack at another paper strip.

Thinking of James did provide some solace, though their conversation earlier that afternoon had not been without its tensions. When she broke the news about Druscilla Carew he let out an expostulation of such outraged dismay that Isobel found herself abandoning all her own worries on the matter in order to insist on its insignificance. Everyone would know anyway soon, she reassured him, while her own stomach twisted at the thought.

'Yes, I suppose they will.'

'In fact, I've decided to tell Ben tonight . . . about going away . . . about you. I've done what you suggested in your letter. We're leaving to stay with my parents tomorrow.'

There was a fractional hesitation. 'So you really are going to tell Ben, you brave thing . . .'

'When are you going to break the news to Juliet?'

'Not sure. Soon. Maybe tonight as well . . .'

'Then we'd be doing the hardest part together . . .'

'Yes, that's true . . . no reason to hang on any longer, I suppose, especially not with nosey neighbours starting to talk . . .'

'I don't care what anyone thinks,' blurted Isobel. 'All that matters is . . . trying to do the right thing, trying to be happy . . .'

'Oh, and we will be, I promise you,' he whispered. 'The place I want us to stay in is exquisite; near the coast, between Ditton and Wetherall, only twenty miles or so from your parents' neck of the woods. "Le Relais", it's called, a couple of miles in from the main coast road. Three stars in the Michelin, a health spa, luxurious suites, total seclusion . . . just what we need.'

'Sounds lovely,' said Isobel quietly, winding the telephone flex so tightly round her fingers that their tips turned a yellowy white.

'Look, why don't we agree now to meet there on Monday evening at, say, seven o'clock? I'll make all the arrangements, they're bound not to be busy mid-week. I'll book us in for three nights, just the two of us, what do you say?' His voice bounced with enthusiasm.

'OK . . .'

'I'll only call in the meantime if there's a hitch.'

She was silent for a moment.

'Will you be able to find it? Are you with me, Isobel?'

'I am, James, I am. Monday at seven. "Le Relais". I'll be there, I promise.' Though more muted in her reaction, Isobel too was now longing to get away, not so much to be with her lover as to have time and space in which to reflect, to regroup for the unspeakable difficulties that lay ahead.

30

The old lady pointed to the 'closed' sign and shook her head. Ben tapped his watch, to indicate that there was still a full minute to go before half past five, and mouthed 'please' with as much charm as could reasonably be mustered in the circumstances.

'I shouldn't,' she tutted, opening the door. 'He'll go mad.'

'I won't keep you long – thank you so much.' Ben stepped past her, smiling with relief. He had half an hour before he was due back in school for the final rehearsal. With the first night only a day away, all he wanted was to see it through.

'Who is it?' growled a voice from a room behind the counter.

'It's a gentleman, dear, he says he won't be long.' The woman winked at Ben and began stabbing at a tray of silver trinkets with a feather duster.

'He'd better bloody not be.' A stooped old man with a shining bald pate and pebble spectacles appeared holding a mug of tea. Through the open door behind him, Ben could see a small television set and a tartan two-seater sofa. His voice had a gentle Northern ring to it, while his eyes glittered with humour behind the thick lenses of his glasses. 'What can I do you for, then?'

'It's this,' said Ben at once, pulling the pink crystal from his pocket and placing it on the counter. 'I want it made into a piece of jewellery. A friend of mine said you might be able to help.'

'Friend? What friend?'

'A Mr Caulder. He teaches—'

'Ah, Dicky, yes – know him well, of course. His lady wife helped in the shop from time to time . . . tragedy her passing on like that . . . terrible tragedy.' He puffed out his cheeks, which were pink with tiny broken veins. 'Not that we've any call for part-time staff these days. I don't care what those politicians say about this feel-good factor business – whatever it is, none of it's bloody coming our way. Is it, Kitty?'

'No, dear.'

'Interesting rock.' Pushing his glasses on to his forehead, he plugged what looked like a small telescope to his eye socket and screwed his face into creases as he studied it. 'Where did you find this, then?'

'Wales. Near a beach. It's been in my coat pocket for weeks . . . been meaning to do something imaginative with it, but I've been so busy . . .'

'Pretty.' The man sniffed. 'And what were you wanting – a brooch, was it?'

'Or . . . I thought maybe a pendant,' ventured Ben, eyeing a glass-topped case of chains in the cabinet next to him. Isobel never wore brooches. 'Could a sort of ring be put round it, with a loop to hang on a necklace?'

'It could.'

'I'd need a chain too.'

'You would.' The man put his telescope in a drawer and got out a pad of paper. 'Sure you don't want a brooch, then?'

'Absolutely.'

'As you wish.' He did a few dark scribbles on the pad with a blunt pencil. 'Like to please, don't we, Kitty? Do you want to choose a chain, then?'

'I'll have that one, please, the one with the smallest links.'

'Got a train to catch?' chuckled the man, raising one grey bushy eyebrow at his customer's evident impatience to be gone. He coiled the chosen necklace into a tidy pile beside the crystal. 'It'll cost you thirty pounds in all and I'll need a deposit. A fiver will do. Be ready by the end of next week, I should think.'

'Great. Thank you very much.' Ben turned to go.

'Don't you want an inscription?' It was the woman, Kitty, who had abandoned her cleaning and was sitting on a small upright chair beside the door, fanning her face with her duster. 'An inscription's always nice, I think.'

'Now, now, Kitty, the gentleman knows what he wants.'

'An inscription – what a good idea.' Ben returned to the counter. 'Round the side maybe, engraved in the ring . . .'

'It'll have to be short,' put in the man, scowling.

'Just "Isobel", I think.' Ben hesitated, blushing slightly, much to the delight of his audience. 'No, hang on . . . how about "Isobel, my love"? Yes, that's it. Is there room?' he added anxiously.

'I should think so. It'll add a tenner to your bill, mind.' The old man smiled. 'Write the name down, then, so I've got the spelling. Full of possibilities is Isobel, like Catherine – or Ewan, for that matter. A right bugger is Ewan, spelling-wise.'

As Ben hurried outside, the shop door jangled shut behind him. He was in a small side street right on the outskirts of Torbridge, full of small, struggling local shops and huddling terraced houses. He was going to have to cycle his very fastest in order to get back to school in time for the run-through. As he swung his bike back on to the road he caught sight of the old lady, Kitty, smiling and waving from behind the smeary pane of the shop window. Ben waved back, his heart thrilling with goodwill towards her and mankind in general.

His two hours of fitful armchair dozing the night before had been followed by a brief but refreshingly dreamless sleep. He had woken with something resembling a sense of purpose, though still accompanied by the feeling that he was clawing his way back from the edge; that every tiny movement mattered desperately in relation to how things would turn out in the end. Snatches of his conversation with Ione Brown criss-crossed lazily through his morning sleepiness, now bringing small surges of comfort as well as amazement. Understanding the past might help the present after all he mused, if tackled in the right way. As the face of the counsellor blurred into Isobel's, he reached an arm across to her side of the bed. But all it found was the warmth of where her body had been. He let his arm rest in the empty space for a few minutes, hardly breathing as he strained to hear the dim sounds of female voices emanating from the kitchen below, of taps running, of cutlery clinking against crockery. And as he listened his heart swelled with love and a new determination to put things right, without further recourse to third parties of any kind.

By the time he got downstairs his family were already halfway out the door. Megan was playing the flute in school assembly and had to be there early for a practice. As he kissed the girls goodbye, he tried desperately to catch Isobel's eye, wanting to communicate at least something of his new-found hope for them all. But she was busy with satchel straps and lunch boxes, dodging behind their daughters as if seeking to shield herself from his reach. She did not meet his gaze until they were at the front gate, and then only fleetingly – more of a blink than a look – before quickly swivelling her face to the road ahead.

All day Ben had been haunted by this farewell glance, by the sheer dismissiveness of it. It made him impatient to get home, impatient to challenge and obliterate the reason for its existence. Instead of dreading the evening's rehearsal he longed only for it to be over. In the meantime, finally doing something about the crystal had made him feel a little better, not because he was naïve enough to believe that Isobel could be wooed back with sentimental gifts, but simply because he knew that at last he was doing something positive. A step in the right direction, albeit taken invisibly and alone.

Pedalling furiously back through the winding side streets of Torbridge, taking every short cut he knew, Ben found his mind skipping to absurdly idyllic images of the little prep school in Hampshire. He had telephoned for the application forms that morning. They would be interviewing throughout the first half of the summer term and would have a decision by the middle of June, the school secretary informed him briskly, before slipping her mask to reveal that she had once had a nephew who sang with the Torbridge choir and retained fond memories of Royles cream teas. Ben had felt ridiculously buoyed by the news, as if such irrelevant connections somehow boded well on his behalf. Remembering the conversation as he rounded the final bend towards Crofton College caused him to break into exuberant song, a silly ditty from one of the girls' tapes that set the handful of boys still loitering on the pavement outside the school's large iron gates giggling into their collars.

Juliet, speeding in the opposite direction on course between retrieving Tilly from a birthday party and Eddie from the scouts, was far too preoccupied to recognise the hunched, dark-headed figure on a bike who slowed and then accelerated over the zebra crossing a few yards from the entrance to the school. Of more immediate concern to Dr Howard's wife were the fresh salmon fillets which had sat in the blast of the car heating for far longer than was good for them, not to mention the bloodied bag of steak, and the tub of hand-whipped ginger ice cream she had bought from the small expensive deli by Mayers Gate. At Tilly's vociferous insistence, they were listening to an Enid Blyton story on the cassette player, an improbable narrative about cave tunnels and treasure, whose literary merits did not stand up well to the pressures of repetition. Tilly, who knew all the words by heart, had turned the volume up and was chanting along with it, omitting nothing, not even the unconvincing barking of Timmy the dog. That Juliet succeeded in maintaining a stoical silence throughout this ordeal was due not so much to motherly tolerance as to a heightened reluctance to provoke confrontation of any kind. Another battle awaited her, for which she knew she would need every ounce of mental reserve.

The Barclaycard bill had arrived that morning, together with a polite letter pointing out that they had exceeded their credit limit for the month and requesting immediate settlement. Thanks to some generous adjustments made during a particularly heavy phase of purchasing shortly after moving house, the limit referred to was a hefty five thousand pounds. The amount by which the bill exceeded this was half as much again. The only resource containing anything like this sum of money that Juliet could conceive of was a special savings account for school fees that James had opened a few years before. Without understanding all the details, Juliet knew that it was an account with a time lock on it, that touching the funds before Eddie was thirteen was not supposed to be allowed and would almost certainly incur financial penalties of the most crippling kind.

Thinking about the showdown ahead made Juliet curiously eager as well as afraid. Preparing for it, as she had done all that day, had reminded her of the once-familiar rigours of facing an opening night, steeling oneself both for certain terror and the possibility of exultation. There would be an argument, of course, ostensibly about the money, but at heart about much more serious things. She knew it was going to take all her cunning and skill, not only as an actress, but as a woman and a wife, to steer them safely through to the other side.

James was having an affair, of that she was now certain. So certain that she no longer even bothered to look for lipstick impressions on his collars or telltale receipts in his suit pockets. It was infinitely more mundane aspects of his behaviour which had aroused her suspicions; like the alacrity with which he had taken to getting out of bed in the mornings, the smug expression on his face as he groomed his hair, the inane whistling as he skipped downstairs for breakfast. Equally remarkable was his recent predilection for relating the events of his day with quite unprecedented and unnecessary detail, as if driven by a sudden need to account for his time. And now a mysterious three-day conference had materialised, only several days away, based at some hotel in East Anglia. James's account of the agendas to be discussed had been thorough to the point of tediousness: a series of seminars and plenaries on the future of the NHS, workshops on fund-holders and trusts, lectures on and from health authorities. He had also taken the trouble to remind her – not once, but several times – that he had once attended something very similar in the past. Juliet, remembering the event to which he referred, had only just managed not to mention that James's involvement on that occasion had been for one day only and that the date had been entered into the diary several months beforehand. Tempting though it was to make him squirm with a few prescient enquiries on the matter, instinct warned her it would be unwise. With his defences up, her husband's conscience would be far harder to assail; she wanted him soft and unsuspecting, malleable in every conceivable way.

By far the hardest aspect of the situation had been containing her curiosity as to the identity of the other woman. To know such a thing would, Juliet knew, make James unforgivable. Far better to keep the enemy a blur, to beat it back before it came sufficiently into focus to represent something so personalised as to be relevant or threatening. What limited speculations she had allowed herself had quickly resulted in the conclusion that it was probably someone much younger. Prime among suspects was the busty new receptionist at the practice, whose arrival James had for some reason failed to mention, and who answered all calls with the silky innuendo of a female overpowered by a nauseating confidence in her own magnetism. But the girl was so absurdly young and pretty that Juliet simply could not imagine her falling for a fifty-year-old, even a relatively dashing, well-preserved one, with a twinkle in his eye and most of his hair still rooted to its follicles.

All the perishables sweating in the plastic bags upon which Tilly was resting her small feet were for supper that night. They would start with the salmon, bathed in a vermouth and cream sauce. The steak would follow, bloody and soft in the middle, just as he liked it, nestling between fist-sized grilled mushrooms and the pretty peaks of a parsnip purée. For dessert she would sprinkle shavings of fresh ginger on the ice cream and decorate the rims of the plates with wafer-thin lemon biscuits that melted on the tongue. As these prospects drew closer, Juliet grew calmer, almost forgetting the initial panic that had overwhelmed her when she recognised the credit company's envelope lying beneath the letter flap on the hall floor, covering the *W* of the *WELCOME* stitched into her doormat. She had stood staring at it for a good two minutes, while her polished parquet floor heaved beneath her feet and the terracotta tints of her walls danced with dizzying black spots. When at last the figure on the bill had been confronted, if not exactly digested, she had rewarded herself with a deep bath, extravagantly scented with the last drops of her best rose oil. She lay in the water for nearly an hour, topping up the hot and inhaling the perfumed steam with long slow breaths that gradually cleared her mind. Afterwards, steaming gently, her flesh mottled pink with heat, she had swept her wet hair into a turban and sat on their bedroom window seat in her dressing gown, letting her breath cloud the view of the garden below. After a few minutes she rubbed a porthole in the misted pane with her fist, and gazed out at their neat arrangement of lawn and shrubs, thinking incredulously of a time, not so very long ago, when all but a patio had seemed to sit between her and the attainment of worldly bliss. The stonework was completed now. Only a dusty circle of leftover sand remained as evidence of all the weeks of wheelbarrows and upheaval. The finished article, with its neat arched inset for a barbecue and low surrounding wall, looked so solid that it was hard to recall the scruffy flowerbeds and shrivelled hedge that had once occupied the same ground.

The view blurred and disappeared as the warmth of Juliet's breath steamed the porthole closed again. It wasn't love which lasted, she thought bitterly, shaking her hair out of the towel and crossing to her wardrobe, it was marriages, sustained by a memory of love. Though uncharacteristically bleak, the notion did nothing to discourage the slow surge of determination now mushrooming inside. If anything it encouraged it. It was a question of understanding the rules, Juliet told herself, as she tugged clothes off hangers and rummaged through drawers. Even if that meant accepting that there were no rules at all.

She got dressed in a plain blouse and shirt for the day, but laid out an altogether different costume for the evening. From the bags still buried under the bed she unearthed the pantaloon trousers, shoes, a cream tank top of knitted silk and the waistcoat with gold buttons. On top of these she placed the least comfortable but most exotic of her bras, an article which, thanks to a heavy dependency on hidden wire, succeeded in pushing her breasts up and together at the same time, presenting them for attention, like ripe fruit on a plate. Last touch of all were her G-string panties, bought during a bygone era of tight trousers, when the curve of her bottom was something she sought to show off rather than disguise. With her clothes sorted, Juliet immediately felt better. Moving now in a brisk, motivated way, she fetched her vanity case of oils and set out a small army of bottles on her dressing table. She paused to trail two immaculately painted nails over the lids and labels, nudging them into new positions as if they were pieces on a chessboard. After a few minutes she settled upon a bottle labelled 'Essence of Nutmeg Oil' and carefully unscrewed the lid. The sweet, nutty aroma smelled good enough to eat. Tiny writing on the side of the bottle confirmed her confidence in her own choice: *Analgesic, aphrodisiac, calming, comforting, elevating, euphoric, narcotic, soothing, tonic (nerve and heart). Mix 3 drops with 1 tbs of sweet almond oil before use in massage.*

'Perfect,' she murmured, closing her eyes, willing herself to believe that with such props all would yet be well in her life. Instead, she saw James as he once had been, felt again his early adoration of her, all that jealous obsession with her body, the dogged patience in the sidelines of her life, his jubilation when, at last, she totally succumbed. Such memories brought both Juliet's fears and her anger more sharply into focus. It was not the shame of a younger rival that scared her so much – though that rankled – as the threat of being left alone. She had done her time as a single woman, experienced enough of its dubious freedoms to know that it was a territory to which she never wished to return. Especially not as an older – as an uglier – woman. For, having tasted some of the power that goes hand in hand with beauty, Juliet knew too well how such influence diminished with age. She could not believe she would find such a husband again. Losing James would mean losing not only security and companionship but also her self-esteem. A disaster from which she had the self-knowledge to realise she would probably never recover.

By the time she got home with her purchases, Juliet had the structure of the evening laid out in her head like a battle plan. Having hurried the children through their homework and shooed them to bed without baths, she set about preparing the food, humming quietly to herself as she moved around the kitchen. When every ingredient had been seasoned or chopped or garnished, she decanted a bottle of claret and set the table, putting a pretty vase of freesias between two fresh red candles. She would feed his senses till they burst, overload him with pleasant sensations until the guilt, the doubt, choked in his throat. She would defeat him with kindness, smother him with spoiling, churn up so much gratitude and pleasure that he would wonder how he ever could – ever should – leave such a marvel. Then would come the money, the trickiest – but potentially the most effective – element of all. The debt had to be both forgiven and recognised for the weapon it was. She needed James to understand that if he wronged her she would bleed him dry, that he could never afford to leave her anyway, because she had him by the balls.

31

Sometimes Druscilla lost the thread of why she did things. There was an airy space inside her head, a vacuum whose emptiness could feel quite a burden, but which at other times served to make her feel uniquely disconnected and free. She had tried to explain it to a doctor once, a long time ago, during the last and worst of her breakdowns. He said having one's face used as a punch-bag left many legacies and that in time the blankness would go away, be filled, like skin closing over a wound. That he was wrong did not bother Druscilla unduly, since as the years wore on what occurred inside her head seemed of increasing inconsequence to anyone but herself. And sometimes it was quite nice not to know why one did things, not to have to bother with the tedium of understanding and logic. At least that was the explanation she gave herself for deciding to give the flower card not to Isobel, as she had promised, but to Ben Tarrant instead.

The note had emerged on Wednesday evening, crumpled but still legible, from down one side of an armchair during a bout of nocturnal spring-cleaning. It stuck to the powerful snout of her dust-buster, vibrating like a trapped leaf until she prised it free. *For my darling, no words can say what I feel.* She read the message out loud several times to the mouth of her Hoover, trying out different inflections and waggling its black head as if hopeful of a reply. Before going up to bed she Sellotaped the card to her front door, as a reminder to return it to its rightful owner in the morning.

After all the exertions of her night, however, Druscilla ended up sleeping through most of the following day. And when she did finally stir from her bed, in order to consume a large bowl of Weetabix and clotted cream, it was already dark. She had just resigned herself to a deferment of her duty when she heard the familiar squeaking of Ben Tarrant's bike brakes in the road outside. The next thing Druscilla knew she was rushing outside in her wellingtons and dressing gown, waving the note at him like a mad thing.

Seeing his neighbour approach in such a crazed fashion caused Ben a moment or two of serious concern. The woman was clearly deranged; but quite harmless, he thought wryly, returning her extravagant gesticulations with a modest wave of his own and an expression that he hoped passed for a smile.

'Out for a run, Druscilla?'

'Only to catch you.'

'Really? I am honoured.' He nosed the wheel of his bike between the gate and post guarding his front garden, his mind still preoccupied with the minor problems needing to be ironed out before curtain-up the following night.

'Isobel is seeing Dr Howard.' She tapped her nose with the note and winked.

'Yes,' drawled Ben, wrestling with his bike, 'we still see a bit of the Howards . . .'

'I mean really *seeing*.'

'Absolutely – of course they are. Now if you'll excuse me.' His left pedal had caught on the gatepost.

'Here's a note from him to her. It came with some flowers.' She thrust the card into his fingers and bolted back inside her house, her heart racing in sudden awe at her own audacity. I've done her a favour, she told herself, when some of the adrenalin had ebbed away, and a small worry surfaced as to which of the Tarrants she might have damaged the most.

Ben studied the writing on the card, chuckled and shook his head. He had just finished locking up his bike when Isobel opened the front door. For a moment the two of them looked at one other, their usually furtive stares emboldened by the dark. Isobel was in leggings, barefooted, with a long dark green shirt that reached to her knees. Her hair was a cloud of orange against the light in the hallway behind. Ben, struck afresh by the beauty of the woman he had married, found himself momentarily at a loss for words.

'Who was that?' Isobel asked, clenching her knees to hide the tremble in her legs.

'Our dear neighbour.'

'What did she want?' She clasped herself with her arms as the shivering moved up her body, dizzy with dread at the thought that Druscilla might have decided to share her sordid secret with Ben after all. It would have been too cruel, that night of all nights, when she herself was primed to tell the truth. She tried to read Ben's expression in the dark. I don't know him any more, she thought desperately, watching him pull the tarpaulin over his bike and noting that he seemed agitated, if not exactly angry.

'She was gabbling about us and the Howards. About you and James, to be more precise.' Ben paused on the doorstep. He wanted very much to say that she was beautiful. But there was so much distance between them still, it was hard to reach across it. He took one of her hands, aware that his head had emptied of all the things he had planned to say. 'You feel cold. Let's go inside.'

'Gabbling?' Isobel whispered, wondering at his calm and allowing herself to be led into the sitting room. Her fingers felt cold and limp in his warm palm.

'Too ridiculous.' He was smiling. 'Implying all sorts of things – some erotic fantasy maybe? But then you know the poor creature better than me . . . always had far more patience in that department . . .' He was rummaging in his pockets, shaking his head in despair. 'She gave me this.' He produced the small white card, no bigger than a bus ticket, and held it up.

Isobel took one step backwards and slowly lowered herself into a chair. 'What is it?' she whispered, knowing already.

'It's a message I wrote to you . . . with the flowers I sent . . . must have fallen out, I suppose . . .'

'You?' There was the briefest, sweetest moment of relief.

'You know I did,' he said gently, coming over to her and crouching at her feet. 'For the anniversary. You put them on the mantelpiece. Carnations . . . Isobel . . .' He tried to pick up her hand but she tugged it away. 'There's so much that we . . . that I . . .'

'You sent the carnations,' she repeated stupidly.

He was looking at the carpet. 'I know I've been hopeless . . .

I don't blame you for not saying anything, for wanting to . . . punish me. I'm aware that I've not exactly made life easy for you recently . . .' He tossed the card on to her lap and got to his feet, determined not to be deterred by the expression on her face. 'Don't think I don't care, Isobel, because I do, very deeply.'

'Care about what?' The handwriting on the card, Ben's handwriting, blurred and shifted before her eyes.

'About everything.' He began pacing the room, clenching and unclenching his fists. 'I've been doing a bit of thinking recently . . . about us . . . about why things have become so . . . hard. Mostly it's my fault, I know . . . I allow myself to get too involved at the school, take on every lost cause that's going . . . and this term has been particularly hard . . . there was one incident especially that almost . . .' He broke off, for a moment overcome by the realisation of quite how long it was since he had shared anything with her at all. Even before the recent bad patch, everyday life had swept them along in its current, creating a semblance of progress and cohesion where in fact there had been nothing of the kind. 'Christ, Isobel, I don't know where to start,' he burst out, running both hands through his dark hair in a gesture of frustration and excitement, utterly overwhelmed by contradicting sensations of empowerment and ineptitude.

Isobel, watching him, felt only the cold brush of despair tiptoe up her back. He had sent her flowers. Flowers for their baby. She hadn't even realised. He was still talking, words pouring out of him.

'I've been feeling so desperate, Isobel, for so long now . . . I didn't want – didn't dare – to tell you . . . I suppose I was afraid what you would think of me if I owned up to some of the things . . .' He was standing with his back to her, one hand holding on to the edge of the mantelpiece above the fireplace. 'Nothing can change overnight, I know that, but at least now I'm beginning to feel that I understand what's been going on, where it all started.' He paused. 'It goes way back, you see. You shut me out.' He swung round to face her, not aggressively, but with the light of inspiration in his eyes. 'When you had the miscarriage . . .'

'The miscarriage?' Shock had slurred her senses.

He shook his head. 'I know it sounds crazy, but hear me

out, please. You see, you were the one who did all the crying, everybody wanted to know how you felt, whether you were coping. Nobody worried about me.' He let out a short laugh. 'Do you know, I actually think I was jealous of you. All those tears you could cry, leaving me without any power to help, without any bloody role at all. Part of me hated you for it. Isn't that terrible? I hated you for suffering so well . . . and then the girls came along, so quickly, taking all your attention, taking you away . . .'

'And does part of you hate me now?' She spoke in a monotone, keeping her eyes fixed on a scuff mark above the skirting board, willing him to answer that he did, in order to take some of the pain of what awaited them away.

'Christ, no. Isobel, no.' He was too absorbed in the effort of unleashing his own emotions to observe the unnatural stillness of her pose, to see that his words were making no impact on her expression at all. 'No, I mean, I got over that – whatever it was. We both got over it, but maybe a little too . . . separately. And it did change things.' He was pacing the room now, lecturing more than talking. 'It pushed us apart. Or at least, it pushed me away from you, back to the old self who had learnt to believe that life was a war that had to be waged alone . . .' He let out a brief self-deprecating laugh. 'Except I'd rather lost the knack . . .' He stopped walking and sighed deeply, shaking his head and looking at the carpet. 'There are other things I should have told you,' he went on gently, 'not because I want sympathy but because, as my wife, you have a right to know.'

'What things?' she whispered, watching her hands twist in her lap and thinking of Aunt Violet.

He swallowed hard. 'There was a baby – my half-sister – who died in the crash that killed my mother.'

Isobel bit her lip, staring only at her twisting hands. Much as such confessions would have meant to her in the past, they could have no significance now. She hooked her fingers together, as if clinging on to the thought.

'It became a big family secret,' Ben continued, interpreting her silence as shock. 'Father's orders. Perhaps keeping it was my way of making up for hating him so . . .' He shrugged. 'I should have told you. I should have told you a lot of things. I didn't because I didn't think it mattered. I thought by keeping silent I could leave it all behind . . .'

'I know all about that . . . about the accident.' She spoke as coldly as she could.

'You know?' He was incredulous.

'Aunt Violet told me.'

'And you never said anything?'

'You never said anything, Ben.' Her voice edged up a note or two, for the first time belying the outward calm of her face. 'You never said anything about anything, until now . . . now, when it's . . . too late.'

'Too late?' Her tone puzzled him. He had imagined something more along the lines of relief, of gratitude even. Wasn't this what all women wanted, what Ione Brown wanted, being true to one's emotions, excavating them from all the dark corners inside? 'Isobel, I'm trying to . . . explain myself to you . . . trying to say I'm sorry. I know I've been difficult to live with, but at last I think I'm beginning to understand why. I'm beginning to understand myself.'

'So you've sorted out the puzzle of your life, have you?' she sneered. 'Well, bully for you, Ben Tarrant. Congratulations. X plus Y at last equals Z.' She was almost shouting. 'But what about me? Where do I fit into the equation? Is my life just supposed to slot into place too now? Is it? And if so, how?' She folded her arms and glared at him, her eyes blazing with anger and tears.

'Isobel, my love,' he whispered, taking a step closer, 'I'm so sorry, I . . .'

'Shut up, shut up,' she screamed, putting her hands to her ears. 'Don't touch me, don't come near, it's all too late, it's all over, it's all over . . . don't be kind, don't you dare be kind to me now, not after all this time . . . please.' She was sobbing, rubbing her eyes with her fists and shaking her head. He tried to touch her but she pushed him away.

'Don't do this, Isobel, please, not now . . . now that we're talking at last . . . sorting ourselves out . . .'

'No, Ben, you're wrong. It's got nothing to do with us, it's all you. You, you, you.' She pushed the wet ends of her fringe from her eyes and took a deep breath. She felt beyond crying suddenly, beyond feeling anything at all. 'And while you've been sorting yourself out, I' – she paused for an extra breath of air – 'I have been having an affair. With James Howard. I was going to tell you tonight anyway.' She got up from the chair and straightened her skirt, tugging it down to her knees. 'I think I might have a drink. Would you like one?' But she didn't move and neither did he.

There was a long moment of silence.

'You've what? . . . You mean Druscilla . . . ?'

'She saw the two of us together.'

'How long?'

'A few weeks.'

'Do you love him?'

'He loves me.'

'Do you love him?'

'He's been very kind, he . . . yes, yes, I love him.' She spat the words across the room. 'He has made me feel . . . oh, never mind. What does it matter? We need to separate, Ben, we have needed to for a while now. I've made arrangements to go to my parents tomorrow . . .'

'How could you?' The question was little more than a gasp. 'How the bloody hell could you . . . with James, of all people?'

'Who would you have preferred, Ben?'

He wasn't listening to her. 'I mean, Christ, Juliet is . . . was your friend . . . how could you?' There was disgust in his voice now. She could hear it blocking his throat.

'I'm not proud . . .'

'Oh good, well at least that's something.' He nodded his head in mock approval, his dark eyes now glittering with all the antipathy she had expected. 'The lady is not proud.'

Isobel reached for her jacket, slung across the back of a nearby chair. 'I do not expect your forgiveness, Ben. I shall never expect that. But a little understanding maybe . . .'

'Understanding? Of your desire to screw a friend of ours? Now that's really rich. Life may not have been the proverbial bed of roses round here, but . . .'

'No, it certainly hasn't.' She pulled on her jacket and tugged open the door. 'All you're feeling now, Ben, is what you've been suppressing for months, for years . . . I'm just helping you admit it. Regard it as a favour.' And with that she strode out of the house, slamming the door.

Druscilla took one timid peek through her curtains before retreating, with some dismay, into the deepest of her armchairs. Imagining more responsibility for such neighbourly goings-on than was in fact the case, she clutched a cat to her chest for comfort, nuzzling its fur with her face. Though the creature purred its appreciation, these gestures of affection were followed by a volley of such virulent sneezing that it leapt from her lap and took refuge under the piano.

32

Isobel walked fast, her hands clenched in the pockets of her jacket, her eyes fixed on the paving cracks beneath her feet. In the quiet of the night, with the darkness all around her, she felt as if she were taking steps merely to keep her balance, like a runner on the moving pad of an exercise machine. Above her, as always, the cathedral spire towered over the skyline of the buildings, its illuminated glory urging attention and reverence. But Isobel did not even glance upwards. She was too locked in her own mind to possess the energy for bestowing the visual world with any meaning at all.

Though she tried to think of James, clinging to the idea of him, images of Ben kept breaking through; disconnected snapshots, bright frozen stills from times long past, from Spain, London, Torbridge. They had begun so well. A charmed love. Only when this carousel hit the episode of her miscarriage did the whir in Isobel's mind slow and clear. Was Ben right? Had things really not been right since then? Had it really been so long? She frowned from the effort not of remembering but of focusing. Usually, looking back to those dreadful months, she thought only of the child she had lost, of her own emptiness. Now she forced herself to recall exactly what Ben had been like, how they had been with each other. She saw him holding the tiny swaddled bundle, heard again the brush of the chaplain's skirts as he left the room, the aching silence afterwards. Then she remembered Ben's dry, dazed eyes, his passive hopelessness, and experienced in the same instant a rush of hatred so strong that the bitter taste of it flooded her mouth. The vehemence of the emotion, never before admitted, shocked her. It was a hatred not just for his helplessness, Isobel realised, but for his very presence. A violent selfish questioning of his right to be there at all. As if her own grieving had indeed been deeper, truer, more worthy in every way. The emotion ebbed away, but the shock remained, fused with a retrospective guilt: for having felt such things of her own husband; for not having loved or wanted him at such a time. Schooled in the belief that an alliance like theirs was an indomitable thing, that any personal crisis could only make them stronger and more devoted, such awfulness had been impossible to own up to, she realised, even to herself. The only faint consolation was knowing that Ben had experienced something similar; that they were jointly guilty both of such feelings and the failure to admit to them.

Making sense of the past offered no remedies for the present, she reflected bitterly, seeing someone approach, and cutting down a side street towards the town hall and Torbridge's main square. The figure had looked familiar. A teacher from the girls' school maybe. Isobel feared recognition above all things; she dreaded the need to talk, to give some explanation for her dishevelled presence out alone so late at night. A light rain had started, a soft drizzle that glittered in hazy clouds beneath the orange glow of the streetlights. When she got to the old black railings skirting St Cuthbert's, Isobel paused, pretending to search for something in her pocket, unnerved by a new set of footsteps half a beat behind hers. But it was only an old man out with a bow-legged hound, both waddling in comic and unconscious symmetry, their noses to the ground. Isobel was about to head for the benched shelter offered by the pleated stone roof of the poultry cross when she noticed that the gate into the churchyard was slightly ajar, as was the door of the church itself. The rain was sharper now, falling not as a mist but in needles of seemingly vicious intent. Seeking shelter rather than religious inspiration, Isobel pushed the gate open and hurried down the short path towards the door.

Archie was on his hands and knees in the vestry swearing profusely, and quite inventively, when he heard the faint but unmistakable groan of St Cuthbert's door hinge being pushed a few inches against its will. Suppressing un-Christian fears as to the likelihood of whoever had entered the church carrying a sawn-off shotgun and a history of acrimony towards ginger-headed priests in jeans and dog-collars, Archie paused only for a moment before continuing with his search. He had lost his crucifix, a small plain silver one which Bridget had given him years before, saved for with money from her Saturday job in the shoe shop. In the light of recent decisions regarding his personal life, mislaying such a thing had seemed so hugely symbolic that Archie had been momentarily tempted not to undergo any search at all. But in the end sentiment had triumphed, boosted by distaste for the sight of the chain dangling empty on his bony white plateau of a chest. The depressing chaos of his bedsit had multiplied dramatically in consequence. Even though two hours of intense investigative activity had thrown up nothing but a handful of loose change and a mysterious, unmissed key.

Searching St Cuthbert's was a last resort as well as a welcome diversion from the still-unsolved problem of how to endure the night. The sleeping pills acquired from Dr Howard worked so well that all Archie's initial relief had quickly been superseded by a terror of dependency. A new routine had established itself in consequence: a routine that involved a prolonged and fatally strained effort to fall asleep, followed by a miserable and uneasy surrender to the promise of oblivion contained in the innocuous white tablets. The result was an entirely new brand of grogginess as company for his working day, a sensation not entirely dissimilar to the challenge of swimming through glue. His eye twitch could now only be held in check by the most exaggerated of frowns. The strain of looking as if he were pondering some universal dilemma whenever anyone was within visual range of his cheekbones was really starting to get him down. He was beginning to feel as grotesquely conspicuous as one of the cathedral gargoyles he had once so admired. Though nobody said anything outright, Archie now flinched at every snigger from the motley gaggle that passed for St Cuthbert's choir, and at every one of Reverend Tully's repertoire of unreadable stares.

Archie was just toying with the unattractive notion of running his hand along the two-inch gap of cobwebbed grime under St Cuthbert's vast wardrobe of clerical vestments when he heard the muted but instantly recognisable sound of someone crying.

Not the sobs of a distraught, machete-wielding male, nor even of an alcohol-sodden mendicant, but – unless his hearing deceived him – of a distressed female.

Filled in equal measure with shyness and charitable zeal, Archie sprang to his feet and tiptoed back into the main body of the church. Here was someone to help, someone to remind him that there were sorrows other than his own. When, from behind the safety of a wide, fluted pillar, Archie established that the someone in question was none other than Isobel Tarrant, a whole host of new emotions flooded his mind. Among them a wicked and most unpriestly excitement that caused him to press his palms together and squeeze his eyes in silent gratitude to the Lord. She was in trouble and God had steered her his way. It was unbelievable. Like a bloody miracle.

Some element of these thrills faded as he made his approach. She looked so forlorn, her hair sticking in wet strands to her cheeks, the shoulders of her thin jacket visibly soaked. And when she looked up, impelled to do so by his polite annunciatory cough, Archie could not help but notice that her face registered nothing but dismay at the sight of him. Her eyes, usually such a crystal green, were red-rimmed and bloodshot. Her lips too looked peculiarly red against the ashen pallor of her skin. The sense of having intruded was so strong that instead of offering help he found himself apologising.

'Sorry . . . I couldn't help . . . I heard something. I was in the vestry.' He wrung his hands and clenched his face tight against the pulse of his tic.

Isobel got out a shrivelled tissue and dabbed her nose, shaking her head.

'There's a box of Kleenex in the vestry,' he ventured, thinking at the same time that any self-respecting hero would have been in possession of a large starched white handkerchief. 'Shall I fetch it?'

She shook her head again and began tearing at the edges of her tissue.

'I say, would you just like to be left alone? I don't have to lock up yet. You can stay for as long as you want – for hours if you like. Won't bother me at all. Loads to do, you see' – he gestured vaguely over his shoulder – 'so you just do as you please.' He turned to go, but stopped. 'Though I know that sometimes people think they want to be left alone, but they don't really, not deep down. I'm like that – pretend I'm fine when I'm not, because . . . well, I suppose because it's kind of embarrassing sometimes to admit to not being fine . . . it's like it's your fault for making a mess of things . . . not that I mean to imply—'

'I'm leaving my husband.' She shoved the tissue into her pocket and shook her hair back in a gesture all the more poignant for its failure to convey defiance.

'Oh dear, oh dear.' An absurd, despicable seed of hope burst inside.

'For all the wrong – but right – reasons.'

'Sounds complicated.' Archie hazarded a small smile, which met only blankness. Now that she had stopped crying she appeared to have gone into a sort of daze.

'It is rather,' she murmured. 'But then love is complicated, isn't it?'

Archie, thinking of Bridget, and his feelings for the woman before him, nodded slowly. Emboldened by the progress of their conversation, he then sat down, not next to her, but one pew away, facing back in her direction. 'It certainly is.' A silence followed during which he racked his hopelessly uncooperative brain for a sentence that might sound wise or endearing. But all he could think of was the outrageous turn of his own emotions, the hope that if he helped her, if he could make her grateful to him in any small way, she might start to feel something in return. 'And there are so many different kinds, aren't there?'

'Kinds?' Isobel stared at him vacantly. She was beginning to feel cold and very tired.

'Kinds of love,' he stammered, his confidence faltering. 'There are different kinds of love . . . for different people.'

'Oh yes . . . how very true.' She stood up stiffly. 'I think I'd better go.'

'Are you sure? I mean, don't you want to talk some more?' He stood up too, careful not to look at her too hard, partly out of shyness and partly to keep the unattractively twitching side of his face out of her line of vision.

'There's nothing to say.' She shrugged her shoulders. 'I have to leave Ben, that's all.'

'Don't you love him, then?' blurted Archie. He did not want her to go. He felt as if they were poised on the very edge of intimacy, that this was his one brilliant, God-given chance to get close to her. Really close. He couldn't bear to feel it slipping away.

She laughed softly. 'Oh, I love him all right. But I've made it so he can't love me . . . I've committed myself to someone else . . . like I said, it's complicated . . . to let another person down too would just make things even worse, don't you think?'

Archie didn't know what to think. He felt a terrible urge to cry. She was walking towards the door, her hair spilling beautifully over the edge of her collar. He wanted to lunge for it, bury his face in it, tell her what he felt. She stopped by the font and for a moment he thought she was going to dip her fingers and cross herself. Instead she bent down and picked something up off the floor. 'Look, a little crucifix . . . someone must have dropped it. Here.' She held it out for him. 'I expect it's being sorely missed.'

He took it from her without a word.

'Heavens, I owe you some money, don't I? That sponsored swim you were doing . . .'

'Walk. It was a sponsored walk.'

'I completely forgot. I'm so sorry . . .' She patted her pockets.

'Don't be . . . for goodness sake, it doesn't matter. It was ages ago.' Something in his tone made her let the subject go.

'I'll be off, then . . . thank you so much, for . . . talking.'

He shrugged and smiled, not trusting himself to speak. As she disappeared through the door, he remained motionless, his fist clenched around Bridget's crucifix, welcoming the tiny stabs of pain as its edges dug into the flesh of his palm. He opened his mouth for an echoing howl of self-pity, but closed it again abruptly. For inside, deep down below the sadness, he felt the feeble glow of a warmth that had been absent for a long time, the dim small light of God's presence, crouching in the darkness of his heart, waiting only for the breath of his faith to fan it back to life. He dropped the little cross in amongst the change in his pocket and trudged back to the vestry to retrieve the keys and begin locking up.

33

Crofton College's *Julius Caesar* was a triumph. The old formula of adrenalin and terror worked its habitual magic on the cast, sharpening the boys' senses and giving an edge to their performances which none of their rehearsals had ever achieved. The pupils and members of the staff attending on the Friday night hammered their applause with such enthusiasm that the actors filed back on stage for two extra curtain calls. On Saturday, when the school hall's handsome oak doors were thrown open to the general public, the atmosphere on stage was nothing short of electric.

Only the director of the show remained unmoved. Watching from the wings, armed with a prompt-sheet and catch-phrases of encouragement, Ben operated throughout both evenings with robotic detachment. The success, so longed for and worried over, felt utterly hollow. Recalling how much it had once seemed to matter filled him with a mixture of incredulity and shame. All that mattered was Isobel, and she was gone. His sense of loss was even worse than the knowledge of her betrayal. Memories of other losses, triggered by the gentle probing of Ione Brown, now slouched out of the shadows in which he had endeavoured to confine them. A pattern was emerging. A pattern that made losing a wife seem painfully inevitable.

Saturday's performance progressed even more smoothly than the first night, animated by a spirit all its own. After a while Ben folded his prompt-sheet away and sat on an upturned crate with arms folded, watching the proceedings from behind the gauze of his own inner despair. Snatches of phrases drifted off-stage and into his consciousness, sounding unfamiliar and fraught with new meaning.

I have not from your eyes that gentleness and show of love as I was wont to have . . .

You are my true and honourable wife, as dear to me as are the ruddy drops that visit my sad heart . . .

. . . if you have tears, prepare to shed them now . . .

'Sir? Do you have a safety pin? The hem of this dress is right down again – I'm scared I'll trip . . .'

It was little Jamie Oates, a rosy-cheeked fourth-former whose initial vehement reluctance to take the part of Caesar's wife, Calpurnia, had been magnificently overcome, to the admiration even of his peers.

'Of course, Jamie, of course,' Ben whispered, patting the boy's head. 'Let's find Miss Harris, shall we? She's got a whole box of the damn things.'

Thanks to a series of such minor demands upon his time, Ben managed to keep a tighter hold on his concentration during the second half. Through a chink in the curtains he squinted at the blurred sea of faces in the audience, unable to stop looking for a glint of Isobel's red hair, even though he knew she was not there. She had fled to Suffolk the previous morning, taking a small holdall for herself and two big suitcases for the girls. Megan and Sophie had tumbled into the back of the car still dazed with sleep, moaning about the cold and the prospect of a long journey. He had kissed them lightly, feigning insouciance, since it was the only protection he could offer, not trusting himself to hug them for fear of breaking down. While Sophie appeared to have swallowed the story of going for a holiday with their grandparents, Megan's black eyes seemed to acknowledge that the break foreshadowed separation of a more terminal kind.

The only red hair that Ben was able to identify was the distinctly unalluring carrot mop of the young clergyman who had been so generous about distributing publicity posters a few weeks before. He spotted him towards the very end of the performance, sitting in the middle of the front row, frowning in grim-faced concentration and absently chewing his nails while Brutus movingly begged for his servant's assistance in running on his own sword. It was only during the final blast of applause, when Ben was leading the last bow on stage, that his eye was caught by two other familiar figures down the far end of the front row, both clapping manically, their hands raised high above their heads, their mouths fixed in grins of appreciation. The Howards. Their knees and elbows touching. He saw James mouth the word 'bravo' before bending his head near Juliet's cheek to catch something she was saying. For a moment the vision of such marital unity was reassuring. Maybe – for some perversely female and whimsical reason – Isobel had been lying? Maybe there was no affair at all? The hope, desperate and pitiable, swelled and died. Ben took a step backwards and dropped his head by way of a bow, before turning with outstretched arms and a mask of a smile to congratulate the cast, holding hands in lines behind him. Then Miss Harris swung the heavy curtains across the stage, muffling the handclaps, which faltered, before finally dying away.

Though Juliet was annoyed with James for wanting to leave so promptly, she did her best not to show it. Determined to nurture their newly brokered peace – still so fragile and tentative – she allowed him to lead her through the mêlée in the hall with as brief a backward glance at the stage as she had once granted her own career. Being in an audience always got her fired up, even when it was a mediocre school play with ill-fitting costumes and scenery done in poster paints. Listening to Calpurnia had been hardest of all. She had had to force herself not to mouth the words, which she had delivered herself many times, croaking most of them through a severe chest infection that lasted for the entire six weeks of a provincial tour. The memory of the cough helped quell any inclination towards nostalgia. As did the diversion of trying and failing to trace Isobel Tarrant in the crowd.

While the crush was bearing them towards the doors, she nudged James in the small of his back with her handbag.

'It really is very odd, don't you think?'

'What, my love?' With so many people about them he could barely turn his head. 'What is odd?'

'That Isobel is nowhere in sight. Whatever can have happened to her? Do you think she's ill? Perhaps we should call in on our way to the restaurant?'

'If she is ill, she won't want us barging in, will she?' James worked his elbows to show that the impatience in his tone related purely to the number of people pressing round him. 'And it would make us late for our table. I could do with a bloody drink after this lot,' he added through clenched teeth, as someone's stiletto ground into the soft leather of his shoes.

'Anything you say,' Juliet murmured, pressing herself against James with unnecessary pressure and using the moment to run her fingers down the back of his right thigh. Believing once more that she held all her husband's dear, predictable emotions in the palm of her hand, she badly wanted to keep it that way. Though things looked set fair, one could never be sure. Indeed, being sure had almost been the death of them, she reminded herself, hooking one finger through a loop in the waistband of James's trousers and giving it an affectionate tug.

A few feet behind them, Archie too had been unable to prevent himself from looking for Isobel in the press towards the exit. He kept catching the eye of Flora Dobbs instead, resplendent in pink and pearls, and fluttering her programme over surrounding heads at any face she recognised. It was heartening to see that most, like him, seemed content either to ignore her or to keep their responses to a muted flutter in return. She had been more predatory than ever since the completion of the sponsored walk, with quite unnatural effusions over the paltry sum of money he had raised and earnest invitations to tea. All Archie's initial guilt about resisting such attentions was diminishing by the day; he was beginning to realise that even priests had a right to say no to people, to preserve some private space of their own.

Having enjoyed the play far more than he had anticipated, Archie was toying with the idea of hanging back to offer Ben Tarrant his congratulations. For once, his hesitation stemmed not so much from shyness as the dubious itch of curiosity that the prospect of such a meeting aroused. He couldn't help wanting to know whether Isobel had really left after all. While the rival man in him longed to see how Ben wore his suffering, whether he cared at all.

As two boys in uniform started to stack chairs and retrieve abandoned programmes, Archie found himself offering to help. By the time they had cleared the hall, quite a party had developed on stage. Music was spitting from a ghetto-blaster, while members of the cast, their faces still smeared with make-up and their costumes in varying states of dishevellment, were swigging from plastic beakers and plunging their hands into bags of food. Archie was on the point of slipping away when Ben Tarrant's voice boomed out across the hall.

'Gatecrashing our cast party now, are you, Reverend?'

Several spotlights were still on the stage and Archie had to raise his hand to his eyes to get any sort of view of Ben at all. 'No, I didn't mean . . . I was just helping clear away . . .' He had to shout above the pulsing rhythms of the music. A couple of boys behind Ben had linked arms and were springing round in circles. 'Thanks anyway.'

'But you've earned it, Reverend . . . very helpful you've been . . . practically a member of the cast. Come on up here, for goodness sake. My wife gatecrashed a cast party to meet me, you know, many moons ago.'

Deliberately ignoring the reference to Isobel, Archie approached slowly, wary not only of being an outsider, but also of the raucous cheerfulness in Ben's voice. It erased all his curiosity in an instant.

'I didn't mean to . . .'

'Shut up, man, and come up here.' He slapped Archie's back as he arrived on stage. His dark eyes blazed with an unnatural light. His smile was tight and fierce. 'There's only orange juice and cider, I'm afraid – not bad in combination actually – and heaps of crisps. Mostly pickled onion flavour, it would seem. Help yourself. And ignore this lot. They'll probably get drunk and then throw up into each other's laps. All part of the ritual. Yours truly has the delightful task of making sure they don't murder each other . . . until the parents return to pick up the pieces. Miss Harris has – with suspicious convenience – developed one of her migraines . . .' Ben appeared to sway slightly as he peered at his watch. 'Bugger . . . one whole hour to go . . . but nice to have another grown-up around.' He handed Archie a cup and steered him by the elbow to a couple of upright chairs in the wings. 'Let's keep an eye on things from here, shall we? Oh, and drink up, we've got litres of the stuff to get through. Think of it this way: the more we drink the less they will.' Ben let out a dry laugh and tipped the contents of his beaker down his throat.

'It was very good,' said Archie quietly, taking a tentative sip of his own drink. 'The play, I mean, not this.'

Ben laughed again, too loudly. 'Glad you thought so. Great stuff, wasn't it? A few young Kenneth Branaghs in our midst after all, eh? The head was relieved, I know that.' He tapped the side of his nose conspiratorially. 'Got to keep the head happy in my business.'

Ben appeared to be even drunker than Archie had first thought. He was talking so fast and furiously that he began to be afraid what the poor man might say. To be so contrastingly sober felt advantageous in a cruel, horribly voyeuristic kind of way. But at the same time there was no question of leaving, not only because of the powerful force of Ben himself, pinning him to the chair with conversation, but because of the largely unattended carousing boys, many of them clearly in a far worse state than their master.

'I say, a pair over there are smoking. Should we . . . ?'

'Oh, let the devils smoke . . . they all do anyway . . .'

While on a mission to find an unopened bottle of cider, Archie mustered the courage to suggest that cigarettes should be enjoyed outside, in the safety of the school grounds. To his astonishment the culprits obeyed at once, reappearing a few minutes later looking windswept and smug. Pleased to see that Ben had closed his eyes, Archie settled back in his chair with a handful of crisps.

'What's your view on adultery, Reverend?'

Caught with a mouthful, Archie was grateful for having a legitimate reason to hesitate. 'I think it's a pity . . .' he managed at last, his throat clogged with salty crumbs.

'Could you do it? Could you screw another man's wife?'

Archie blushed crimson, feeling suddenly quite transparent, as if Ben had guessed the truth of his feelings for Isobel, and was venting some of his own bitterness by deliberately making him squirm. 'I . . . I'm afraid we all could. Probably.'

'And what does your God say about that, eh?'

'He forgives us.'

'Oh, bloody marvellous.' Ben began a slow clap, looking round for an audience that wasn't there, since most of the boys had disappeared to take advantage of Archie's impromptu off-site smoking regulations. 'And what about us poor mortals? Are we just supposed to take the forgiveness route too?' Ben sat up and glared at him, his face twisted with anger and pain. 'My wife's left me, you see, Reverend, so I'm doing a spot of research into the matter. Turns out she's been fucking – sorry, having an affair – with another man, something of a family friend as it turns out . . .'

'I really don't think . . .' Archie stood up.

'Oh, come on, surely you can do better than this, Vicar. If God doesn't come up with some decent answers then therapists are going to steal all the business. The couch is the modern alternative to the confessional, you know. Feels good too, for' – he drew in his breath – 'oh, at least four, maybe five minutes afterwards. But understanding things can't stop them *happening*, can it? Especially for those of us who've reached the understanding stage rather late in life.' Ben picked up his empty cup and crushed it between his hands. He had said as much to Ione Brown the evening before, when her quiet acceptance of his decision to pull out of any further sessions had provoked him into being unforgivably rude. Instead of confessing to the very real fear of making himself even more vulnerable to her than he had already, he had launched into an emotional diatribe against professionals who peeled back the onion skin of other people's lives and constructed nothing in their place. She said that such construction was for him to do and people like her could only help to point the way. At which point he had disgraced himself and all his arguments by slamming the phone down and sobbing into a cup of cold tea.

'Don't you think you've had enough . . . ?' suggested Archie gently, now seriously worried by the expression on Ben's face.

'Enough? Oh yes, I've had enough, all right.' Ben lunged for the bottle of cider and made an ugly show of swigging from it, spilling a few drops on his shirt front in the process. 'And I suppose Isobel had too, one way or another . . .'

'She must have had her reasons, I suppose,' Archie muttered, flicking away a crisp with the tip of his shoe. He wondered where she had gone, but did not dare ask. Since their encounter in the church his feelings for Isobel had reached a new pitch of confusion to do with trying to adore something that was so plainly imperfect. His fantasies did not work so well with a woman who cheated on her husband.

Ben let out a short laugh. 'I'm sure she did. I'm sure she did. Reasons to do with me, no doubt . . . I never stopped loving her, you see, I just forgot I needed – forgot how – to show it . . .'

'Perhaps if she realised that—'

'What, and then I just forgive her, do I?' Ben clicked his fingers. 'Just like that.'

'Perhaps she has to forgive herself first,' suggested Archie quietly, responding to an uncharacteristically intuitive flutter of inspiration that blew across his mind from nowhere, as sweet and subtle as the whispering in his heart after Isobel had left the church. With it came a vivid recollection of her crumpled misery. She had not seemed like a woman in love, with herself or anyone else. It struck Archie in the same moment how curiously coincidental it was to have stumbled into intimate conversations with both Tarrants within such a short space of time. Curious to the point of being designed. Ordained. The ember of faith flickered again inside, helping to ease the pain of what he was relinquishing. Fantasy was a figment of the imagination after all, he reminded himself, fuelled by the dubious powers of enzymes and hormones, and the unfathomable mysteries of human psychology. He did not know Isobel Tarrant enough to love her. He never had. The best – the most Christian – tribute to his affections would be to help her in any way he could. 'I think forgiving oneself can be the hardest thing of all. We can't move on until we've done it . . .'

'Maybe not,' drawled Ben, staring hard at his companion, wondering through the fug of his unhappiness how young freckle-faced curates acquired such wisdom. 'That's quite a twitch you've got there,' he remarked suddenly, which stopped Archie in mid-yawn, bringing a blaze of colour to his cheeks.

He quickly slapped both hands to his face and attempted a casual laugh. 'Oh, it's nothing really . . . gets a little worse when I'm tired . . .'

'Eye-strain,' muttered Ben, rolling down the sleeves of his shirt and beginning, ineffectually, to try to rake some order into his hair.

'I beg your pardon?'

'Eyestrain,' he repeated, more loudly. 'See an optician.' He stood up, now diverting his attentions to the untucked ends of his shirt. 'Look here, sorry if I've been, you know, aggressive . . .' He rocked back on his heels and caught hold of the edge of his chair to steady himself. Behind him, his students had collapsed into stupefied and silent cameos of disarray. A few had even fallen asleep. The tape of music had stopped and been left unreplaced.

'You haven't been aggressive . . .'

'Bloody liar,' growled Ben, glaring in a way that managed to convey affection.

Archie grinned back at him. 'Would you like me to stay until the parents—?'

'No, no. Run along, please.' Ben picked up an empty cardboard box and embarked on a slow, shuffling tour of the debris littering the stage. When Archie started to help he found himself seized quite roughly by the elbow. 'It's OK, Reverend, I can manage now. You're a good man, a very good man, but I want you to go home. I know I'm pissed, but I can manage – I'd prefer to manage alone. You've been a big help but now I want you to bugger off,' he whispered, but so kindly that Archie knew he was being thanked.

He strolled the mile or so through town back to his digs feeling more at peace with himself than he had for months. Instead of bolting inside, he paused before putting the key in the lock, and gazed up at the vivid, surreal triangle of the cathedral spire towering above him, noticing for the first time the halo of fuzzy light that clung to its outline, like a shadow illuminated in the dark. The surge of joy that flooded through him almost knocked him off his feet.

Though sleep remained its usual elusive self, there was no suffocating panic that night. For once the darkness seemed full of comfort and companionship. After a while an easy stream-of-consciousness-style prayer began of its own accord, focusing not on himself, but on the Tarrants. Archie had forgotten the exquisitely uplifting pleasure of genuinely wanting someone else's happiness more than his own. Riding on the crest of such sensations came the relief of knowing that he had moved on at last, that he was no longer locked in a time warp of self-obsession and disappointment, that he was ready to get on with the job of helping rather than needing help. With a little easy detective work he would find Isobel – wherever she was – and tell her exactly how things stood. They were both evidently wretched without each other. He would offer his services as a go-between, someone neutral who could make both positions clear. All Archie's own longings paled into insignificance beside the Christian nobility of what he intended to do. He would reunite the Tarrants even if it killed him. He could feel God willing him on inside.

34

Slipping into the usually irritating straitjacket of her parents' domestic routine had proved strangely comforting. It removed the pressure of trivial decision-making and provided them all with a structure to get through the day. The girls responded particularly well to the extra attention and discipline, which made Isobel realise how badly she had allowed things to slip at home. Mothers weren't designed to have emotional crises, she reflected ruefully, while gazing at but not reading the Sunday newspapers during a rare spell alone; there simply wasn't the time. Her parents had taken the children to church, leaving her with meticulous instructions concerning potato-basting and the preparation of vegetables. The carrots had to be sliced thinly instead of chopped into her usual careless chunks, and the French beans, once topped and tailed, were to be cut into equal halves. Instead of offering her customary resistance to the inflexibility of such absurd family codes of culinary practice, Isobel agreed with a meekness that highlighted her greediness for a spell of abdicating control.

The relief of leaving Torbridge – of leaving Ben – was immense. Though his pinched face still haunted her, she was grateful to be removed from the incessant, hopeless need to try to do something about it. For there was nothing to be done. She had done him a terrible wrong. Not just by throwing herself at James, but by misreading the entire situation so badly from the start. That she had failed to acknowledge the flowers he sent on the anniversary of the miscarriage – to have assumed they were from another man – was so awful that Isobel could still hardly bring herself to think about it.

But behind such regrets resided a deep anger. The memory of Ben's neglect of her, the months of coldness, however justified she now perceived some of the causes to be, still stung. He had been selfish, of that she had no doubt, brooding over his own troubles without any thought as to how it felt for her, being left alone on the other side of his silence. That this silence somehow related to problems brewing from as far back as the outcome of that first disastrous pregnancy was something with which she was still struggling to come to terms. Having assumed all along that she was the one labouring to absorb her grief, it was something of a shock to discover that Ben was as deeply – but so differently – wounded himself. She realised now that all his clumsy impatience with her misery, his apparent eagerness to get on with their life, had blinded her to everything else. She even wondered whether the arrival of Megan, such a distracting joy at the time, hadn't come too soon; whether having a second baby so quickly had helped to hide the fact that they weren't yet fully – or jointly – over the loss of their first.

Isobel sliced the carrots viciously, wishing she could stop her thoughts wheeling backwards when all she wanted was to focus clearly on what lay ahead. She had James to think of now. Their tryst, only a day away, loomed large, filling her with a confusion of hope and dread. Though she still grasped at the possibility of their sharing a future together, the reality of it seemed more and more improbable. Only the wildest, most ardent love could propel such a drastic rearrangement of their families. And while she feared that James's emotions reached such a pitch, she was growing increasingly aware that her own fell far short of it. Realising the extent of her misjudgments as regards Ben had made everything much harder, much more complicated. There was no justification any more, no self-righteous zeal to fuel her betrayal. Yet James loved her. He wanted to make a life with her. Could she let him down as well?

She was staring out of the kitchen window, transfixed by the resilience of a bright regiment of tulips under the incessant siege of a stinging wind, when the church party returned.

'How's the gravy?' enquired her mother at once, expertly looping her apron over the robust perm of her hair and seizing the oven gloves from off her daughter's shoulder. 'Did we make a roux?'

'No, we did not. Sorry, we forgot. We're quite hopeless,' apologised Isobel, rolling her eyes comically for the girls' sake and then doing her best to listen to their two simultaneous but conflicting accounts of the morning's religious adventures. All younger members of the congregation had been presented with crosses made from palm leaves. Competitive efforts to describe this high point, however, resulted in the precious articles themselves being used as martial aids across the kitchen table.

'Now, now, you two, that's enough,' shouted Isobel, losing her temper at last, and shooing them out of the kitchen.

'Stir the gravy, there's a dear,' said her mother, handing her a wooden spoon. 'George is on sherry. Do you want one?'

'No thanks.' Isobel concentrated hard on her allotted task, inwardly marvelling at her parents' studious inability to refer directly to the reason for her visit. It was almost as if by ignoring it they hoped to trivialise the matter sufficiently for it to disappear altogether. All her tentative attempts to explain the severity of the situation had so far been greeted with tuts and arm-waves of dismissal, together with mutterings about it being nobody's business but their own. On the couple of occasions she had steered the girls to the telephone to ring Ben, her only punishment for not grabbing the receiver herself was two raised eyebrows of disapproval and knowing parental glances batted across the room.

Watching her mother scamper between sink and oven now, Isobel was uncertain whether such stoical reticence was something for which she should experience gratitude or vexation. That her parents both cared very deeply about what was happening was not in question. All their pink-cheeked Sunday morning vigour sprang, she knew, not from the fresh East Anglian air, nor from the stirring words of their local priest, but from a state of suppressed emotion. How would such feelings be vented, she wondered nervously, when it became clear that their daughter was already involved in a relationship with another man? The thought made her stir the gravy so vigorously that several thick chocolate-coloured drops splashed on to her mother's immaculate white hob. For all their funny ways and implied criticisms, her parents had, she knew, grown quite fond of Ben. More significantly they both shared a puritanical like-it-or-lump-it approach to matrimony, treating all deviations from such a creed – by friends and public figures alike – with impatient and withering contempt.

'So you're off tomorrow, are you?' Her mother stabbed the shoulder of pork with a two-pronged fork and levered it on to a serving dish.

'Yup.' Isobel found a small lump of flour and chased it around the edge of the saucepan with her wooden spoon.

'I see. And back on Wednesday. And we're not to know where.' She set the serving dish on the table and put a carving knife beside it.

'If that's all right. I'm sorry, it's just . . .'

'Fine. We'll say no more about it, then.' Betty Hitchings took off her apron and folded the oven gloves into a neat rectangle before disappearing to summon her husband and granddaughters to the table.

35

Ben spent most of his Sunday sleeping off an excruciating headache and trying to resist phoning Isobel. It was up to her to take the initiative, he told himself, thinking at the same time how much he would hate to be ensnared in conversation with either of her parents. So far the girls had phoned him twice, on each occasion giving hurtfully cheerful summaries of how they were spending their time and with no suggestion that they should hand the receiver over to their mother. She had obviously briefed them well beforehand, Ben decided grimly as he tussled with the double duvet, sticking arms and legs in wild and unnatural poses in a vain attempt to find a position conducive to sleep.

Eventually, hunger lured him downstairs, where he finished off the last of the bread and cereals on which he had been subsisting since Isobel's departure. Though the fridge was quite empty, he had not yet been able to find either the time or the inclination to shop. Having plied his system with instant coffee, he forced himself to tackle the correspondence which had been accumulating on the hall table, an unpromising pile of brown envelopes whose sole redeeming feature was the application form for the headmaster job in Hampshire. For a few brief moments Ben allowed himself to be seized by the conviction that the post offered the way out of all his dilemmas, a way forward on his own. He kissed the form and waved it over his head in an attempt at celebration that quickly fell flat. Not so much because of the realisation that there would be scores of other excellent candidates, but because it dawned on him that he was still banking on Isobel coming too. The emptiness of the house curled round him like the breath of an icy wind. She was gone, but he was the one in exile. Forgiveness was all very well, he thought miserably – recalling snatches of what the kindly priest had said – but not always relevant. Isobel wasn't available to be forgiven. She had run away, to plan a future that did not include him. The thought of James Howard – a thought which Ben realised he had subconsciously been doing his best not to confront head-on all day – hit him like a punch to the stomach. Convinced he was going to retch, he hurled himself dramatically in the direction of the sink, where he stared at the soggy remains of some cornflakes clogging the plug-hole and waited. But nothing happened. The feeling ebbed away, taking with it the nausea, and leaving an expected residue of puzzlement. The Howards had looked conspicuously united. Was the hypocrisy of the man so developed that he could behave like that in public with his wife when he was planning to leave her? The thought created a quite absurd combination of hope on his own behalf and apprehension on Isobel's. Loosening his grip on the edges of the sink, Ben returned to his seat at the kitchen table, telling himself that his wife deserved everything she got and it was no longer his business to worry about her. But his emotions continued to disobey him, spurred on by two slanting and smudged rows of old-fashioned typing informing him that his pendant was ready for collection sooner than expected and asking that the balance of thirty-five pounds be paid as soon as convenience allowed.

Seated only a few yards away, at her own kitchen table, Druscilla was studying a list of properties to rent by the sea. Brighton seemed to hold the most possibilities in her price range, though many of them were flats with shared gardens. The property agent, after raving about the dearth of rentals in roads like Fox's Crescent, hadn't seemed nearly so enthusiastic or friendly in person. At the memory of the man's visit the day before, Druscilla shuddered and gripped the edges of the paper more tightly. She hadn't liked the way his beady eyes had appraised her home, sniffing at things she held dear, pushing round her private space as if he had a born right to be the judge of it; all the while committing indecipherable mutterings into his little tape recorder. The cats hadn't liked it either, especially when he spent so long in their room, nudging cushions and mattresses out of the way in an attempt to assess the state of the walls.

Though Druscilla had told the animals – and the property agent – that a change was as good as a rest, that she had always wanted a spell by the sea, that most likely they would all return after six months and carry on just as before, the truth was very different. Nothing would ever be as before. Life had turned sour, as it always seemed to, in the end. And so suddenly too. The first phone call had come on Friday morning, when she was rushing round looking for empty plastic bags to take to the shops. There wasn't any noise exactly, nor even any breathing; just the sense of someone there. A few moments after she replaced the receiver it rang again. When she answered, more gingerly this time, she was greeted only by the same thick silence. The experience was so unnerving that she fled from the house without any bags at all. And without her handbag too, which proved rather more of an inconvenience, though thankfully her keys had been in her pocket. The comfortable vacuum of her existence had been broken, and Druscilla felt all the terror of it. Just when she was feeling safe the phone would ring again; and though she told herself to ignore it, somehow she was unable to. Suspicions as to the origin of the calls had initially focused on the Coombes – her neighbours to her left – who had never been polite enough to hide their dislike of her and whose stair-pounding made the precious pictures on her walls vibrate. But then a less easily contemplated possibility had planted itself in her mind, arising from the deep dark waters of her past and the knowledge that nothing – that nobody – could be run away from for ever.

The sudden inspiration of dialling 1471 was rewarded only by the disheartening message that the caller's number had been withheld. She thought of contacting the police, but rejected it in the same instant. Bitter previous experience had taught Druscilla to expect no favours from such people. Nor did the idea of changing her number offer much hope. He – for she was sure it was a he – knew where she lived, she felt certain. In thinking through her limited options for escape, Druscilla was alerted for the first time to the alarming degree of her own alienation. Only Isobel Tarrant had ever found time for a smile and a word, and now she had gone, taking her beautiful children with her. The conviction that her involvement had triggered this departure did little to lighten Druscilla's state of mind. Whatever had possessed her to give the note to Ben she could not now imagine. At the sight of him over the last few days, all stormy-looking and striding, she scuttled back from the window, fearful of whatever daggers of blame his expression might hold. Though she did not really think him the type for hate-calls, she had nonetheless whispered his name a couple of times into the silence on the telephone, just in case. With such preoccupations it took all Druscilla's determination to digest small print about gas central heating and ventilated lavatories and to scrutinise the tiny, inadequate photographs of places that might provide a new refuge. Many of the nicer-sounding ones said pets were not welcome, which made her so cross that she put a big black cross in the margin together with three exclamation marks of disapproval. She had just completed a series of these when the shrill ring of her phone set her nerves fizzing with apprehension. Taking deep breaths, she tiptoed into the hall, picked the receiver up very slowly between two fingers and slipped it under the hairsprayed curtain of her hair and on to her ear.

'Hello. Anybody there?' said a cheerful male voice.

Druscilla was so relieved that for a moment she could not speak. She nodded vigorously instead, putting her hand to her throat as she fought to catch her breath.

'Hello?' said the voice again, less certain this time.

'Who is it?' enquired Druscilla, looping the flex round her fingers.

'Reverend Heighton-Jones . . . I popped in a couple of weeks ago . . . you kindly treated me to some biscuits. I spilt a few coffee grains on your kitchen floor,' he added meekly, by way of a further prompt into the silence on the other end of the line.

Laughter, the hysteria of relief, burst into Archie's right ear. He held the receiver at arm's length for a moment, shaking his head in despair. The woman was a complete crackpot.

'Oh, Reverend,' she cooed, 'I can't tell you what a nice surprise this is . . .'

'Sorry to disturb your Sunday afternoon, Miss Carew—'

'Call me Druscilla, please.'

'Ah yes, Druscilla, exactly . . . the thing is . . . I was just wondering if you would happen to know of anyone who could put me in touch with one of your neighbours.' He coughed nervously. 'I need to get in touch with Isobel Tarrant and did not want to bother her husband . . .'

'She's left him,' interrupted Druscilla flatly.

'Yes, I am aware of that . . . but do you know where she—'

'What do you want her for, Reverend?' she asked slyly, some of her old curiosity blossoming at the scent of intrigue.

Since it felt impossible to explain the ambitious philanthropic reasons for wanting to contact Isobel to anybody, let alone her inquisitive neighbour, Archie made the sign of the cross on his chest and told an outright lie. 'I have a couple of books that belong to her, that's all. I'd like to know where to send them.'

For a moment Druscilla toyed with the deliciously meddling idea of confiding the name of Isobel's lover to the vicar. She drew in her breath and managed to swallow the temptation away, aided considerably by a recollection of recent events. 'I can't say for sure, but I believe she has gone to stay with her parents in Suffolk. I don't know the address, but maybe directory enquiries could help . . .'

'What is their surname?'

'Now I'm afraid you've got me there . . . I've no idea.'

'Oh dear.'

He sounded genuinely forlorn. 'The simplest thing would be to ask Mr Tarrant himself . . . or . . .' Druscilla hesitated. 'I suppose you could always try her friend, Juliet Howard, who lives in Ilcombe.' She spoke very slowly and carefully, inwardly congratulating herself on her powers of discretion. She would not betray Isobel again. 'Her husband's Christian name is James. I expect they'll be in the book.'

'I might just try that, then. Thank you so much for your time . . .'

'Vicar?'

'Yes?' Archie spoke with blatant and quite un-vicarly impatience, oblivious of the lifeline his phone call presented.

'Well, goodbye, then,' she muttered, deterred by his tone of voice.

'Goodbye, Miss Car—, I mean, Druscilla. And thanks awfully.'

When the other calls started again a little later, Druscilla took the phone off the hook before making herself a mug of hot milk and taking her black pen and list of properties upstairs. The three cats curled amongst the chaos of bedclothes blinked lazily at her as she came in, their claws sliding out like knives as they stretched.

'It's no good looking like that, my lovelies,' she scolded, pulling a wide-cabled jumper on over her clothes and negotiating a space between them on the bed. 'There'll be none of Mummy's milk for anyone that sulks. We'll find a lovely place to hide, you'll see,' she crooned, stroking each animal as it lapped from her mug, before taking a greedy slurp herself and feeling comforted as the warm liquid snaked its way down inside.

36

On seeing no evidence of James's car, Isobel decided to while away the time by going for a walk. She was almost one hour early and did not relish the idea of checking in on her own. With the clocks having been put back over the weekend, it was not yet dark. A suggestion of summer seemed to lie in the cool brightness of the evening and in the way the sun warmed the colours of the grass and trees. Le Relais, which she had vaguely heard of but never visited, looked more like a grand family home than a five-star hotel. In the centre of the semicircular gravelled drive in which she had parked was a small round fountain comprising a single cherub blowing water from a long horn. The entrance to the hotel itself was a narrow porch, tumbling with the green ropes of ripening wisteria. On either side of it an immaculate jigsaw of grey stone formed the walls, interrupted only by dark-timbered windows, each one adorned with its own flower box of exploding colour.

On walking back out of the gates, Isobel passed the rustic arrow of a signpost she had almost missed from the road, with the words *Le Relais* carved across its middle. Understated to the point of illegibility, the sign of a truly affluent business, she thought wryly, crossing the road towards a five-bar gate and the start of a promising pathway along the edge of a field. She quickly discovered that the evening was colder than it looked, especially when the sun dropped behind the rim of a distant wood and brisk wind appeared from nowhere, edging its way up under the hem of her coat and in through the cracks in her clothes. She bunched her hair about her ears for warmth and curled her fingers tight inside her pockets. She would walk to the end of the next field, she decided, before turning back. But as she pressed on, her determination not to return until James had arrived began to be superseded by a greater concern that he might appear in her absence, see her car and worry where she had gone. The end of the second field was further than it looked and the ground was growing unpleasantly muddy. After a few yards of stepping from tussock to tussock in the interests of preserving the appearance of her shoes, Isobel at last acknowledged the pointlessness of her journey and turned back. It was already a quarter to seven. The sun was gone for good now and had been replaced by a menacing steel wall of cloud. A few minutes later a drizzle started, compelling her into a fast walk that gradually became a run, as a dim panic welled up inside. Earlier indulgent sentiments about not trampling upon the fragmentary carpets of bluebells were all quite forgotten as she raced back along the last stretch of path, her hands and face still icy but her body growing hot from the exertion of running. Poor James, she thought, her heart thumping. The decision she had prepared for him was bad enough; not even being there when he arrived would make it look as if she didn't care at all.

A pretty string of yellow lights lit up the hotel sign and a nearby tree. There were others along the gutter line of the main building, like a trim of gaudy icing round a cake. Eagerly, Isobel sprinted the last few yards across the road and up the drive, pausing only to brush her loose hair behind her ears and to wipe her face with the back of her hand. She almost laughed at the thought of what a sight she must look, wondering with some hysteria whether James would mind, whether it might make the blow she was about to strike any easier to bear. He was the kind of man, as she had discovered, who appreciated perfume and hair that behaved, the kind of man who liked high clean heels and painted nails. Only very recently had she realised that the small extent to which she had obliged such tastes had been nothing but an act, nothing to do with how she wanted to live her life at all. Never my kind of man, she reflected bitterly, marvelling not for the first time at how unhappiness had so utterly warped her perspective on the world.

It took several minutes for Isobel to establish that James's car was still not resident in the drive. A smudged chalk board saying *Extra Parking To The Rear*, propped casually amongst some bushes, offered fresh hopes that were quickly dashed upon the discovery that the space referred to contained nothing but an old wooden handcart and a tractor wheel sprouting pansies. Faced with little alternative, Isobel scurried back round to the main entrance and went inside. A cosy sitting room of a reception area greeted her, complete with a roaring fire and cartoon hunting prints on the walls. The instant she entered, a well-groomed young man in a dark suit appeared from nowhere, crooning banalities of welcome and commentaries upon the ugly turn in the weather. 'I presume madam would like to check in?' he said, keeping his eyes on her as he reached out to press the bell on the unattended reception counter to their left.

Isobel nodded uncertainly, wondering suddenly what name James might have used on her behalf.

'Our receptionist will be with you in just a moment. Will you be wanting a table at dinner this evening?'

'I – I'm not sure. I should think so.'

'Excellent.' The young man slipped a gold pen out of his breast pocket and swung his clipboard into action. 'Will that be a table for one, madam?'

'Er . . . two. A table for two.'

'At what time?'

'Eight thirty,' she hazarded, seeing from the handsome grandfather clock beside the door that it was already almost a quarter to eight.

'We shall look forward to it,' he announced, carefully returning the pen to its lodging place and clicking his heels. 'And here is Elspeth to take care of your room reservation.' Looking perceptibly relieved, he sped away down the corridor, ducking under a low beam and a sign saying *Restaurant & Bar*.

Elspeth, who wore a badge advertising her name in gold letters, offered Isobel a stiff grin of welcome and reached under the counter for a large leather ledger.

'Could I have your name, please?'

'Howard,' replied Isobel with considerably more confidence than she felt, stepping forward to tinker with a small stand of pamphlets detailing sites of local interest.

'Ah yes, here we are. Two nights, double—' The girl stopped

mid-sentence and frowned. 'That's odd, it appears to have been cancelled.' She smiled apologetically. 'I've only just come on duty, I'm afraid, so I'll have to find out what's going on. I'm sure we've still got a room if you've changed your mind.'

'Cancelled?' repeated Isobel, staring at her stupidly, a colourful fact sheet about a nearby stately home dangling from her hand.

'Oh, hang on a minute . . . my colleague has left me a note here explaining all about it. Don't worry,' she added, seeing the expression on Isobel's face, 'I'm sure it will all be fine.' Her voice had a pretty Welsh lilt to it that was somehow soothing. Isobel relaxed a little and smiled back.

'What does it say?' She put down the pamphlet and rested her elbows on the counter.

The girl's pale young face creased into a frown. 'It says there's a letter for you . . . oh yes, here we are.' She produced a long white envelope and handed it across. 'Came by courier this afternoon apparently, a little after the reservation was cancelled. But like I said, we've lots of room at this time of year . . .'

But Isobel was already turning away, staring dumbly at the slanting loops spelling out her name. Slowly she made her way to the armchair in the furthest corner of the room and sat down. For a moment she was tempted to drop the letter into the flames unread. It was obvious what it would say. It was obvious he was not coming. Any relief she might have felt was overcome by horror at her own obtuseness; not only for having failed to guess this outcome herself, but actually having worried – of all things – about being late. On closer inspection the roaring fire turned out to be a gas-fired simulation of the real thing, complete with faked coal embers and crumbling logs. Quite unsuitable for burning letters or anything else.

'Excuse me? Would it be possible to turn the heat down a bit?'

'Of course, madam.' Elspeth scampered out from behind the counter and fiddled with an artfully concealed panel of knobs in the skirting board. 'If you need anything further, madam, don't hesitate to ring,' she added with a look of pity that made Isobel quail inside. 'A drink perhaps . . . or a cup of tea?'

'I'll let you know . . . thank you.'

When the girl had gone, Isobel ran her finger under the envelope flap and pulled out the single folded piece of paper inside.

Seeing the body of printed script she felt the first prickings of real disappointment. The handwritten opening and closing only added insult to injury, like the two-word scrawl on Christmas cards from friends one never saw.

Monday, 8 April
My Dear Isobel,
What will you think of me? If I wrote sorry a million times I know it would still not be enough. Believe me when I say I wish with all my heart that it could have worked. You are such a special person. I can only say how privileged I feel to have been allowed so close to you.

She groaned quietly to herself. It was going to be even worse than she had imagined.

It would be hard to explain all the detail of what has occurred during the course of the last few days. Suffice it to say that Juliet and I seem to have reached a new understanding with each other. Please find space in your heart to wish us well.

I thought about phoning you at your parents', but was worried I might stir up yet more trouble, since I know you had not explained the situation in full to them. Biking over this letter seemed the only safe way to get in touch. Since the hotel is only a relatively short drive from your parents' place, I know you will not be stuck for somewhere to go once you have received it.

We had a good time, Isobel. Can we remember it that way?

I'm afraid I have to end by requesting one humble favour. Juliet, while being cognisant of the fact that our marriage has come through something of a 'bad patch', is not to my knowledge aware of our affair. She has her suspicions, I know, but none of them focus on you. Would it be too much to ask you to assist me in keeping our secret from her? It would make things very hard for me otherwise.

I can only wish sincerest good luck to you and Ben. I am sorry that you are both so much further down the road towards separation. But perhaps it was meant to be and will turn out for the best. Who knows, maybe we can all become good friends again one day!

With all fondest wishes,
James

Isobel left the hotel without bothering to inform Elspeth or any of her colleagues. Instead of turning back in the direction of her parents' village, she headed east towards the coast. The rain seemed to be coming horizontally at the car, and with such force that her windscreen wipers barely had time to clear a view before it was shattered by a fresh onslaught. She drove slowly, partly because of the weather and partly out of shocked preoccupation with what had happened. Abhorrence at the cowardice of James's chosen method of dealing with the situation was exceeded only by disgust at herself. At the thought of all her recent agonising over how to protect his feelings she almost laughed out loud. James Howard had the welfare of his own emotions well in hand, she thought grimly, and required no help from her or anyone else in looking out for them.

Telling Juliet was not something she would ever have seriously contemplated anyway, for the simple reason that it would have caused additional and unnecessary pain. Although a more vulnerable creature might have needed warning about the finer features of her husband's personality, all Isobel's instincts and knowledge on the subject of Juliet Howard reassured her that she would be more than equal to the task of coping with James, on this and any such similar occasions in the future.

Since she had already resolved not to return to Torbridge until the following week – and then only to pick up a few more belongings – the chances of running into either of the Howards were mercifully thin. Testing though it would be for all concerned, Isobel had decided to prey on her parents' hospitality for a while longer. It was the only way of creating the time and space in which to work out how she and Ben would lead their separate lives. Tempting though it was, common sense warned her that too much had been destroyed for her to grant herself the indulgence of thinking in any other terms.

37

A lively and unexpected chat with a young curate from St Cuthbert's with an unpronounceable surname had livened up Juliet's Sunday evening considerably, though it did bother her later that night and during the course of the following day that she had failed to quiz him more directly about his reasons for needing to contact Isobel. News of the Tarrants' break-up, received via James that afternoon, had left Juliet feeling somewhat shaken, not to say offended. For Isobel not to have given even so much as a hint as to how bad the situation was cut very deeply. As her one-time closest friend, Juliet felt she had every right to feel thoroughly cheated.

Such disappointments had been partially made up for, however, by James's surprise announcement on Monday morning that he would not be attending the conference after all, but would take a couple of days off work instead. He spent an hour or two pottering in his study, before salivating over the simple tuna salad she prepared for lunch and then surprising her for a second time by declaring his intention to collect the children from school and take them to a Disney extravaganza at the cinema. Suppressing motherly knee-jerk reactions about such indulgences being more appropriate for birthdays or weekends at the very least, Juliet had pronounced herself delighted and settled down to enjoy an indolent afternoon.

Since she never quite bridged the distance between sofa and ironing board and then managed to fall asleep in front of *Oprah*, it turned out to be even more indolent than she intended. Worried that she would not even have supper ready by the time James and the children returned, she scurried round her pretty pine kitchen, hurling chicken legs, vegetables and stock cubes into a casserole dish with unseemly haste. As she did so, Juliet found her thoughts flitting back to the milestone of a meal she had prepared with such contrasting care the week before. It had been so much easier than she had expected, she reflected, with a happy sigh, pouring in a generous splash of red wine before fitting the casserole lid and placing it in the oven. Almost as if James had been looking for a way out. She paused, knives and forks in hand, as details of the evening came back to her, feeling again the excited terror with which she had played her part.

The candles on the table had surprised him, as had the lingering kiss with which she greeted his arrival at the door. Aware that he was appraising this new turn of events, taking in the stunningly provocative look of her clothes, the delicious smells seeping out from under saucepan lids, she had said nothing at first, but simply taken him by the hand and led him into the kitchen.

When he tried to speak she put a hand over his mouth, whispering, 'Not now, just enjoy.' He sipped the whisky she gave him, eyeing her with curiosity over the rim of his glass, watching as she moved around the room, stirring and tasting and adjusting all the elements of their meal. Aware of his eyes, aware of his interested bewilderment, Juliet savoured every moment. As the sense of expectation mounted, so did her confidence in her own desirability. It was a long time since she had tried to seduce her husband.

When she saw the whisky was almost gone, she turned and faced him, leaning forward on the back of a chair so that her breasts pushed upwards through the flimsy material of her shirt and the longest, loosest curls of her hair fell forward over her shoulders.

'The children are asleep, the meal is ready when we want it . . .'

He protested then, shaking his head and smiling. 'I don't think . . .'

'I'm going to remind you why you married me,' she said quietly, taking him by the tie and leading him up the stairs, 'before you've had too much good wine and food to appreciate such things.' He had giggled like a guilty schoolboy, offering up protestations, but weakly and through smiles, so that she knew that the first hurdle had been overcome. Before making love she massaged him with the nutmeg oil she had prepared, kneading and teasing his flesh with slow suggestive movements, relishing in spite of herself the feelings of power flowing through her palms. Through a great effort of will, which good sense warned her she would have to learn to exercise many more times in the future, Juliet managed during the course of this exercise to keep all images of possible rivals firmly out of her mind. If she wanted him enough, she had to forgive him, she reminded herself, abandoning the oil and tipping her head forward so that the curly tips of her hair floated across his back.

When at last they arrived back in the kitchen, in dressing gowns and exchanging the flushed happy glances more commonly associated with young lovers, she had lit the candles and set about serving up the first course of her tremendous meal.

'Am I missing something here?' James asked after a while, laughing softly as she poured a teaspoon of wine into his glass for tasting. 'Is my birthday early this year?'

'No, it's more important than that.' For the first time nerves threatened to have an adverse effect on her performance.

'More important, eh?' He raised one eyebrow and smacked his lips appreciatively at the claret. 'I say, that's good.'

'We are celebrating the first day of the rest of our marriage,' she declared, aiming for a tone that she hoped sounded both solemn and fond. 'I know I've been losing you and I want you back.'

'Losing me?' James, who had gone along with the evening so far with a combination of tolerance and pleased surprise, experienced his first frisson of real worry. It dawned on him that his wife might have a hidden agenda of some kind, that a little more than the easy reassurance of sex was required of him.

Her round blue eyes, glittering under the clever enhancement of eyeshadows and coloured pencils, never blinked. 'Yes, losing you. And . . .' She paused for full effect. '. . . you have been losing me.' Juliet paused again, thinking that a lover of her own would have been easier to confess to than the piece of paper folded under the lee of her side plate. 'I have been very unhappy, James. And when I am unhappy I do foolish things . . . like spend money.' She put down her knife and fork and slowly pulled the bill out from its hiding place. Her nails, richly red and round-tipped, looked striking beside the whiteness of the paper.

'What's that?' he whispered, now scowling with worry.

'This?' She dangled it between thumb and forefinger over her plate. 'This is the evidence of my unhappiness, James. I want you to be understanding about it. I want you to recognise the part you played in bringing it about.'

'What on earth . . . ?' Before she could stop him he had reached across the table and snatched the bill from her. For the first few moments he just gasped, his jaw agape in a caricature of horrified dismay.

'A woman scorned,' she said quietly, threateningly. 'And if you leave me ever again – in any sense of the word – I will make you pay. I promise you, James, together or apart, I will make you pay. I swear it.' Having delivered her ultimatum, Juliet allowed her voice to quiver more endearingly during the course of the next sentence. 'Because I love you, you old fool. And I will fight to the death rather than surrender you to anyone else. Because' – her voice was higher now, cracking with emotion – 'because we are good together, we know how to make each other happy, because I wouldn't be with anyone else for the world. And I'm sorry – desperately, desperately sorry – about the money. I was just so miserable and alone and trying to cheer myself up and get at you all at the same time . . .'

James, struggling with the shock not only of a demand for several thousand pounds, but also of the implicit revelation that she knew of his affair with Isobel, took an unseemly gulp of claret and shook his head from side to side. 'It's just so much. What did you . . . ?'

'It was clothes,' Juliet muttered through a hiccough of a sob. 'Most of them are still in bags with the receipts . . . I've asked if they'll take them back and they said maybe. They don't usually give cash refunds,' she added meekly, beginning to clear a space for dessert, 'but said they might be able to make a bit of an exception with some of the more costly items.'

'Well, that's something, I suppose.'

She shot him an anxious glance, unsure whether he was expressing genuine relief or merely being sarcastic. But James was the picture of distress, shaking his head as he clasped and unclasped his hands.

'What I'm saying, I think, is that I'll be good if you will,' Juliet continued quietly, setting out the swirling finale of ginger ice cream decorated with biscuits and then going round behind him to place her hands on his shoulders. 'I don't know who she was and I don't want to know. As far as I'm concerned it's over. And I'll try to get some of the money back, I promise,' she blurted, 'and if I can't, I'll earn it. Even before I qualify I can start to charge a little for a massage, begin to build up a clientèle . . . Shelley wants us to go into business together, run our own beauty therapy shop . . .'

'Steady on there . . .' he interjected, sounding decidedly unsteady himself. 'One thing at a time, eh?'

'Do we forgive each other, then?' she asked in a small voice, sliding her fingertips down into the front of his dressing gown and resting her chin on his shoulder.

'Oh, Juliet, I—'

'Just say yes and we need never talk about it again.'

'Yes,' he growled, taking her hands and pressing them between his own. 'Silly sparrow, of course I love you.'

'Always?'

'Always,' he agreed, telling himself in the same instant that the business with Isobel had probably run the most stimulating part of its course anyway, and wondering how many other husbands would be let off so lightly for sexual misdemeanours. It was only money after all, and maybe not even too much if the shop did the decent thing. A small price to pay for a marriage that he now realised he had never really wanted to jeopardise in the first place.

Juliet smiled to herself as she recalled the way they had both tucked into their ice-cream desserts afterwards, marvelling at the wonderful simplicity of knowing what one wanted and recognising the most effective way of bringing it about. And they had felt so close ever since, not in a fake forced way, but really deep down inside, where the bedrock of their commitment lay. The only pain was the vigilance, she reflected with a sigh, as the crunch of rubber on gravel alerted her to the fact that the cinema party had returned. She tweaked back the dining-room curtain and watched James get out of the car and clap his hands with impatience at the children. She would always be watching him now, she realised with a start, not just with her eyes but with her instincts, listening for the inflection that sounded wrong, for the first pulse of unnatural affection that would warn her that it was all happening again. It was not a happy thought and she made up for it in the vehemence of her greeting as he stepped through the door, gripping his neck so tightly that he let out a small, surprised cry of pain.

38

Ben stood at the end of the bed staring down at the motionless figure of his aunt. Her frail frame caused barely a ripple amongst the bed covers. On her bedside table was folded a small white handkerchief with a lacy trim and a full glass of water. Slowly he let his eyes roam around the rest of the room, taking in the modest array of belongings and mementos on the shelves and dressing table. Like a selected museum of relics. Even the brush-and-comb set, arranged at perfect equidistance from the hand mirror, looked like articles on display rather than existing for any practical use. Seeing their familiar mother-of-pearl backs and the single tooth missing from the comb, fourth from the end, Ben felt the first tremor of real emotion. Aunt Violet had had tremendous hair; long and fair and thick as a horse's tail. She had brushed it one hundred times a night, occasionally before his sleepy, mesmerised eyes, beating it down in strong swift movements and then whipping it up and round her clever fingers into a sort of knot that managed to stay in place until the morning.

'Can she hear us?'

'We think so.' The nurse smoothed an imaginary crease from the counterpane. 'Unless she's asleep, of course. Sometimes it's hard to tell. But she does speak from time to time. Cup of tea?'

'No thank—' began Ben automatically before realising that a cup of tea was in fact exactly what he wanted. 'That would be great. Milk, no sugar.'

When they were alone Ben approached the bedside cautiously. Watching his aunt drawing small, barely audible breaths through the crack between her thin grey lips, he felt all the pointlessness of even beginning to try to make up for all his ingratitude, for his inability to act upon the extraordinary surges of passionate admiration that seemed to characterise his affection for her. She had found him hard to love too, he knew; the role of surrogate mother, forced upon her by the selfishness of an absent but adored brother, never having suited her very well.

He felt angry at her too, for choosing such an inconvenient time to start her dying, for adding to his wretchedness about Isobel. For making him feel so damned guilty.

A small groaning noise was coming from the back of her throat. Repelled, and a little scared, Ben bent over and picked up three of the limp, lumpy fingers lying near him and held them lightly in his. 'I'm sorry,' he muttered.

The nurse bustled back in carrying a cup of tea and a small plate of biscuits. 'Thought you looked like you could do with something,' she said with a bright smile, 'it being most folks' suppertime. Stay as long as you like. There's a phone booth downstairs when you want to call a cab for your return journey – down the corridor to your left, past the sitting room. If we had the space I'd offer to make you up a bed for the night, but I'm afraid we're chock-a-block at the moment. There's always an armchair if you fancy a doze. I'll be downstairs if you want me, or you can find Nurse Dudley who's on duty down the corridor – third on the left past the lift.' She paused to cock her head fondly in the direction of the patient, now silent once more beneath her grey shroud of a counterpane. 'A dear, really, beneath all that huff and puff. Has she no other relatives?'

Ben swallowed. 'Just me.'

After the nurse had gone he couldn't bring himself to hold the fingers again. The least he could do, he felt, was not be a fraud, not make a big show of something he could not quite feel. Instead, he crossed to make a closer study of the bookshelves, sipping his tea and wolfing biscuits with a relish that felt quite inappropriate. It was nine o'clock on Monday evening and, as the nurse had correctly guessed, Ben hadn't consumed anything by way of a meal since lunch. Though he had managed two bags of shopping on the way home from school, he had made little headway in unpacking them. The call from the home telling him of Aunt Violet's stroke had interrupted a catnap in front of the early evening news, a guilty, fitful doze which had served as a diversion not only from the mayhem of the kitchen, but also from the increasingly burning need to speak to Isobel. He was missing her more every day. And the girls. It seemed incredible that only five days had passed since they had left. It felt more like a lifetime. The Easter holidays, now only one day away, loomed large, shimmering with difficult and unresolved dilemmas.

While waiting for a taxi to whisk him to his aunt's beside, temptation had vied with self-pity, as Ben tussled with the decision as to whether or not to dial the number in Suffolk. A dying aunt was a fair pretext. But then, it was his aunt and not Isobel's. He knew only too well how she had always resented visiting the home; and with the easy vista offered by hindsight, Ben could well understand why. Another responsibility taken on and shirked, he thought regretfully, picking up the receiver and slamming it down again, as all his longing hardened into bitterness towards himself.

Amongst Aunt Violet's books were several that looked familiar, including a large leather-bound atlas with a torn spine. Putting down his cup, Ben reached up and carefully slid it from the shelf.

To My Darling Vi,
You see, the world is not so large after all,
Your devoted brother, Albert. Christmas 1956

Seeing his father's extravagant handwriting, sweeping across the flyleaf with all the brash confidence that had made him as resented as he was successful, caused his son an unexpected shiver of pain. He closed the book abruptly, suppressing and despising the sense of quite illogical expectancy which the sight of Aunt Violet's possessions had triggered in him. There were no keys to understanding life, except within one's own head. If the last few months had taught him anything it was that. The image of Ione Brown flickered in his mind, bringing with it the usual confusion of anxiety and gratitude. Talking to her had opened a lid that would not now be closed. The Pandora's box of his past. Self-knowledge till the cows came home, he thought grimly, slotting the atlas back into place. And none of it had so far done anything to make him – or anyone else – any happier. Being repressed and dysfunctional had been far easier, he reflected with a wry smile, as he turned away from the bookshelf and reached absently into his jacket pocket. His fingers closed around the brown envelope he had collected from the jeweller's that afternoon.

'Bloody thing,' he muttered, tearing open the envelope and pouring the chain into the palm of his hand. Closing his fingers round it, he quickly crossed the room, lifted the lid of a small green suede jewel box and dropped the pendant inside. Briskly dusting his hands together, as if to dismiss the matter and his own sentiments for good, he returned to his aunt's bedside.

'Who is it?' she croaked, making him jump.

'It's me, Ben, Aunt Violet.' He sat down and patted her arm. 'How are you feeling?'

'Who?'

'Albert's son,' he reminded her quietly.

'Where's that girl?'

'Which girl would that be?' He wondered for a moment if she was referring to one of the nurses.

'Lovely hair. Red hair. Nice voice.'

'Isobel?'

'Where is she?'

'She's . . . not here.'

'I want that girl who visits. I've not been nice to her—'

'Oh, I'm sure you have.'

She was twitching the sheets with her hands and jerking her head. Her eyes fluttered open and closed again, as if searching for something they could not see. Alarmed, Ben pushed the red button in the wall above the bed.

'She seems a little upset,' he explained apologetically, when the nurse hurried in. 'I wasn't sure . . .'

'What have we here, then . . . ?' The nurse lifted the twiggy wrist for a pulse and punched some air back into the pillows.

'She's been asking for someone . . .'

'Has she? Well, that's nice. Is it someone you can contact?'

'Er . . . maybe.' He coughed and mouthed the words 'How long?' across the bed.

The nurse shrugged sadly. 'Hard to say,' she whispered. 'Days maybe . . .'

'I'll certainly do my best, Aunt Violet,' Ben said loudly, picking up his coat from the back of the chair. 'Will you call me if there's any change?' he added in a whisper to the attending nurse, before gently easing open the door and slipping outside.

It was a relief to leave the room, though the smell of medicine and floor polish was, if anything, even stronger in the corridors. As he passed the open door of the sitting room on his way to the telephones, Ben saw two rows of empty armchairs being lectured to by a man on the television. He hurried past, averting his gaze, suddenly dreading his own fate as an old man.

39

It rained all night, not just across East Anglia, but over the whole of southern England. Archie, sitting on Tuesday morning in the luxurious rear seat of a coach that had more features than the interior of an airplane, shook his head in wonder at the streaks of silver flooding cutting through the fields flying past his window. Thinking of the summer to come and the drought that had so preoccupied weather experts the year before, he said a short silent prayer about rainfall and reservoirs, before extracting a cheese-and-pickle bap from the bag on his lap. He had found himself in a state of almost constant prayer over the last couple of days, jumbled stuff, mostly about gratitude for being grateful. God didn't mind jumble, he was sure of that. He could feel the pleasure of him burning inside now, like hunger, only stronger. After his recent sustained inability to feel anything except misery, the wonder of it was breathtaking.

Almost equal pleasure had been derived from addressing the more practical problem of his eyesight. A half-hour visit to the Chapel Street optician's the previous afternoon had resulted in the acquisition of some gratifyingly erudite, wire-framed spectacles, containing lenses empowered to accommodate the very different requirements of his eyeballs. The eyes had been working against each other, the optician explained cheerfully, blinking over the top of his own tortoiseshell frames, resulting in prolonged and considerable muscle strain. After only a few hours, Archie had noticed a difference: the twitching still came and went, but less regularly and with none of its customary ferocity. With the curious cohesion that life sometimes allows, this diagnosis had been followed by the first good night's sleep that he had known in months. The small brown bottle of Dr Howard's little white pills was now set to gather a nice coating of dust on the window sill above his bed. Though Archie planned, eventually, to consign them to the grimy interior of his kitchen bin, he had decided for the time being to let them play the useful role of psychological fail-safe, a safety net should the need arise.

Having seen off the bap in four or five mouthfuls, Archie reached into his bag in order to pull out his latest acquisition from the library. Though a trifle bashful at the thought of being seen in possession of a book like *Anna Karenina*, his new-found confidence made him determined to give the thing a go. Any enquiries on the subject would have met with a stout defence of a curate's right to improve his knowledge of Russian classics. But what Archie really sought was more understanding of the emotional complexities of Isobel Tarrant in particular and the female psyche in general. The memory of his first proper meeting with Isobel in Torbridge library was still vivid; especially the carelessly bright way in which she had mentioned the book's theme, and his own absurd shyness in trying to respond. Any assistance Tolstoy might offer on the perplexing question of fully fledged female passion could, Archie believed, only strengthen his capacity to handle the meeting that lay ahead. Quite what Isobel's parents were going to make of a Torbridge priest striding up to their front door he hardly dared imagine, though he had deliberately worn full battledress – as he fondly called his cassock – in the vague hope of giving himself something of a flying start. As the moment drew ever nearer, he cowered most at the prospect of confronting Isobel, worrying that she might think him interfering instead of kind. Defused though his passions were, Archie could not bear to think of her not liking him at all.

Druscilla Carew's recommendation had proved a highly fruitful means to information. Juliet Howard not only surrendered the address of Isobel's parents without a moment's hesitation, but also seemed extremely eager to discuss her friend's circumstances in some detail.

'Yes, she's gone to her parents, without a word to anyone.

James only found out quite by chance. That's my husband. He's a doctor at the Stanton Street practice.'

'Ah,' said Archie, some of his enthusiasm for conversation instantly dampened by the revelation of this minor social connection. While not consciously apportioning blame to anyone but himself, he retained few positive memories of his consultation with James Howard.

'The marriage has broken up. Been on the rocks for months – she had a lover, apparently,' went on Juliet. 'A lover, for goodness' sake. Isobel Tarrant. None of us can believe it.'

Archie tried to interrupt her with a view to concluding the discussion, but Juliet had swept on.

'And those poor, poor girls, caught between them, as the children always are in these circumstances. And such a *nice* family too . . . positively frightening to see it all fall apart . . .'

'Absolutely,' Archie had cut in with mounting desperation, sensing all the impropriety of discussing the Tarrants' misfortunes in such gleefully scandalised terms. 'And thank you so much. Goodbye—'

'Goodbye, Reverend . . . what was it?'

'Heighton-Jones.'

'Ah yes. St Cuthbert's, did you say?'

'That's right.'

'So they haven't yet managed to pin African face-masks round the apse?'

'I beg your pardon?'

'Totem poles instead of altars. I thought you were under threat from the ethnic arts people?'

'Oh no, I mean, yes, we were. Plans have been shelved. We've been saved – for the time being.'

'Wonderful. I hope we meet in person soon. Though we usually go to the cathedral – if we go at all . . . Goodbye, Reverend. So nice to have talked to you.'

Remembering the conversation, Archie squirmed in his bus seat. She might be a friend of Isobel's, but he hadn't liked the sound of her at all.

To Archie's dismay, he found his new novel hard going, largely on account of the unsympathetically extravagant emotions of Anna herself. As the coach sped on, its fat wheels spurting like water mills through the dripping roads, Archie found himself concentrating less on the rollercoaster ride of Anna's sensibilities and more on the simple pleasure of skimming his newly reinforced eyes effortlessly over the lines. So accustomed had he become to the blurring and jumping of letters on a page that being restored the simple gift of perfect sight felt nothing short of miraculous.

After an hour or so he gave up completely and pulled out his second and final sandwich – the one he had vowed to keep until lunch-time – and told himself he would eat half. It was beef and horseradish, on a doughy bread with crusty doorstep edges. He chewed quickly, staring with a wild and happy heart at nothing in particular while the rain coursed down his window. Views of pretty floods or anything else had been blotted out by the grey curtain sweeping from sky to earth. But I still know the prettiness is there, he mused, lingering on the notion with pleasure, sure that he had found yet another small but revealing analogy for the visibility of God to troubled souls. There but sometimes hidden, he murmured, stifling a fruity burp and settling back to close his eyes.

40

Spending Monday night in a seaside bed and breakfast did little to raise Isobel's sense of optimism for her own future. She felt washed up and quite beyond repair. The thinking time – once so longed for and talked about – had produced such vague and fruitless circles of regret and self-recrimination that she left her room shortly after dawn in search of distractions. It did not feel possible to go scampering back to her parents just yet, like the failed child that she was. Instead she had a greasy cooked breakfast and a mug of lukewarm coffee in a café that smelt of fish and then set out for a stroll along the beach. Apart from a bounding Labrador, being roared at by a distant owner, the sands were empty and grey. The waves snarled at her as she walked by, like foaming animals straining at the leash. After a while, she took her shoes and socks off and walked with her feet in the icy water, wishing the numbness could seize her heart as well as her toes. Staring out towards the grey bands where sky met sea, she found herself understanding the attraction of stepping into it, of wanting to merge with the nothingness that it seemed to contain. The incoming tide embraced her ankles, then slid back towards the sea, pulling the sand from under her toes and leaving the instep of each foot stranded on little humps that dissolved beneath her weight.

From nowhere the Labrador appeared at the water's fringe, its tail flicking water as it pumped the air, its drooly jaws clamped round a large stick. It plunged towards where Isobel was standing and deposited the stick a few feet from her left hand. For a moment she watched absently as the piece of wood bobbed and started to float away on the swell of a receding wave.

Seeing its toy in danger of disappearing, the dog gave a frantic yelp of encouragement.

'Oh, bugger it,' she muttered, reaching for the stick and hurling it as far as she could back towards the shore. In the exertion of doing so, she lost her balance and fell backwards. For a moment there was nothing but cold and shock. Then the palm of one hand met the hard pebbly ground and in an instant she had levered herself upright again. Amazingly, only one leg, half her back and an entire arm suffered the calamity of being entirely drenched. The dog, having retrieved its trophy, raced away towards the sound of a piercing whistle, leaving Isobel to wade back on to dry land, now laughing breathlessly – and a little hysterically – at her own foolhardiness. A trail of dark drips marked her path across the beach and back up to the road. Her hair, dampened and frizzy from the moist salty air, stuck in clumps to her cheeks and neck. Catching sight of her reflection in the polished glass of an amusement arcade a few minutes later, Isobel clapped her hand to her mouth in a mixture of horror and real amusement. No wonder she had been getting strange looks. A few yards on from the arcade was a hairdresser's. With a rush of determination to achieve at least one positive thing that morning, however superficial, she pushed open the door and stepped inside.

In spite of the look on the girl's face, she stuck to her guns. 'I want it all off. Right down to the last inch. And I'm a bit pushed for time.' She smiled briskly and looked at her watch. 'So if you wouldn't mind . . .'

'If you're sure . . .'

'I'm sure, thank you.'

'Would you like to keep the hair?'

'Keep it? Whatever for?'

'To make a hairpiece, or as a memento . . .'

Isobel laughed. 'Oh God, no, I wouldn't. I don't want any mementos at all, thank you.'

The hairdresser, who was usually renowned for her sales patter with even the most awkward customers, remained quite silent while she saw to Isobel's request. Sensing an agenda that was quite out of her realm, she kept her eyes on her scissors instead of her client's sodden clothes, trying to keep her expression impartial as each coil of shining copper flopped noiselessly to the ground.

Before embarking on the drive back to her parents', Isobel changed into dry clothes and bought a large green headscarf from a charity shop. As well as introducing her to the phenomenon of cold ears, to have so brutally cropped such an obvious asset felt like an act of honesty; anyone could see now that she had nothing to hide behind, no camouflage for her insecurity. That is was indisputably ugly felt most important of all.

'Ugly on the outside, ugly on the inside,' she declared to the wing mirror, grimacing at the egg shape of her skull and the crimson tips of her ears. Her eyes, exposed in the bare pale frame of her face as never before, glittered with new resolve. 'Not the Ophelia sort anyway,' she muttered, giving the sea a parting scowl as she turned along the road that led away from the coast. At the thought of seeing the girls, Isobel allowed herself a broad smile; her first for days. Both the traffic and the weather deteriorated steadily as she continued her journey inland. On the final stretch of motorway, she was caught up in a tailback of traffic that lasted for several miles. Impatience at this unforeseen delay was instantly humbled by the sound of sirens wailing in the distance. The line of cars on her side of the road was completely stationary, while on the other side there were no vehicles to be seen at all. Leaning back against the headrest and half closing her eyes, Isobel prepared to wait. A minute later she opened them again, her attention caught by a stunning scissor of azure blue opening in the sky ahead, directly above where she imagined the cause of the delay to be taking place. With the rest of the world still so thunderously black, it looked like a crevice of light in a darkened room.

After a good half-hour the traffic started to move again. The cars appearing on the other side accelerated away with evident relief. A couple of miles later bollards, police signs and a scattering of broken glass told Isobel that she was about to pass the scene of the accident. Feeling she shouldn't look, but wanting to anyway, she glanced left and saw a coach tipped over on its side. Two badly dented cars were behind it. To her right, several yards' worth of snarled metal road fencing told a little more of the story. The number of uniformed helpers and official cars parked round the damaged vehicles underlined still further the grave scale of what had occurred. Shaking her head in dismay, Isobel sped into the clear road opening ahead of her, empowered by a fresh sense of her own good fortune. Remembering the bleakness of her thoughts on the beach that morning, she felt quite guilty. There was so much to live for after all, even for foolish women with broken marriages and pitifully hazy notions as to the nature of their own ambitions. It was just a question of seizing this new phase in her life by the scruff of its neck and shaking some sense into it, she told herself, pushing off her headscarf and stroking the soft brush of her hair. She would get over Ben, with time. Maybe, one day, she might even be able to laugh at the calamitous sequence of misunderstandings and misfortunes that had driven them apart, at the awful fiasco of seeking answers in the arms of someone like James Howard.

The crevice of blue had opened into a great canyon. The stream of yellow sunlight pouring from inside made the dark wet roads shine like polished obsidian. For the last couple of miles Isobel drove faster than she should have, spurred on not just by the brightness of the day, but by the pleasurable prospect of surprising the children by her early return, of putting some of her new determination to the test.

41

'Now that's what I call odd,' remarked Juliet, flicking the page of newspaper in front of her with her fingertips and then scowling at the jagged shoreline of her week-old nail varnish. It was Wednesday morning, and James, having enjoyed two days in the company of his family, was returning to work.

'Hm?' Never at his conversational best before eight o'clock on any day, he glanced first at his wife, then at the kitchen clock and finally at the egg still submerged in frothy water in a saucepan on the stove. Having safely waved the children on to the school bus, Juliet, attractively enveloped in her peach housecoat, had confessed to a firm but loving intention to provide her husband with the nourishment of a cooked breakfast. Keen as they both still were to foster every show of affection, no matter how mundane or small, James had falsely pronounced himself delighted at the prospect and had been regretting it ever since. 'How long did you say it would take?'

'Four and a half minutes. Two to go,' she added, keeping her eyes fixed upon the paragraph of newsprint in front of her. 'This really is too much . . .'

'What is, my love?' he asked dutifully, after casting a surreptitiously sceptical glance across the table. Juliet was not often absorbed by newspaper headlines, least of all those splashed across the inside pages of the *Torbridge Gazette*. 'Another bomb?' For a second or two his thoughts lingered with something like nostalgia on Torbridge's brush with terrorist explosives earlier in the year. He remembered holding Isobel's hand, the look of surprise in her wide green eyes.

'James, are you listening?'

'Loud and clear.'

'It's all about that vicar chap, the one I told you about – the one who rang on Sunday night. Listen.'

DEATH MYSTERY OF TORBRIDGE VICAR

The only fatality of yesterday's Suffolk motorway coach crash has been identified as Reverend Archibald Heighton-Jones, a twenty-two-year-old curate from Torbridge's own St Cuthbert's. His parents were called to Barstone Hospital to identify the body, which they have taken to their parish in Cheshire for burial. 'He was a fine and holy man,' commented Reverend Tully, 'called to God far sooner than any of us would have hoped or expected. Our hearts go out to his friends and family.' That his employee had apparently claimed to be too sick to attend to his parish duties in Torbridge that morning was a matter on which the Reverend was unprepared to comment. A fellow passenger confirmed that the young trainee vicar was carrying no luggage apart from a picnic lunch, a pair of spectacles and the novel Anna Karenina. So it seems the secret of the itinerant vicar is one that he will carry to his grave. His replacement at St Cuthbert's has yet to be announced.

'Poor chap. And a man of passions, obviously, if his taste in reading is anything to go by.' James left the table to peer anxiously at his egg, too distracted by such pressing dilemmas to make any connection with the red-headed curate who had consulted him about insomnia a few weeks before.

'Of course, of course, but don't you see?' Juliet was so excited she could hardly speak. 'It all fits.'

'What fits?' James retorted with some impatience, now seriously concerned both for the welfare of his breakfast and his time schedule for the morning.

'All that stuff about wanting to send her books was nonsense. He was going to visit her.'

'Visit who?'

'James, don't be dim. Isobel. He was going to visit Isobel Tarrant.' Juliet slapped the table with the palm of her hand and pushed past him to the saucepan. 'There's no other explanation.' She transported the egg, its surface turbulent with cracks and entrails of yellow and white, to a rabbit figurine of an eggcup, before – somewhat unnecessarily – batting it on the head with a teaspoon. 'Everyone's saying Isobel had a lover. Well, I think it must have been this priest. He had a lovely voice – and no doubt a lovely body to go with it.' She handed him his breakfast and folded her arms with a challenging humph of satisfaction.

James quickly busied himself with picking off fragments of shell. 'Don't be ridiculous, darling – I mean, really . . .' Inside, the yolk was dry and quite solid, as was its surrounding cushion of white. As he chewed he could feel little bits of it sticking between his teeth.

'It's the only scenario that makes sense. Listen.' Juliet held up her fingers and counted off each component of her theory. 'The two of them have a clandestine affair; when Ben finds out, Isobel panics and runs off to her parents'; then the vicar – lovelorn and despairing' – she rolled her eyes with relish – 'calls me to find out where she is and goes running after her. And ends up getting killed for his pains. It's too romantic for words, like something out of a great tragic' – she spread her arms for added emphasis – 'love story.'

James opened his mouth to scold his wife for being so absurdly imaginative and then closed it again. He ran his tongue round the clogged edges of his teeth before smiling. 'You are a genius, my sparrow, did you know that?'

'Yes, I did, actually.' She sat back down beside him and sighed deeply. 'It just goes to show, you never have a clue really what's going on in other people's lives. You think you know someone and then' – she clicked her fingers – 'pow, you discover something that makes you realise you never did at all.'

'Like the Tarrants, you mean,' he said carefully.

'Exactly. All that time the four of us spent together . . . it's weird . . . it's like we never really knew each other at all.' She sighed again. 'But I do miss her – Isobel, I mean. We did have a lot in common, once upon a time.'

James abandoned his egg to put his arms round her. 'You've got all your Ilcombe friends now and that Shelley woman.'

Juliet pushed him away with a brusque kiss and began clearing the table. 'Of course I have. I'm not complaining. I'm very happy with my lot – now.' She shot him a little look as a reminder of the subject she had vowed never to mention again, before picking up the newspaper and folding it in half. After only a moment's hesitation she then turned and dropped it into the bin, where it subsided amongst an avalanche of eggshell and yolk crumbs.

42

Though reputedly still breathing, Aunt Violet was showing few signs of life by Wednesday afternoon when Isobel raced up the green-carpeted stairs two at a time for her turn at the bedside. The physical deterioration was a shock. Her skin seemed to have shrunk to her bones, sinking round each curve and nodule of her skeleton like shrivelled clingfilm. Without the support of dentures, the jaw and cheeks looked pitifully deflated; quite incapable of defiance, thought Isobel sadly, recalling all the acerbic comments to which she had once been subjected with a surge of affection. After the nurse had left, she stood quietly by the bed for a few minutes before retreating to a chair to fiddle with her rings and wonder quite what she was expected to do.

Thanks to her hair – or rather the lack of it – her homecoming in Suffolk had proved something of a trial. Though her parents managed to contain their astonishment with a few murmurs and a stoically tight-lipped determination not to appear shocked, both Sophie and Megan howled at the sight of her and for quite some time afterwards. The news about Aunt Violet did little to alleviate such tensions. Though it felt churlish, Isobel could not repress a certain incredulity at having been summoned to the bedside, Aunt Violet's rambling and spiky conversation having done little to suggest that she might ever be called upon to play such a potentially dramatic role. The fact that her last few visits had served as a loose geographical alibi for meeting James Howard added a further twist of complicating guilt to these emotions. Remembering how beadily the old bird had eyed her sometimes – her uncanny knack of saying the most unsettling things – Isobel had even caught herself wondering if she was being called to attend a dreadful final tribunal of some kind; whether she was to be subjected to quavering judgments for having allowed old bad cycles of hurt and betrayal to recur.

In spite of such apprehensions, there was never any question of her not complying with the request. Her only condition was that Ben should be contacted and warned off being there himself. Though her parents clearly thought this an unnecessary cruelty, Isobel remained adamant. She feared what might happen to all her new-found courage at the sight of him; she feared, above all, the thought of his disdain, of seeing once more the look of repulsed disappointment that had burned in his eyes upon the revelation of her affair with James. Seeing her daughter's determination, her mother had finally agreed to phone Ben to make the terms of the visit clear. But as she left the room to do so, the grim expression on her face revealed for the first time the full extent of Betty Hitchings' consternation at what was taking place and her despair at being so powerless to do anything to prevent it.

Upon seeing the old lady, Isobel had immediately felt ashamed of all her earlier apprehensions. What little remained of Aunt Violet's energies was clearly being channelled into far more fundamental matters than delivering tirades upon the misdemeanours of relatives. Feeling both relieved and strangely let down, she eventually abandoned her chair and began to wander round the room much as Ben had the day before, tinkering with ornaments and speculating about their origins and the sentiments attached to them. When she reached the dressing table, Isobel picked up the comb and gently ran her thumb down the uneven row of teeth. Pushing her headscarf back off her head, she stooped in front of the mirror and slowly pulled the comb through her hair, still intrigued by the way the crop of her fringe now grew vertically upwards, like the glossy bristles of a soft brush.

Two cups of tea and one hour later, Isobel felt she had earned a stroll in the grounds. As she walked, she peeled off her scarf and cardigan and slung them across her handbag. The day had warmed up considerably since her arrival, though the manicured lawn and rich foliage surrounding it still gleamed from their recent rich diet of rain. After making two circuits, her eye was caught by a gap in the hedge and a narrow path that seemed to lead towards some greenhouses, their glass roofs just visible through the trees. Upon following the path, however, she found herself being led round the back of the greenhouses, past a large compost heap and out into a scrubby area of land that contained the fenced-in square of an old tennis court. Tufts of grass and dandelion clocks had pushed their way up through the lines in its rugged face and one net post slanted dramatically towards the ground, like the death-dive of an uprooted tree. Isobel pushed her way inside through a broken gate and began an idle tour of its perimeter, keeping half an eye open for rotten balls and wondering how many decades had elapsed since any had been in use.

When Ben got his first proper view of his wife she was leaning with her fingers looped through the rusty mesh of the fencing surrounding the court, staring outwards. A woman in a cage, was his first thought. And in the same instant he felt a searing stab of responsibility for the part he had played in putting her there. Only then did his senses register the full horror of her hair.

Unaware that she was being observed, Isobel abandoned her pose and absently kicked at a stone with the toe of her shoe. She watched as it bounced along the faint dusty image of a baseline and out through the open gate by which she had entered. When she saw Ben, she stopped abruptly and threw down her bag.

'You weren't supposed to be here.'

'I know.'

'You promised.'

'I know. I lied. I wanted to see you.'

'Well, now you've seen me.'

'You've cut your hair.'

'Full marks for observation.' She reached down and tugged her scarf free from the tangle of her bag straps. Letting Ben, of all people, see her ugliness was hard. Worse than standing naked before the scrutiny of strangers. He had loved her hair. Once, a long time ago, he had held strands of it to his face as he slept. Isobel twisted the scarf round her hands and wrists, glowering at the effort of not putting it on. 'It's my head.'

'Yes,' he said quietly, 'I know. How are you?' He plunged his hands in his pockets and looked at his shoes, as if such distraction might make the burden of any answer she had to offer easier to bear. 'How is . . . James?'

Isobel rolled her eyes and picked up her bag. 'I've no idea. He's back with Juliet.'

'I see,' he whispered, wishing she did not look so sad.

'Apparently she knows nothing of my involvement with James and I for one am more than happy to keep it that way. Seeing the threat I must have – however briefly – posed to their marriage, it seems the very least I can do.'

'And what about our marriage?' he faltered, still seeing only her sadness and hating James Howard for being the cause of it.

'I think that was a casualty long before any of . . . this, don't you?' She cleared her throat and tightened her grip on the strap of her bag. 'Now, if there's nothing else . . . I have come here – in case you had forgotten – to comply with the dying wishes of your aunt. I know we have a lot to talk about, but if you don't mind I'd rather not do it here.' She swept past him and began marching back towards the house, half hidden through the screen of trees behind them.

'Wait – Isobel, I . . . I've got your post.'

She stopped and turned, her voice scornful. 'My what?'

'Post,' he repeated faintly, feeling pathetic as he reached into his jacket pocket for the couple of letters that he had grabbed as he was leaving the house.

'You could have sent them on . . .' she began; though the remark did not prevent her from coming back towards him, holding out her hand. 'Thank you.'

'She looks bloody awful, doesn't she, the old thing?'

Isobel nodded.

'Has she said anything to you yet?'

'Nope. Can't think what it was all about.'

'She said something about not being nice to you . . .'

'Did she?' Isobel was so surprised she smiled. 'Well, I . . . how funny and how unlikely.'

'Wasn't she nice to you?' he asked, with real concern in his voice. 'You never said . . .'

'I never said a lot of things, and neither did you . . .' she began, before checking herself and letting out a small sigh. 'Oh God, I don't know . . . I suppose she sort of picked on me a bit, let off some steam – nothing serious at all.' She shrugged. 'Funny old thing. Who's the other Isobel, by the way?'

'The other Isobel?'

Admitting to her nosiness made her flush. 'I was rooting around in her jewel box and . . . well, I found this pendant thing inscribed to an Isobel. I couldn't help wondering who she was.' She shrugged and turned to leave him once more. 'I thought you might know. It doesn't matter.'

Ben opened his mouth twice before managing to project any sounds from it. 'No, there's only you. Only one Isobel.'

Something about his tone made her stop and look back.

He cast his eyes to the ground, suddenly overcome with emotions for which he could find no adequate verbal expression. But she still loves James, he reminded himself, clenching his jaw to steady his voice. 'The contents of all her jewel boxes will go to you anyway – and the girls, of course. There's no one else. There'll be no money to speak of – it all went on paying for this place.' He nodded in the direction of the house.

'Well, that's nice,' Isobel murmured, realising for the first time that she had been so absorbed by her own emotions that she had failed to notice his. He looked neither bitter nor disappointed, as she had expected, but preoccupied and utterly downcast.

'You'd think dying might provide some answers to *something,*' he burst out, spreading his arms in dismay. 'I mean, when I got here I actually found myself hoping for a better understanding of . . . oh Christ, the past, I suppose, and why everything happened as it did . . . but in fact it's just a bloody anticlimax, isn't it? There's nothing to understand, no deathbed epiphany, no visions for anybody except perhaps bloody John of bloody Gaunt—'

'John of Gaunt?'

'In *Richard II* – prophetic urge as he's dying – mind you, that doesn't do any bloody good either—' Aware that he was ranting, but that she was listening, Ben careered on, all his instincts telling him that though the door was closing fast, he might yet slip his foot into the gap to stop it shutting completely. 'The bad stuff just happens,' he continued, 'and before I've always let it – not fought it – or at least fought it inside by pretending it wasn't there. And I kind of thought you'd taken me on those terms, that you had fallen for this unbreakable, self-driven thing, and so I guess I wanted to keep it that way, because if you saw the mess inside you wouldn't . . .' He broke off, angry with himself for the tremor in his voice. 'So I kept a tight control over myself and part of that was controlling you, not letting you . . . flourish.' He threw his hands up in despair at the inadequacy of the word. 'I trapped you as much as I trapped myself.'

Isobel, shuffling her clutch of letters, swallowed hard, though her mouth was quite dry. Having expected any angry rantings to be on the subject of James or marital infidelity, she was astonished at the turn the conversation was taking, and fractionally encouraged too.

'I drive people away from me, don't I?' he snarled, his dark eyes blazing. 'Apart form my pupils, of course. But then they're easy because they go home at night, taking most of their troubles with them. But people that matter, I drive away. It's my big speciality. Like my father—' He caught his breath before continuing, his voice tight and calm. 'For whom, as you know, I was barely able to feel any affection at all.' He shook his head. 'God, how the past throttles the present . . .'

'Only if you let it,' she put in quietly, picking at the corner of a stamp.

'The only person I've ever felt really close to . . .' He swallowed. '. . . is you . . . until . . .' He clapped his hands, making her jump. '. . . our baby . . . there's another death that didn't make any sense – life's full of the bloody things, had you noticed?' he added, flashing a dark smile. 'And all I could do was feel jealous of your sadness – God, Isobel, you were so bloody good at being sad.' He laughed bitterly. 'Jesus Christ, it's funny, it's actually very funny.' His laughing echoed round the empty tennis court beside them. 'Because you see I've learnt how to be miserable now, all right. But now is too late . . .' He threw his head back, whooping at the sky.

'Stop it, Ben, please,' she begged, appalled.

Putting his hands up, he made a show of trying to swallow the laughter away. 'Do you know, I have even been driven to seeking professional help – I actually saw a counsellor who confirmed all my worst fears—'

'A counsellor?' Isobel was so surprised she dropped her letters.

'Amusing, isn't it? What's even better is that this one and only session – this great hopeless bid for psychological self-reform – took place just the day before you elected to break the news about dear James. I mean, if that isn't funny I don't know what is.' But he wasn't laughing any longer. All he could manage was an attempt at a smile, which Isobel, staring hard at a tree as she braced herself for the barrage of recrimination that would follow, failed to observe.

But instead of recrimination, there was silence.

'The fact is I want you back, Isobel, and don't know how the hell to go about it, how to persuade you that I'm worth a second shot, that I'm worth more than . . . James.'

'More than James?' she repeated dumbly, her mouth dropping open in disbelief, while her heart leapt with a hope she had thought to have abandoned for good. 'I need persuading of that, do I?' she went on archly, recovering herself. Though, as she stooped down to retrieve her letters, she was careful to keep her chin to her chest so that he would not see the wobble in her lower lip.

'Don't you?'

The scurrying figure of a nurse suddenly appeared in the shrubbery behind them, waving her arms and shouting.

'Oh, there you are . . . could you come? We think . . . it might be time . . .'

'Oh heavens, we'd better be quick.' Isobel, with a spurt of guilt, began to trot back up the path.

'We had indeed,' he called, striding after her. 'Who knows what dying revelations we may have missed – more family scandals, buried treasure or hidden deeds to magnificent homes . . .'

'Ben, shush,' she scolded, having to suppress a smile as they caught up with the nurse.

'So you two found each other, did you?'

'In a manner of speaking,' said Ben, giving Isobel a funny look which she pretended not to see.

'I'm so sorry, but your aunt seems to have taken a turn for the worse. You'd better come with me.'

43

But Aunt Violet was to prove as uncooperative in dying as she had in living. Conceding, almost apologetically, that the immediate crisis seemed to have passed, the nurse left the old lady's chief mourners-in-waiting eyeing each other with some awkwardness from opposite sides of the bed.

'This will only be my second death,' remarked Isobel after a while, 'of someone to whom I feel any attachment at all. That's quite lucky, I suppose, isn't it, for a person who's been on the planet as long as I have?'

'All of thirty-one years, isn't it?'

'Thirty-two.'

'Ah yes, thirty-two.'

'Do you believe in heaven, Ben?'

'Not for a moment.'

'Not even for Toby?' It was the first time she had said the name out loud to him in years.

'Well, all I can say is, if that's where he is then I only wish we could warn him who's on the way,' he replied, making a face at the figure of his aunt, whose shallow breathing was now being conducted with her chin thrust at the ceiling, as if to facilitate the passage of air.

'This is awful. I'm not sure I can bear much more.'

'You're not thinking of going, are you?' he said quietly.

'Maybe.'

'Please don't. I . . . need you, Isobel.'

'I was just beginning to adjust to the idea of not being needed at all, by anyone ever again. And of not needing anyone myself, for that matter,' she added, frowning at him.

'But Aunt Violet might give a sign any minute – something to show why she wanted you here. You obviously meant a lot to her.'

'Don't you dare start flattering me now, Ben Tarrant,' she retorted, leaving the bedside and wandering over to the dressing table. Seeing the chain of the pendant hanging out of the jewel box, she pulled it free and dangled it at him.

'This was what I was talking about. *Isobel my love*, it says.' She squinted at the tiny print inlaid in the silver. 'And it's even spelt my way too. Don't you think that's peculiar? A pretty heart shape . . . and it's got a sort of shiny new look to it too compared to all the rest of this stuff.' She fished out a pair of enormous pearly paste baubles and held them to her ears. 'What do you think?'

Ben scowled furiously shaking his head. 'You look like a tacky Christmas tree.'

'How sweet of you to say so.'

'But the hair's growing on me, though, if you'll pardon the expression.' They both laughed, and then shot guilty looks at the bed.

'This won't do at all,' she whispered, spinning the chain round her hand and suppressing another smile.

'This will do just fine,' he countered, sitting back in his chair, savouring the realisation that he did not need to own up to the ownership of the rose crystal, that he could woo her without needing to resort to sentimentality or dramatic gestures of any kind. All that they had once shared was still there, dormant, but wonderfully alive. 'In some countries they dance at gravesides every year to celebrate the life of the person who's gone. They drink vodka and tell rude jokes.'

'Do they, now?' She slipped the necklace over her head and made a face at herself in the mirror. 'Well, the vodka part sounds promising.'

'Isobel . . .'

A look from her almost silenced him. A look generated by the fear that they would get it wrong, that some slip of a remark would throw them off course again.

'Would you like to live in Hampshire?'

'I very much doubt it.'

'I'm going to apply for a job . . . headmaster of a small prep school . . . I couldn't do it without you.'

'I want to study Spanish with the Open University.'

'You could do that too—'

'All those smelly little boys.' She screwed up her nose.

'And smelly girls too – it's mixed.'

'Oh God, look, she's moving her mouth, Ben – she's trying to say something.' Isobel leapt back across the room and bent her head near the withered face. As she leant over the bed, Ben took the opportunity to seize her hand.

'I'm sorry for what I did to you – to us – Isobel—'

'Shush, I'm trying to listen,' she whispered, trying and failing to tug her hand free.

'I know how much of it was my fault—'

'If you carry on like this I'll think I deserve no blame at all,' she retorted, looking up at last and relaxing her fingers in his.

They kissed, with some awkwardness, across the bed, and with such absorption that when Aunt Violet did at last open her mouth to embark upon a dying utterance, they did not even notice. The nurse, appearing a few minutes later at the open door behind, blushed scarlet and tiptoed away to tell her colleagues. A lively and impromptu tea break ensued, during which a range of ribald but by no means ill-intentioned opinions on the unexpected nature of the visitors' behaviour were gleefully exchanged. Beneath the sheer thrill of these speculations hummed a deep gladness, which the nurses themselves would have found hard to define, but which perhaps derived from a general sense of the irrepressibility of the human spirit.

An air of something like triumph lingered in the hushed, scrubbed corridors of the home, even after Ben's bashful but solemn face appeared round the office door to announce that his aunt seemed finally to have breathed her last. While the nurses moved around the bed, the Tarrants stood a little to one side, their heads bowed in respectful silence. After a moment or two they linked fingers, tentatively at first, but with increasing confidence, until their two hands were as tight as a clenched fist. Within the small circle of this private embrace each sensed a world of forgotten possibilities, a world powered with enough determination and desire not only to accommodate the burdens of the past, but also to allow stirrings of hope for what might lie ahead.